The Wonder of Knifemaking

WAYNE GODDARD

Published by

krause
publications

700 E. State Street • Iola, WI 54990-0001
Telephone: 715/445-2214
Web: www.krause.com

To place an order or receive our free catalog, call 800-258-0929.

For editorial comment and further information,
use our regular business telephone at (715) 445-2214.

Library of Congress Catalog Number: 99-68101
ISBN: 0-87341-798-4

Printed in the United States of America

Contents

Introduction

In the corner of my garage sits an old anvil and a hand-crank forge. They were gifts from my grandfather. That might be why I was assigned to edit this book.

Like all other books at a publishing house, this one was assigned to me. That I had some interest in knifemaking made me a prime candidate for putting the photos in order and making sure all the text was clear. It turned out to be quite an easy job, thanks to Wayne Goddard's skill.

Something happened as I reviewed the pages and adjusted the artwork. The feeling that I wanted to build a knife started to grow. And, thanks to Goddard's writing, I felt for the first time that I could really build a knife. This book is that good — that clear—that easy-to-read.

Any knifemaker of any skill level will learn from this book because Goddard answers the questions knifemakers have actually been asking for years. Questions like: "Which is the best steel for camp knife or a Combat Quality Blade? How do I forge a dagger? Should I burn gas or coal in my forge? Should I grind my blades or forge them?" are all addressed in this one book. The answers are direct and easy to understand.

It took 30 years of work for Goddard to gather all this knowledge, now it's all in one place, ready to help you become a better knifemaker. Enjoy.

Kevin Michalowski
Editor

Foreword

I first met Wayne Goddard in 1977 in Sacramento, California, while sitting among a group of fellow pocketknife collectors. This Oregon maker saunters up, shows us a photo of himself standing beside a 6-foot folding knife, and introduces himself as a full-time knifemaker. In those days a full-time knifemaker was a very rare thing. However, it was not so rare if you knew Wayne. In a field in which few can survive as full-time knifemakers unless their spouse has a well-paying job, Wayne Goddard has thrived. He has thrived because he has the rare gift to be able to look through the fog of hype and promotion and actually see what is going on in the hand-made knife business; where it is going in steels, in design, in form, and in marketing. That is vital as a full-time knifemaker, and it is achieved by very few.

Wayne is far more than just a good knifemaker. He is a knife designer for manufacturers. He is a writer, and, above all, he is a teacher. While attending an Oregon knife show in the 1970s I watched Wayne demonstrate sharpening a knife during a seminar at that show. It made quite an impression in me, in both the clarity and dynamics of Wayne in a teaching situation, and the rapt attention he commanded from his audience. In those days I was owner of *Blade Magazine* and producer of the Blade Show, and it was Wayne's seminar at that April show in Oregon that prompted the idea of seminars at the Blade Show.

Later, at *Blade Magazine* we started amassing a large number of technical knife questions. These were questions that only a knowledgeable knifemaker could answer and there was no doubt where those questions would go. They went to Wayne Goddard, because I knew Wayne would provide the readers concise, easy-to-understand explanations of what are normally difficult-to-understand (and sometimes dry) topics.

There's nothing dry in any of Wayne's explanations. He is just as upbeat and enthusiastic about some new type of steel as he is about explaining how to set up a forge with a hairdryer and a barbecue grill. And he writes as clearly as he speaks. That ability is put to good use in the columns he writes for *Blade Magazine*. He is constantly working and experimenting and researching to broaden his knowledge of knife making, and then he turns right around and gives that knowledge away through his writing. He has made may otherwise dry topics alive and exciting, and at the same time broadened the knowledge of a whole generation of knife enthusiasts. To me, that is a notable achievement.

On a personal note, Wayne also achieved what I would have thought was impossible. In a two-week stint at the Bill Moran ABS School of Bladesmithing he taught this writer how to hand-forge a blade that would withstand the tests required by the ABS for Journeyman smith ratings. The two weeks of my life invested to study under Wayne was time very well spent.

You will discover that the time you spend reading this book will be time well spent for you, too. Stay sharp.

J. Bruce Voyles

July, 1999

Dedication

To my wife, Phyllis, who made it possible for me to be a knifemaker.
Thank you for making what I have achieved much easier.

Wayne

Acknowledgments

Ken Warner and Bruce Voyles first encouraged me to write about knifemaking. Ken published my first article in *Knives '86* and Bruce published my article on knife testing in *Blade Magazine* in 1990 which led to the Q&A feature in 1991.

Many thanks go to *Blade Magazine* editor, Steve Shackleford, who continues to publish my columns and always makes me sound sensible.

Ed Fowler is my island of reality in what sometimes appears to be a make-believe world of knives. Thanks Ed for making a priority of creating real knives for real work.

Thanks to my dedicated and patient editor, Kevin Michalowski, for helping this book the best it could be.

Most importantly, my sincere thanks go to all the readers who have sent in questions over the years. I especially appreciate those who have taken the time to help me get back on the path when I got lost. This book is for you.

Chapter 1

KEEP IT SIMPLE

It was my rebellion against "high tech" that led to the *Blade Magazine* series "The $50 Knife Shop". The purpose was to present knifemaking with simple tools and methods. This is a stark contrast to the headlong rush towards complicated (and often expensive) tools that are quite common in the handmade knife shop of today.

I tell my students that if they can't learn to do it with simple equipment, they may not ever do it long enough with fancy equipment to get good at it. I've often heard new makers say that their knives would be better if they had better equipment. I have also watched their frustration level raise when they do get better equipment and find that it will still take many hours of practice to get the skill necessary to do good work.

Every so often the phone rings and it will be someone who wants to get started making knives. When I'm not too busy I invite them out to see my shop and get acquainted. I remember one young man who walked in, took one look around at all my equipment and said words to this effect, "I won't be able to make knives, I can't afford all this stuff!" I told him that it could be done with much less equipment and even described to him the meager equipment I had when I moved to my present location in 1970. I explained that it had taken me more than 35 years to accumulate all that I had. He could not be convinced otherwise. He was going to have a lot of equipment or none at all; a simple start was not for him.

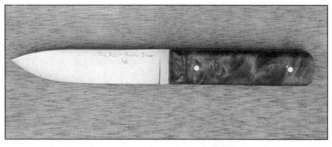

The stock-removal knife made in the *Blade Magazine* series "The $50 Knife Shop." It was made with lawnmower blade steel, scrap maple burl and a bare minimum of equipment.

That experience and others where the shortage of tools and information was hindering people from getting started, reinforced my desire to be able to teach knifemaking on a very basic level. This led to my experiments in the use of primitive methods. My success with the project proved that all that was necessary was the desire to do it. It might be considered almost un-American to accomplish something in such a primitive manner. A simple start is not for everyone; it is for those rugged and inventive individuals who coined the phrase "Yankee Ingenuity." The most important ingredient for success with simple methods is to have a sincere desire to do it. I like to call it; "having the want-to's."

Perhaps the most sensible part about a simple beginning is that as the skill level increases more and better equipment that allows higher production can be obtained. I've seen many new makers who were frustrated by having good equipment but no skill to go with it. It would be like giving a 3-year-old kid a Stradivarius violin and then expecting to hear something that sounds good. On the other hand, you can give a master violinist almost any old fiddle and he can make sweet music with it.

SETTING THE PRICE MEANS KNOWING YOUR TRUE COSTS

I am often asked about the method used to establish a price on one's work. I base my method on time studies and operating expense over the 26 years I've spent as a full-time maker. Multiply the hourly wage you want to make by four. Multiply that figure by the hands-on hours spent on a knife. That answer gives the selling price.

Put it like this: If you want to make $20 per hour, that's $20 X 4 = $80. If it takes you four hours to make the knife; 4 X $80 = $320 as a selling price for the knife.

This should allow you adequate income to pay for materials, insurance, maintenance, advertising, show expenses and a million other things. Don't forget to pay your taxes.

The skills necessary to produce knives having superior workmanship, strength and cutting ability are learned with much practice. Books, videos, classes and machinery are only a starting point. I recently did some calculations and came up with the following: Let's say it takes the beginner 10 hours to make a knife; and assume that they will have to make at least 100 knives to become efficient. It will take an investment of 1,000 hours to learn the fundamentals. Assuming that their time is worth $15 per hour it means an investment in dollar/hours of

$15,000. A pretty good set of knifemaking machinery can be purchased for less than $3,000. What I'm getting at is this; a wise person will consider both the investments in time and money necessary to learn the skills of knifemaking.

HOW I GOT STARTED
MAKING KNIVES

An old-time blacksmith gave me a formula for using an oven-tempered lathe rasp to make a knife. In 1963 I found a lathe rasp, but then I needed a grinder. So, I built one. It wasn't much of a machine but it worked well enough to grind out my first knife and quite a few more. Parts are as follows: 1/3 hp - 1750 rpm, Westinghouse washing machine motor, a grinding wheel adapter and wheel from Sears, a plywood base, and an old cookie sheet for a guard. (See the photo of the reconstruction of that grinder.)

I call it the Good News / Bad News grinder, GNBN for short. The good news is it only cost $5 to make. The bad news is it's not much of a grinder compared to a $2,000 belt grinder. It is good enough to make the knife shown on the previous page. It can also be set up as an abrasive saw and that's something the $2,000 Belt grinder can't do.

I didn't know it at the time, but that knife got me started on my life's work. There were those who liked that knife well enough to have me make one like it for them. If that wouldn't have happened I might not have made any more knives.

The guard is steel, the handle slabs are Oregon Myrtlewood, and I made the rivets out of 1/4-inch bolts. (See photo.) I ground it out very carefully from a lathe rasp just like the formula said. I tempered it at 375 degrees F in the kitchen oven. Careful grinding was necessary to keep the edge from being softened from overheating. (The edge-holding ability of most carbon and carbon alloy steels can be ruined by heat caused by careless grinding with wheels or belts.) The grinding wheel marks were smoothed up

with the disk attachment on an electric drill. Back then my idea of a fine finish was somewhere between 60- and 80-grit.

That first knife never did sell. It seemed that everyone wanted the "improved" workmanship of the subsequent models. By the end of that first year I decided it would be a good one to keep. I figure it is by pure luck that I still have it. I'm glad to have that knife because it helps me prove some points with new or want-to-be makers. It shows that a knife can be made with a $5 grinder and an electric drill. It clearly shows that I had no real, natural-born talent for knifemaking. I believe that the main requirement is a strong desire to do it. Years of hard work and practice will get a maker a lot closer to success than any talent they may have at the start.

This is the first knife I made back in 1963. I must have ground on that piece of steel for 15 hours. The grinding wheel was cheap and I didn't know how to dress it. The 1998 version of the grinder had a state-of-the-art Norton ceramic grit wheel and things went much faster. The wheel was worn out on a saw sharpening machine and just the right diameter for the washing machine motor grinder.

The only knifemakers I was acquainted with learned most of what they knew from me. They figured out some new and different ways to do things and I would usually try their methods if it looked like a better way of doing it. I had very little money to purchase equipment and I wouldn't have known what to get anyway. I made knives the only way I could figure out how to get the job done. This type of beginning may not be the best way to get started but I've never regretted it. I've always been thankful for all the things I learned by doing it the hard way. I learned to solve problems on my own, and that included how to make most of my own equipment. My primitive beginning makes me very grateful for all the tools I have to work with today.

At this writing, I've been in my present location for 29 years. When we moved in, all of my equipment fit neatly on a 4-foot square, homemade table that I bought at a thrift store. I had a grinding wheel mounted on a ball bearing arbor for roughing the blades in. I smoothed up the marks from the grinder with a disk sanding attachment on an electric drill. A washing machine motor turned my buffing wheel. A second electric drill mounted in a drill press adapter furnished a crude but workable method to drill holes. Everything else was done with a small vise, a coping saw, a carpenter's wood saw, metal cutting hacksaw, files, sandpaper and sharpening stones. That was 1970 and I had made several hundred knives by then. A few of those early knives are in my collection, and they aren't too bad if you consider the tools I had to work with. I first started using a belt grinder in 1972, and it was one I made out of junk parts. It didn't work very well but it was a big improvement over the sanding attachment on the electric drill.

PITFALLS FOR THE KNIFEMAKER

It isn't enough to have some good designs, use the best materials and to know how to make a good knife. It does not depend on having a specific type or brand of belt grinder. In addition to the physical skills, it takes a certain amount of business skills to succeed as a knifemaker. Some of these are only learned by trial and error and with the passage of time.

There are a number of pitfalls for the new or experienced maker. The knifemaker who eliminates the most pitfalls will have the best chance to be successful. I made some of these mistakes myself, therefore I write from firsthand knowledge. Some of the most common pitfalls and some possible solutions are as follows:

1. An unrealistic shop rate. In my opinion the overhead on a one-man operation is such that the shop rate needs to be higher than that of most job shops that employ many workers. The knifemaker working alone is the Head Janitor, Maintenance Foreman, Production Manager, Bookkeeper, Delivery Person, and in the spare time he or she makes knives. (Some days that's the way it seems.) In 26 years as a full-time maker, I doubt that I average five hours a day, of hands-on time making knives. The rest of the day is taken up with other necessary duties. That means that the value of a knife made in one day will have to equal the hourly wage you expect, plus pay all expenses necessary to keep the business going. That is how a shop rate is calculated and it's a necessary thing to have figured out if there is to be money coming in equal to the wages plus expenses.

   When I look at knives made by a maker that I am unfamiliar with, I can usually tell from the prices if the maker does it as a part-time job. The knives will usually be priced for less than they could afford to if they were doing it for their sole support.

   I have rarely over-estimated the time and materials necessary to complete the one-of-a-kind custom knife. I have adopted the policy of telling the customer that it will be no less, but no more than so many dollars. This is the only way I have been consistently able to be profitable on the custom, one-of-a-kind orders.

2. Do not take things in trade for knives that have to be made in the future. This can be worse than abusing a credit card. Play it safe if you make trades, only do it for knives that you already have finished. This will keep you from getting in the deep hole that I've seen more than one maker get into.

3. Don't try to work beyond your skill level. There have been times when I could not deliver knives on time because I got talked into trying a project that was beyond my skill level. When a knife project goes bad it is hard on one's nerves and one's patience. If you have a deposit on the project it puts on extra pressure that isn't needed.

4. Taking deposits. General advice; don't do it unless you are very careful. I quit taking deposits with new orders 15 years ago and it was one of the best things I ever did.

   Most of my orders are for Damascus knives and I handle it is this way. When I have the blade welded up, heat treated and tested I ask for 50 percent of the total. I then finish the knife, expecting the balance about the time it is completed. This system is working pretty well.

5. Promising out more work than can be actually done. This comes from getting publicity, which often brings in more work than can be reasonably scheduled. There is a certain amount of security in having a backlog of orders, but the down side is the added responsibility to manage a delivery schedule, and manage any money taken in as deposits.

6. Lack of business training. Most of us knife-makers, if we knew anything about business at the start of our knifemaking careers, would probably have gone into some other line of work. I can speak for myself that I started out without any real plan other than to make the knives. I had made knives on a part-time basis from 1963 to 1973 and by then my wife Phyllis and I both felt that the thing to do was give full-time knifemaking a try. We had her income from a full-time job to fall back on while the knife business got going, and we needed it.

My plan was to make knives and not much thought was put into any other aspect of enter-ing the new business. The knives that were inside of me were trying to get out, and mak-ing them was the only way to relieve the prob-lem. From the business standpoint, that may not be the best reason to start an enterprise. From the practical application standpoint it is a good reason. The headaches that come with the bookkeeping end of the business were far from my mind.

Success will come quick and easy for only a few. To most others, including myself, it means working long hours with not much pay. I read this somewhere, "No one ever mastered anything in 40 hours a week". When it comes to knifemaking, I would agree. The desire to create the things we call knives is what kept me going even when my ego and pocket book were as flat as they could be. I am a knife-maker because there is nothing else that I wanted to do for the last 36 years. This is the best reason I have for what I do.

SOME GOOD REASONS WHY MAKERS SHOULD ATTEND KNIFE SHOWS

Months of anticipation, burning the midnight oil and then wondering if I was doing the right thing were over. Phyllis and I were finally on our way to our first knife show. It was the summer of 1972 and it was a long drive to Kansas City but the '67 T-Bird ran smooth and fast.

The Knifemakers Guild was having it's show in conjunction with the Missouri Valley Gun Collectors Association. It was the first time the Guild had a separate room exclusively for its show. The Guild was to have a business meeting before the show to decide on the rules for admission into the Guild. I was more than a little nervous wondering if they would let me in, but they did. That was as a proba-tionary member, I went back in 1974 and was accepted as a voting member.

That show in 1972 was small by today's stan-dards, but all the big names of the period were there. There were approximately 40 tables and before the show was over I was acquainted with almost everybody. My records show that we sold three knives for a total of $150. That's not much when compared to sales at the shows today, but it

brings me to the first, and what I think is the most important reason for the new maker to go to shows.

Reason #1. The contacts that you make at a show will almost always be worth far more than the dollars you get for your knives. The knife world will not know what you are doing if you stay at home. For example, at that 1972 Guild show some of the people I met were Sid Latham, and Butch and Rita Winter. Sid was working on an article on hunting axes for *Field & Stream*. I was one of half a dozen makers who had hunting axes at the show, therefore I was included in the article which came out in the May 1974 *Field & Stream*. I had gone full-time in May of 1973 and by the time the article on hunting axes came out my backlog was running around two to three months. My backlog was out to two years by the time all the orders came in from the hundreds of letters that we answered from the ax article. You heard it right, two years work from one article! Sid also included me in his book; *Knives And Knifemak-ers*, Winchester Press, 1973. That book seems to be in most large libraries and I still get calls every year from people who read it and have no other exposure to hand-made knives.

Having fun after dinner at a *BLADE* Super Show in Atlanta. Left to right: Barry Gallagher, Ed Schempp, Mike Draper, Josh Smith, Lisa Smith, Phyllis and Wayne Goddard, Wade Colter and Rick Dunkerley. History was made twice that day. Josh became the youngest and Audra Draper was the first lady to gain Journeyman Smith status in the American Blade-smith Society. Photo by Audra Draper.

One of the knives we sold was a Nessmuk-style hunting knife, which Butch and Rita Winter added to their collection of Guild Member Knives. That knife was photographed and appeared in the Bates and Schippers book, *The Custom Knife*, 1973. I said all that to make my point that even though that show in 1972 was not a success from the financial standpoint, the long-term benefits of the exposure from the articles and books was very valuable.

Reason #2 . To gain and maintain a proper per-spective as to where you and the rest of the trade are. Before the 1972 Guild Show I had seen very little of the best work that was being done at that time. It was all there. By the time the show was over I knew exactly what I needed to do to improve my knives. I also was starting to get a clear picture of a specialty that I wanted to peruse. The tips and techniques I gained from the makers there were well worth the cost of the trip. You should remember that at that time there were no magazines or books telling how it was done. In the early 1970s, if you were going to learn new "stuff" you either had to work it out yourself or find a maker to show you. My desire to teach and share comes out of those early years. I will forever be grateful to Bob Loveless, Lloyd Hale, Gil Hibben, Corbet Sigman and Bob Ogg who were the source of my inspiration and, at the same time, totally unselfish and free with information.

Reason #3. The variety of customers that you acquire will give you a broad base for your business. The day when a maker could stay home and do enough advertising to keep busy may be over. My personal observations seem to show that the most

My version of a photo of the Eiffel Tower.

successful makers combine sales from advertising and shows to gain the broad base necessary to keep busy.

Reason #4. It allows you a market for "show" or "Art" type knives that would not sell in your hometown. I get to do what I want when getting ready for a show, which is usually more fun than working to strict instructions. The knives that I make for a show are made as if I was making them for myself; and as such, they are more of a true expression of my art than turning out standard models. That one peculiar design that had been festering in my mind for some time now has a chance to come out and be a reality. Most knives shows have some type of competition for knifemakers, and I take it seriously. Working on a knife for a competition allows me to do my best work, and not worry about whether the knife will sell or not. The quality of the fit and finish becomes the motivation for the work. I do my best work when it becomes a labor of love and all thought of money is aside.

Reason #5. You get to see the country. Phyllis and I were talking one day about our knife business and she mentioned that we had gotten to see a lot of cities and much of our great country, just from going to knife shows. We cherish our memories of New York City, Orlando, Dallas, Kansas City, Atlanta, Los Angeles, San Francisco, Knoxville and Paris.

Reason #6. Selling knives is the lowest priority on my list of reasons. We all want to sell knives at the shows, but it sometimes takes a few shows or years for a maker to figure out what sells and what does not. Instant success is not possible for most of us. Do not give up after a few shows, those who are successful never gave up on their ideas and dreams.

One final thing: It's not a reason for going to shows, but a secret that I am willing to share to help you have a successful show. Lay out a good variety in styles, sizes and price ranges. I have never gone to a show where I thought I had all my bases covered in this area. Sales are always better when we have a good variety. If you have a whole table full of hunting knives, there will be nothing for the buyer of miniatures, axes, Bowies, fighters, camp knives, folders and etc.

Update: I wrote this article before the Internet was established as a great way to do business. In Reason #3 I stated that I believed it was necessary to combine advertising with shows to keep busy on a full time basis. I want to modify that statement by saying it may be possible to keep busy full time with only a web page.

I've had a web page for two years and it has been successful even though I usually don't have very many knives in stock. I'll be giving the Internet more of a test in the future. I'll be cutting back on the number of shows attended and hopefully get some stock built up to advertise on the web page. If I get an excess of knives on hand that don't sell from the web page I can always find some knife shows to attend.

DEVELOPING A
UNIQUE STYLE

Bruce Bump of Walla Walla, Washington writes:

If you had your knifemaking career to do over, would you make your own style of knife or the customer's style? I know that you're doing your own thing now but would your knives have sold back when you were as unknown as I am?

Answer: Part of developing a style of your own would be to have good designs. I might as well express some opinions on that subject while I'm at it.

I decided to see what Webster's New Collegiate Dictionary had to say about style. I had to get down to the fourth definition before it applied to your question: "distinctive or characteristic mode of presentation, construction, or execution in any art, employment or product, especially in any fine art; also quality which gives distinctive character and excellence to artistic expression." I like that definition; that Webster fellow had a real smooth way with words.

From the time I made my first knives in 1963, I always made some based on customer designs as well as doing my own ideas. It was easy to sell knives back then because everything I made seemed to look good to my customers. Hardly anyone I knew had ever seen a handmade knife or one that was well-designed.

I got to see a lot of well-made and beautifully designed knives at my first Knifemakers' Guild Show in 1972. I came home from there and got serious on my workmanship and designs. I made a lot of headway during my two-year probationary period. By 1974, when I got my voting status, I'd begun to have a style of my own. I didn't know it at the time but I can see how my style developed when I look at my old photo books. Learning which shapes and curves would work together on a knife was the bonus that came with developing a style of my own.

My style didn't develop much until I went into knifemaking full-time and started making a lot of knives. It's hard to explain the evolution of my patterns but it went something like this: I'd make one or more of a pattern and usually nothing seemed like it needed changing. A time would always come when I would look at a pattern or a finished knife and some part of it would look too fat, too thin, too curved or too straight. I'd make a change, usually going too far. As I progressed, my changes that would've been in fractions of an inch changed to the width of a pencil line. I can't explain the way I decided what needed changing other than it just didn't look right.

Making knives to a customer's drawing was a valuable experience because it helped me learn what a good design was. Most of the customer ideas weren't too efficient when it came to what a working knife should be. Some of the customers figured that out by themselves and came back for a design that would work.

It was the occasional good design from which I learned the most. All of this was a very important part of my development as a designer. When I got to the

The knife at the top shows an example of unique style in a folding knife. I originated the use of wood or Micarta® for bolsters on crown folders back in 1981. The beautiful knife below it is an excellent example of good design. Patrice Plasky of France sent me a drawing of the knife and I made it for him. The knife had curves I had never thought of putting on a knife. They're all in the right place to give the design a nice, flowing appearance. Every part of the handle shape has a function in allowing a firm grip in any position. The construction was integral bolster, wire damascus with a full-taper tang with ivory handle slabs. Making it was a giant step in my development as a knifemaker. I'll never forget all those curves and still sneak some of them into my own designs. Thanks, Patrice.

point where I had confidence in my designs, I would often talk a customer out of his impractical idea in favor of one of mine that I knew would work.

When it came to handle thickness, length, shape and such, it seemed that I had to make a certain amount of knives that didn't work to figure out what did work. When I made a knife that didn't feel or look appropriate, it meant I wouldn't make another one like it. There's a lot to be said for using one's own knives to do some real work.

I see many knives being sold as hunting pieces that have square corners on a too-thin handle. Blades are often too wide or too thick and of a clumsy shape. I hope you believe me when I say that most such knives wouldn't be made the way they are if the maker had actually ever done any work with them. Part of my style is to round everything off real well, and I suppose I do that because I remember the blisters I got using one of my knives that had a thin handle with square corners.

Your life experience, background and motivation will influence the style you develop. These factors will determine if you make real or make-believe knives. I define a make-believe knife as one that's designed on paper and made without any evolution as a working tool. My opinion is that most lasting designs evolve and aren't necessarily the result of an original idea.

I realize that probably 90 percent of handmade knives will never see much use for serious work. You may be able to make a good living turning out knives that are all fangs, claws, reptile parts and buggy eyeballs. There's a market for that and you'll not need to worry about the knife holding an edge, being balanced or having proper edge geometry.

You might consider what the market share is for different types of knives. I went through the November '98 Blade magazine and classified every knife shown into one of six categories. The following figures show what type knives are being featured in articles and advertisements, but may not be a true indication of what is actually being sold: tactical (folder and fixed)-108; sport/hunting (folder and fixed)-31; elegant folding knives-30; traditional (folder and fixed)-29; Bowies-22; and art/daggers-16.

I keep a loose-leaf notebook titled, "The Good, Bad and Ugly." In it is a collection of photographs and also pictures from magazines and catalogs. It's my textbook for teaching design. A picture is worth a thousand words and, with examples, it's easy to point out distinctive styles as well as effective and ineffective designs. It would be good for you to start a book that contains your drawings and ideas. Stick any pictures of knives you like in it and then spend time trying to figure out why you like them. Keep the ugly knives in it too, just so you'll remember not to make them. Good luck with developing your unique style.

SAFETY IN THE KNIFE SHOP

Eye protection is of the utmost importance. We can get by without fingers and other body parts, but the miracle of vision would be a bit more difficult to do without. Safety glasses should be worn at all times in the knife shop. A full-face shield should be worn for drilling and grinding operations. Don't forget about the smithy. The forge fire puts out harmful rays that are stopped by the proper lens or shield. I wear a facemask when forge welding, it has a Jackson #8042 DK GR 040 shield in it. I've cut off the bottom part so I can see to forge without lifting it up. Only the top part is necessary for looking into the forge.

I see a lot of makers working with facemasks or safety glasses on but no hat. A soft brim hat that comes well down over the top of the glasses stops the stuff that comes over the top of the face shield. Don't forget to brush or vacuum yourself off after grinding and keep your fingers out of your eyes. If you get a piece of grinding grit in your eye you can sometimes tickle it out by gently working the opposite eye (eyes closed of course). The eyes are programmed to work together and the movement of the fingertip on the unaffected eye will often work the grit out of the affected one.

Someone suggested using a magnet for removing metal slivers from the human eye. Before you do that, look at the metal stuff under your grinder with a strong magnifying glass or 40X Radio Shack microscope. You'll find metal chips that look like microscopic screws, fish hooks and whale harpoons. The ones shaped like that should be extricated very carefully by a professional. If you have someone to help you and they determine it's a straight little sliver of steel the magnet might just work. I said it might work, but I'm not recommending it! Even if the sliver comes out there is still the danger of infection. A spark is a white-hot chip of steel. More often than not they stick to the surface of the eye. Grit from a belt or wheel is easier to deal with.

In 36 years of making knives, and 10 years in saw manufacturing and tool grinding I've only had to have one piece of metal taken out of my eye. I'll credit the stupid looking soft brim hats I've always worn while grinding. (See photo.) In that instance, I thought I was well protected while I was gumming a huge circle saw. We made a headgear that looked like something you would wear in the desert. It was a full face-shield with about six layers of shop towels wired and duct-taped over the top and down the back. The machine had a 2-horsepower motor turning a 1-inch by 14-inch wheel and I was throwing sparks for 20 feet in all directions. I saw an orange speck coming and I was so interested in watching the spark that I didn't close my eyes. After bouncing it's way through the inside top of the face shield it hit the inside of my safety glasses and made one more bounce right into my eye where it welded itself in place. The doctor had to deaden my eye and pry the metal particle off the surface. Not fun! The spark had gotten in through a hole that had burned through the top of my "lid." If I had worn my floppy hat under the hood I would have saved myself that trip to the doctor.

Beware of the Sharp Things

The things we make are made to cut and sometimes they cut us. It was a cold winter day back in

Proper attire for looking into the mouth of the "Dragon". A floppy hat, colored facemask, welders gloves and a leather apron. Photo by Gene Martin.

1974. My double garage was my shop and the garage door didn't keep out much of the winter air. I was finishing the last of an order for four miniature knives. There were three Bowie style knives and the fourth was an Arkansas toothpick with a blade of around 2-1/2 inches. The blade had straight edges right down to the needle-like point. I had wrapped the blade with a layer of paper towel and masking tape while I did the detail work on the lugged guard and pommel cap. After finishing the handle details I unwrapped the blade and proceeded to wipe the whole knife clean. I became aware of something on the floor between my feet and when I looked down I realized it was a small puddle of blood. Seeing blood when there is no one else around is always quite a shock to my nervous system. It had to be mine so I first looked at my front side and didn't see any blood coming out of anything there. I then looked at my hands and saw that my left index finger was cut to the bone on the side next to my thumb. The cut was just about even with the first joint and was putting out a lot of blood so I put pressure on it with my fat little thumb. I laid down the miniature, which was still in my right hand and headed for the house to put myself back together.

I washed up real good with Army surplus surgical soap and put a nice-looking gauze bandage on it and enough tape so that I wouldn't be tempted to bend it. I healed up just fine and to this day that is the worst cut I've gotten from knifemaking. I hadn't made any effort to sharpen the blade that cut me. It got that sharp just from buffing out the thin blade. I'm not just sure how I did it but the little blade was sharp as a razor. It made it's cut and I didn't even feel it. After that I got in the habit of dulling any knife that got sharp as I was working on it. I keep a small flat on the edge until the very last thing. I then set up the sharpening angle with a fine belt.

If I am going to work on the handle of a knife that has been sharpened I make a protector "boot" for the blade. First, the blade is wrapped with toilet paper and then a couple layers of masking tape. The paper layer keeps the sticky goop from the tape from getting all over the blade. I then put several additional layers of tape along the edge. When the protector boot is put on right it can be taken off and put back on. Be careful not to get grit in under the paper and then close the vise jaws on it.

The Most Dangerous Machine in the Knife Shop

The buffer gets my vote because it has the habit of grabbing a blade and throwing it right back at the person who stuck it at the wheel. Buffer safety starts with the way it is mounted to the bench. In my opinion it is not safe to have a buffer sitting directly on a table or bench. The buffer base should be set on a board that is out from the bench. The reason is that anything that is tossed down by the inertia of the wheel can bounce back and then be propelled by the wheel in the direction of the opera-

tor. Several layers of carpet or one of rubber conveyor belting on the floor under the buffer will protect any object propelled down by the wheel. It will also keep blades from bouncing up the way they do after they hit cement. I was holding a folding knife blade with my bare fingers to buff off the wax used in the logo etching process. The blade was caught by the wheel, made the trip to the cement floor, bounced up directly into the face of the wheel. The blade was again propelled to the cement, however, this time it bounced up and the point stuck in my fat little finger. It was then that I decided it was more intelligent to hold the blade with ViseGrip® pliers.

I run stitched buffs that start out 10 inches in diameter at 1,750 rpm. Turning the wheel at 3,400 rpm will do the job faster but the added danger is not worth it for me. I'll run a 6-inch wheel at 3,400 but nothing larger. The reason for using the stitched buffs is that they aren't as grabby as loose buffs. I keep about the last two rows of stitches cut so that the surface is not so hard. There are times when a hard face is desirable but most of the time a softer edge is better for getting in corners where the guard meets the blade.

I dress my wheels at an angle because it makes it easier to get the corner of the wheel into tight places. (See drawing.) It also allows more "reach" with longer work pieces. Before mounting, a new wheel has the corner cut off with a huge pair of scissors that were made to cut carpet. Once mounted the wheel is dressed with a rake made by driving nails through a piece of plywood. The scissors will then be used to smooth it up.

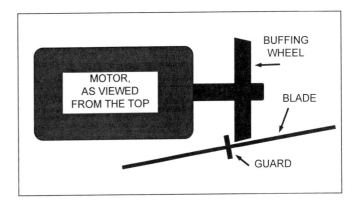

Knives with a double guard are probably the most dangerous to buff. My habit is to have everything finished prior to attaching the guard and that eliminates serious buffing after assembly. A friend who I taught to make knives got in a hurry and mounted his buffer directly on a bench. A dagger got caught by the guard, bounced off the table back into the wheel, was propelled around and directly through the palm of his hand. The cool thing was he had a helper take a photo of the mess before pulling it out. It took $3,000 in medical bills and several months recovery time before he was back to work. (That $3,000 was at mid-1970s prices.)

The buffer should have a guard over it. Even if nothing is ever propelled around the wheel and into your face it is nice to have the fluff and excess compound going down to the floor instead of in your face. My guards are made out of plywood, glued and screwed together. My theory is that a knife blade propelled around the wheel might stick into the wood before it gets to me. A lip at the front of the guard can be adjustable so that it can be lowered when the wheel gets worn down.

Safety with Saws

I've always been uneasy around table saws, probably because I don't use one enough to have confidence in what I'm doing. I know of several serious hand injuries that occurred when a table saw was being used to rough out handle slabs. One injury happened when a board split and kicked the sharp part back into the hand of the operator. Another injury happened from just getting the hand into the blade. I recently had the opportunity to spend a month around some reconstructive plastic surgeons and queried them about shop tools. Every one said the saws were the most dangerous shop tools. At the time there were three men in that ward who had one or more fingers reattached. The most injuries were from the hand-held circular saws, next were table saws and last were the radial arm saws.

Band saws don't seem to account for too many serious injuries. I have seen damage to the arm of an individual who was running one without a guard; somehow he got his left arm in the return side of the saw. Split fingers are the usual result of not using push tools. Simple pushing tools will eliminate most risk. Always keep the top guide, which should have a guard on the front of it, right down close to the top of the work. Cutting round material is risky because the blade will spin the part. I've come close to having my fingers pulled into the blade when this happened. A solution for this is to clamp the round section into a "V" block arrangement so that it can be safely cut.

Electricity

All equipment should be properly grounded and the wiring should be checked for ground faults with a detector. A periodic check of all power cords is essential. Always be sure that a moving part of a machine is not contacting the power cord. Keep power cords off of the floor, especially under the buffer and workbench. More than one knife blade was damaged when it was dropped on a power cord and subsequently shorted the power while burning a hole in the blade.

Drill Press

The first hole drilled by the novice drill press operator will usually result in a broken or chipped drill bit. It takes a certain amount of pressure to make a drill bit cut, but if that pressure is not decreased when the drill is about to break through the underside of the steel it will either grab the steel or break the bit. The trick is to learn to listen and feel for the moment to slack off on the pressure so the drill will not bind up as it breaks through the underside. The most common injury from the drill press is caused when the drill bit grabs a blade or handle slab and causes it to spin. See the drawing for a simple clamp arrangement to keep a blade or handle slab from spinning. Micarta and brass are especially prone to grab a drill bit. Grinding or honing the rake angle of the cutting flute to make it closer to zero will keep the drill from grabbing when it breaks through the underside of the material being drilled.

Grinder

Abrasive grinding wheels present a different type of danger in that they can break if misused. Guards need to be in place and tool rests kept adjusted close to the wheel. When there is excess space between the tool rest and the face of the wheel it becomes a hazard because the fingers can be caught and pulled in by the inertia of the wheel. Disk and belt grinder tool rests present the same danger and need to be kept in adjustment up close to the disk or belt.

A belt grinder set up for hollow grinding presents a different danger. The area where the belt meets the top edge of the wheel can catch the point of a knife or the guard and propel the knife into the body of the operator. When a blade catches between the belt and contact wheel it will usually make one complete revolution and often catches the hand that was holding the work.

Sharp new belts are safer than dull belts. A sharp belt will do more damage in a given amount of time but control of the work piece is important. Dull belts take so much pressure that little control is possible. I've stuck fingers or knuckles into a dull belt far more often than I have with a sharp one. Be aware of the edge of the belt, the coarse belts act just like a band saw blade, fine belts act like a knife. When the splice on a belt becomes loose it can catch the blade and propel it towards soft body parts. Stop the machine and inspect any belt the very moment it makes any strange noises. It's not too bad to get slapped around by a fine-grit belt, but a coarse, heavy belt is another thing.

First Aid Kit

I keep a few bandages and a tourniquet in the shop. The tourniquet is out of an industrial first aid kit and can be applied with one hand. I hope I don't ever need it but it's ready to go just in case. The macho thing is to keep working with a dirty rag wrapped around a cut finger. My advice is to stop what you are doing and take care of the cut, no matter how small. The worst infection I ever got was from a small cut that I put a Band-Aid on without cleaning it up. My habit was to apply masking tape over the Band-Aid if it got loose. I often would not check under the "dressing" for half a day or more. That time I had trapped alien bacteria under the dressing and before I was done I had to get some antibiotics to clear it up. After that experience I treat even the smallest cut with respect. I want to wash a cut up real good before applying a dressing. I'm lucky enough that I've never had to be stitched up from a knife cut. It is also good to keep current on tetanus shots.

Safety with Work Knives

I had a leatherwork knife I made that had a round section of elk antler for a handle. I was using it to cut the stitches on a new buffing wheel one day. I laid it on the bench so I could pull the loose strings out of the wheel. It rolled off, and stuck into my running shoe and nearly severed the little toe on my right foot. As soon as I got the bleeding stopped I took the round handle and ground it rectangular. It just never dawned on me that a knife with a round handle was dangerous because it could roll off of a table or bench and stick in my foot.

Air

The stuff we grind on isn't going to do our lungs any good, so it's a good idea to either wear a real good respirator or rely on a good suction system to keep the air clean. If you use a shop vacuum it should vent to the outside, otherwise it will recycle the smallest particles. I've got a primitive "clean air" system. A 12-inch diameter exhaust fan is built into the wall directly behind the belt grinder on which I do all my roughing. It pulls out 90 percent of the dust created and blows it out on my scrap pile. A bucket of water under the belt catches anything that goes down and the fan gets most of the rest. Another "breeze box" fan is mounted in the same wall and between the two of them the air in my shop stays nice and fresh. The Willamette Valley of Oregon has a mild climate and the front or back door of my shop will be open most any day of the year. If it weren't for the open doors and fans I would surely need a vacuum-type system. I do have two shop-type vacuums that I use when grinding micarta and wood like cocobolo. I'm set up for wet grinding on pearl and micarta and that is nice because no dust is made, just the mess from the splash.

Safety in the Smithy

I was having a conversation with Jim Fagan at the ABS School in Arkansas. Suddenly he slaps the side of his neck and says, "Something bit me!" Blood was trickling from between his fingers so I took a look and found a crescent-shaped cut. Realizing that he had been hit by a flying piece of metal, I had all the students stop work and gather up all the

hammers from the shop. Inspection of the hammers found one that was missing a piece that exactly fit the shape in Jim's neck. Inspection of the anvil that the hammer was being used on showed three or four dents where the hammer had missed the blade being forged. The hard face of the hammer meeting the harder face of the anvil had raised a spall and finally it was propelled off into space to find a new home. We fixed all the hammers and anvil edges that were spalled, which eliminated half a dozen accidents waiting to happen. Chisels, hot cuts and any tool that is struck by a hammer should be checked for spalls and if any are found the whole surface should be removed by grinding.

Knives and Vises

Leaving a knife in vise is asking for trouble. Always take the knife out when not working on it. When working on the handle always use a protective "boot" on the blade. Cardboard or just layers of paper towel, napkin or toilet paper with masking tape over the top works just fine. When you have to work on a blade it is best to make a board to support it. The point of the blade is kept back a little bit from the end. If you tangle with a blade supported in that manner the damage will be far less.

Safety with Gas

About 20 years ago I was torch-cutting some big saw blades into blade blanks. All of a sudden there was quite a loud explosion. It was at my left side where the acetylene bottle was sitting. I quickly turned off both bottles and grabbed the fire extinguisher but there was no fire. I checked all the gas and oxygen fittings with soapy water and found no leaks. Then I began to think that perhaps the hot slag had ignited either a loose firecracker, primer or .22 cartridge, any or all of which could have found their way to the back of my shop. After thoroughly cleaning the floor and checking all fittings for the second time, I went back to cutting. It was about three minutes later when the same explosion happened again. This time I was at a little different angle and thought I could see the acetylene bottle rise up 2 inches and set back down. I've never had my heart jump-started but this must have come close. This time the regulator was removed and the bottle taken outside and set on its side where I determined that it was leaking at one of the plugs in the bottom. Every since then I look over every new bottle real well.

I had the oxygen/acetylene outfit inside the shop at that time. I checked with my insurance agent and he said if I had burned my place down, my fire insurance wouldn't have covered it. I moved the oxygen/acetylene outfit out back and got my insurance agent to look over my shop. He didn't see anything he didn't like. My homeowner's plan would not have covered all of my shop equipment so he sold me some extra insurance to cover it all.

When I built my first propane furnaces I checked every safety source I could find. I had the natural gas company come out and survey what needed to be done to use natural gas for the forges. I have a gas forced-air furnace and water heater and a fairly new meter. They explained that I would need hard plumbing to within six feet of the furnaces and a shut-off valve. I'm still burning propane because I will have to move 4,000 pounds of steel in order to have the plumbing done. That's one project I'm not looking forward to.

Final Words on Safety

The results of an accident survey in a woodworking magazine were very interesting. In almost every instance of serious injury there was a few seconds before the accident when the individual was aware that a chance was being taken and that they could be injured. They made the choice to continue and the results were an injury. Chances are not worth taking, so stop and think of a safe way to do the job. Stop and think through any new process and always ask for advice from those with experience.

Chapter 2

THE MYSTERY AND MAGIC OF STEEL

We can only speculate as to how ancient man first made iron, and then how, from the iron, he formed knives and tools. The methods used are understood today because many ancient iron-making furnaces have been excavated; a few of which had the "bloom" intact. The bloom is the end product of reducing the ore by use of fire. The bloom is also called sponge iron because of its resemblance to a natural sponge.

According to Genesis, 4:22, Tubal Cain was "an instructor of every artificer in brass and iron." This means that mankind has been working iron for about 6,000 years. An iron blade, probably 5,000 years old, was found in one of the pyramids of Egypt. I read somewhere that the Earth's crust is 7 percent iron. There are places where you can pick up relatively pure iron ore off the ground. Iron meteorites were also used by early ironworkers.

Sometimes the iron is in the form of black sand, which was a favorite source of iron for the sword-makers of Japan. Once the iron ore or black sand was collected, charcoal for fuel and a source of air was all that was needed.

Bellows made from animal skins are quite ancient. The Oriental method was to use an air pump, either round or square. Both methods would supply enough air to heat the charcoal fire to a temperature sufficient to reduce the ore into an impure form of iron. The earliest smelters may have been simple pits in the ground with clay tubes for the air supply. Later the smelters evolved into larger-capacity furnaces made of earth and clay.

The cross-section drawing (see illustration) gives a general idea of the type of furnace that was built of earth and which had a clay liner. The furnace would first be fired with charcoal to warm it up and then alternating layers of charcoal and ore were laid up and burned out. After several hours, smelting was complete. Some sources say the earliest furnaces were not tapped but that the bloom would be removed after it had cooled down. In some cases this meant tearing down the furnace. The bloom was a porous, metallic mass that was primarily iron but with some parts containing carbon in varying amounts.

I have a video of contemporary African steel makers that shows this process. The furnace was built into a hillside. In the most primitive operations the bloom was forged out at a temperature that we would call a welding heat. They used a large rock for an anvil, and another rock swung by a strong man was the power hammer that forged the bloom into a rough bar. The rough bar would be forged out, folded and forged enough times at the welding heat to solidify and homogenize the iron. The narrator on the video said that this method has been in use for at least the last 1,700 years. A later development consisted of breaking up the bloom and sorting the pieces according to the apparent grain size or hardness, then using the different parts for varying things. The process we know as pattern welding may have started when it was discovered that some of the layers created in the folding process were of a different appearance than the others. This would have been the result of welding together bars made out of material from different parts of the bloom.

The charcoal or coal fire can be reducing, oxidizing or neutral. The oxidizing fire has an excess of oxygen; this type fire will cause the surface of the steel to form scale and gradually be consumed. When there is an excess of carbon, iron has the capacity to absorb it at the right temperature. When iron absorbs enough carbon to cause it to harden, it becomes known as steel. The folding and welding process in the right type of fire would have given the iron enough carbon to become steel. This is probably what led the ancients to figure out how to make steel from iron.

Only in the last several hundred years has it been discovered that it was carbon alloying with iron that would cause it to harden when quenched into water from a "cherry red" heat. Along the way it was discovered that iron could be "steeled"; this we call carburizing. When iron is heated with different organic materials containing carbon such as horn or hoof trimmings, leather filings, charcoal or leaves it absorbs carbon and becomes steel. Over a number of hours the iron absorbs the carbon that remains as the organic material burns up. This led to the making of blister steel, shear steel and cast steel.

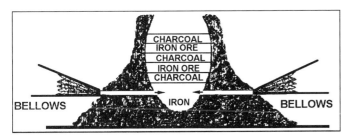

Cross-section view of a primitive iron-making furnace.

Somewhere in history it was discovered that some forms of iron were harder than others. It was only a matter of time before it was possible to narrow the variables and produce blades that had comparatively good edge-holding ability.

The ancient method of "steeling" an iron bar left it with an outer shell that would harden in water, yet the core could have been anywhere from soft to springy. Carburizing would be the modern terminology for steeling. During the process of forge-welding small bars of steeled iron together to make a larger bar, the material was refined and the carbon was diffused more equally through the bar. Welding together bars of dissimilar carbon content most likely led to the discovery of the layered look that appears after etching, and the eventual development of pattern-welded steel. Blister steel was a later development where iron was carburized in large quantities. The surface of the carburized bars formed blisters during the process, thus the name. Blister steel was used for some tools; however, a higher grade of material was made as follows:

Blister steel bars would be stacked, forge-welded together, drawn out, sheared into smaller pieces, restacked and forge-welded once more. The finished product of this process was called shear steel. When the shearing, restacking and forge-welding was repeated, it was called double shear steel. When forged, finished out and etched, old shear steel saw blades make beautiful knives. The pattern is a subdued layer look with a few surprise squiggles, and a very clear and sharp temper line. (See photos)

Sheffield owes its fame as a steel-making center to Benjamin Huntsman, a clockmaker from Dorchester, England. In 1740 he was searching for better quality steel for his springs and pendulums. He discovered that shear steel, when melted in a crucible and cast into ingots, made steel that was much more uniform in composition than blister steel or shear steel. Steel made by the new process was called crucible or cast steel. Another type of crucible steel was made by melting wrought iron with charcoal and fluxes. The modern version of Wootz steel is made by melting in a crucible a pure form of iron and a suitable source of carbon. (See photo of cast Wootz cakes made by the "Wizard of Wootz," Al Pendray.)

Wootz cakes and billets made by Al Pendray. The cake at the right has been cut in half to show the crystalline structure.

Top and bottom show two examples of markings on Sheffield knives. The center is from a hatchet.

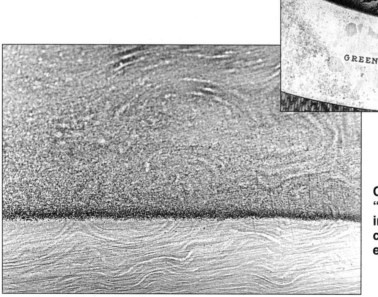

Close-up view of a blade that shows the "damascus" pattern caused by the layering that is a result of the shear steel process. The band at the bottom is the hard edge portion of the edge-quenched blade.

It is interesting to note that the new material did not find acceptance by the Sheffield cutlers who claimed that it was hard to forge. After the French cutlers began to use it, their Sheffield counterparts began to realize its value as a blade material. Crucible cast steel was the highest quality material for knives in its day, but it would be no match for steel made with modern methods.

WHAT IS STEEL AND WHAT DO CERTAIN ELEMENTS ADD TO IT?

Steel in its simplest form consists of iron, carbon and manganese. Steels containing only these three alloying elements are known as carbon steels. When a particular steel type contains more than these three elements it is classed as an alloy steel or tool steel. Tool steels are special-purpose alloy steels and have their own classification system. Carbon and alloy steels are classed by a number designation system: 1084, 1095, 5160, 52100, etc. Tool steels have a letter prefix: A-2, D-2, W-l, 0-1, etc.

The most important alloying elements in carbon and carbon alloy steels used for knives are carbon, chromium and vanadium. All steels contain manganese (Mn). However, manganese is not considered effective as an alloy element until added in an amount over .40 percent. Manganese is in all steels because it is necessary to make the steel sound when first cast into the ingot. Manganese also makes the steel easier to hot roll or forge.

The effect of a specific alloying element on steel is rather complicated because of the ability of one alloy element to boost the value of the other alloy elements in the steel. The value of a particular element when used alone may be 5 and yet when combined with one or more elements may be 8 or more. The accompanying chart shows the common alloy elements used in knife steel and their effects on the steel.

Carbon (C) makes the steel hard. The more carbon steel has, the harder the steel (the hardness giving it the ability to hold an edge).

Chromium (Cr) is a strong carbide former and improves the steel's ability to be hardened. The hard carbides formed promote wear-resistance. When the chromium content is 13 percent or more, the steel can be classified as stainless.

Vanadium (V) is also a strong carbide former when found with chromium in 50100-B and 6150. The only real difference between W-l and W-2 (see the Steel Specification Chart) is the .20 percent vanadium added to W-2. After working with these two steels, I can verify the positive effect of a little vanadium in a steel type.

Practically all tool steels contain small percentages of silicon (Si), .10 to .30 percent and for much the same reasons that manganese is used. As an alloy element silicon is almost always used with manganese, molybdenum or chromium.

Nickel (Ni) increases the steel's toughness. It is found in L-6 (sometimes used for saws) and in amounts up to 2.75 percent in other saw steels. The strongest blades I have tested were made of saw steel, bearing witness to the usefulness of nickel as a toughening element.

Tungsten (W), the "W" stands for wolfram (an alternative name still used for tungsten). Tungsten increases wear-resistance somewhat in high-carbon steel when added to the extent of 1.50 percent. Four-percent tungsten in 1.30 percent carbon steel causes the steel to be so abrasive-resistant in the hardened state that it is very difficult to grind. When added in amounts of 12 to 20 percent with chromium or in an amount of 6 percent with molybdenum, tungsten gives the steel the property of red hardness. (These steels are known as high-speed steels.) The red hardness is important in cutting tools that have high operating speeds. The heat generated at these speeds would draw the hardness out of carbon steel cutting tools. Few makers work with high-speed steel because it is so expensive and difficult to work. High-speed steels make an excellent knife where cutting ability is important and strength is secondary.

The last alloy element we will consider is molybdenum (Mo). It imparts somewhat the same properties as chromium and tungsten. It gives the air-hardening steels, such as A-2 the ability to harden in air. In large amounts and in conjunction with chromium, it imparts secondary hardening characteristics to the 154-CM/ATS-34 family.

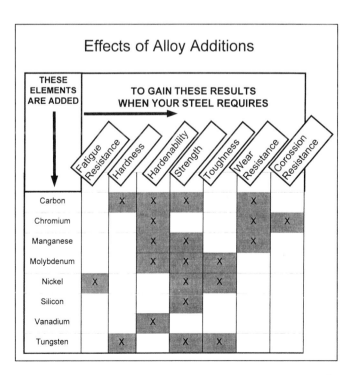

Effects of Alloy Additions

THESE ELEMENTS ARE ADDED	TO GAIN THESE RESULTS WHEN YOUR STEEL REQUIRES						
	Fatigue Resistance	Hardness	Hardenability	Strength	Toughness	Wear Resistance	Corrosion Resistance
Carbon		X	X	X		X	
Chromium			X			X	X
Manganese			X	X		X	
Molybdenum			X	X	X		
Nickel	X			X	X		
Silicon					X		
Vanadium			X				
Tungsten		X		X	X		

COMMON TOOL STEELS

	C	Mn	Si	Cr	Ni	Mo	Co	V	W
W-1	1.00	.35	.35	/	/	/	/	/	/
W-2	1.00	.35	.35	/	/	/	/	.20	/
W-4	1.10	.30	.50	/	/	/	.25	/	/
W-5	1.10	.30	.25	.60	/	/	/	/	/
W-7	1.00	.30	.30	/	/	/	.50	.20	/
O-1	.90	1.60	/	.50	/	/	/	/	.50
O-2	.90	1.60	/	/	/	.30	/	/	/
O-6	1.45	1.00	1.25	/	/	.25	/	/	/
O-7	1.25	.35	.35	.60	/	.20	/	/	1.75
A-2	1.0	/	/	5.00	/	1.00	/	/	/
D-2	1.50	.40	/	12.00	/	.80	/	.90	/
D-3	2.25	.35	.25	12.00	/	/	/	.20	/
D-5	1.40	.30	.60	13.00	.50	/	3.30	/	/
D-6	2.00	.80	.35	12.00	/	/	/	/	1.2
D-7	2.35	/	/	12.00	/	1.0	/	4.00	/
L-3	1.00	/	/	1.5	/	/	/	.20	/
L-6	.70	/	/	.75	1.50	.25	/	/	/

CARBON AND CARBON ALLOY STEELS

STEEL TYPE	Number	Example
Plain Carbon Steels	10XX	1095
Manganese Steels	13XX	1350
Nickel Steels	2XXX	2340
Nickel Chromium Steels	3XXX	3150
Molybdenum Steels	4XXX	4140
Chromium Steels Low Chromium Medium Chromium	5XXX 51XX 52XX	50100-B 5160 52100
Chromium Vanadium Steels	6XXX	6150
Silicon Manganese Steels	9XXX	9160

THE STEEL DETECTIVE

Your friend just handed you a piece of steel that someone gave him that was said to be "real good steel." He wants a knife made out of it. I don't mind looking at such a piece of material but I am reluctant to put much labor into making a blade out material that I don't know how to work. Mystery steel is usually not worth the time it takes to learn how to heat treat it unless there is not a lot of the material available at a very reasonable price. It is always best to use high quality, new steel.

The junkyards of the world contain many objects made of excellent steels for making knives. Some can be utilized for stock removal knifemaking but most will need to be forged to get them into a size suitable for knifemaking. Springs, ball bearings and races, saws, files and planer blades are the most common junkyard materials used for knives.

A simple quench-test that will determine whether a certain type of "found" steel will be suitable for knifemaking. Heat a piece of the steel up to non-magnetic and let it soak for half a minute or so and quench in water. Check it to see if it got hard by trying to break it with a hammer. Please wear gloves and eye protection while doing this. If it breaks like glass it is probably worth working up a couple of test blades to see if it tempers out all right.

POSSIBLE STEEL TYPES OF FOUND OBJECTS

(This collection of "possible" steel types has been gathered from many sources, over a long period of time. It should be considered for reference only.)

Axles, crankshafts 1045 or other alloy steels with .035-.060 carbon.

Harrow discs: 1080

Hay rake teeth: 1095

Transmission shafts: 4140

Ball Bearings: Most are 52100, but some are stainless steel and others are HSS.

Many roller bearings are 4815, (Low Carbon, nickel alloy, carburizing grade, they're hard on the outside, soft in the middle). The races will usually be made out of the same material as the rollers or balls. While most roller bearings and their races are case hardened, not all are. It's necessary to forge them out and then do a quench test to see if they get hard all the way through. Roller bearings and races that get full hard may be 52100.

Saws, band and circle, L-6 type, make the toughest knives of anything I have worked with. Always quench test saws to make sure they will get good and hard, not all saws will make good knives.

Files: Most are 1 percent simple carbon steel, (No other alloy elements). Nicholsen Black Diamond files are 1.25 percent carbon and that's enough to make them an excellent material for knives with superior

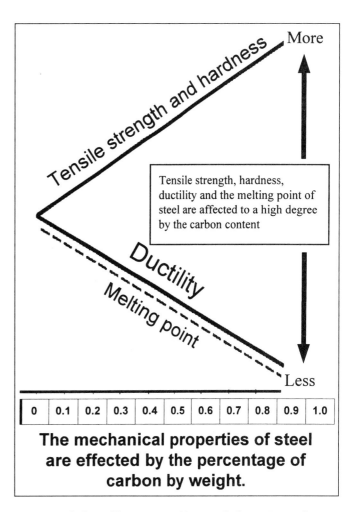

Tensile strength, hardness, ductility and the melting point of steel are affected to a high degree by the carbon content

| 0 | 0.1 | 0.2 | 0.3 | 0.4 | 0.5 | 0.6 | 0.7 | 0.8 | 0.9 | 1.0 |

The mechanical properties of steel are effected by the percentage of carbon by weight.

cutting ability. Chain saw files and the triangular files used for saws are probably 1.25 percent carbon. Automobile coil springs before mid-70s are 9260. Automobile coil springs after mid-70s are 5160H. Coil Springs: (Might be any of the following.)

1095 Simple carbon steel, no alloys

4063 Molybdenum Steel

5160 Chromium Steel

6150 Chromium Vanadium Steel

Leaf Springs: (Might be any of the following.)

1085 Simple carbon steel, no alloys

1095 Simple carbon steel, no alloys

4063 Molybdenum Steel

4068 Molybdenum Steel

5160 Chromium Steel

Most coil springs from automobiles, train cars and the like are 5160.

6150 Chromium Vanadium Steel: If a truck spring seems extra hard to work and shows a temper line when hardened it may be 6150 chromium/vanadium steel.

9260 Silicon Manganese Steel: Extra tough, but not the best for edge holding when made into knives. Cadillac used 9260 for some time after the others switched but now uses 5160H.

Planer blades: May be D-2, Chrome vanadium (50100-B), or one of a number of High Speed Steels.

Snap Rings and lock washers are probably 1065.

It is good for the ecology of our planet to recycle materials but I always teach my students to buy new bar stock and learn to work with only one steel type until the steel and its heat treat is mastered. It will cost less than one dollar per knife to buy new 1084 or 5160 bar stock. You will usually have to buy a whole bar and that will run $25 to $45 depending on the thickness and width. It is the labor that makes knives cost what they do. Steel is cheap, so buy good quality material.

TESTS FOR STAINLESS STEEL

A quick test for stainless is to use the type of cold-blue solution used to touch up firearms. Clean the part to be tested and apply a drop of the cold-blue solution, an immediate color reaction rules out the part being stainless steel.

Check it with a magnet, if it attracts the magnet it may be martenistic stainless, which can be hardened by quenching.

If the stainless is nonmagnetic it is most likely an austenitic stainless and that means it cannot be heat-treated.

Not too common is ferritic stainless. It is magnetic but not hardenable by heat-treatment. It is used in high-temperature applications where strength is not the most important factor.

HE COULDN'T BREAK IT

It was 1983 and I was just getting into forging. I was doing a lot of experimenting with selective hardening by using a torch to soften the back of the blade. I had a lot of stock removal blades around and would use them to experiment with. I had given one of my stock removal blades made of band saw steel a soft-back draw with the torch. It was a butcher knife blade with no handle. The blade was about a 9 inches long. It was what I called Mountain Man Camp Knife, the type of knife I have made ever since I got started in 1963. I had flexed that blade 90 degrees several times and straightened it out with a hammer.

I had that test blade with me at one of the first BLADE shows in Cincinnati. Gil Hibben was talking to me about forging and asked if I thought it made a better knife. I handed the blade to him and asked if would like to break it. (He assumed it was forged.) He put the tip of the blade on the floor with his foot on it and pulled on the tang. It bent past 90 degrees but did not break. He seemed surprised so I took the blade and straightened it out by reversing the bend. He thought forging was a good thing and then I had to tell him that it was a stock removal blade. The strength was a combination of tough steel and proper heat treating.

HOW I ACCIDENTLY LEARNED ABOUT 6150 CHROMIUM VANADIUM STEEL

It was a big, thick leaf out of a truck spring and if I remember right I bought it 15 years ago at a yard sale. It was obviously new because it still had paint and symbols on it and was much too clean to have ever been under a truck. When I got ready to work it, I split it into four pieces with the oxygen/acetylene torch.

My battle plan was to forge one piece of it into a Bowie knife with a 15-inch blade. As I got started forging I realized that it was harder to forge than if it were the 5160 I usually use for large knives. At first I thought it was because of the 3/8-inch thickness but as I got it worked down at the edge it was still harder to forge than 5160. I was beginning to think that it was not 5160 as I assumed it would be.

After the finish forging, normalizing and annealing I ground it to prepare it for heat treatment. For heat treatment the blade was heated in my home-made gas forge. I used a magnet to judge the low end of the critical temperature, let the temperature climb a bit more and did an edge quench in my "Goop." Goddard's Goop is a mixture of paraffin, cooking grease and dirty hydraulic oil.

As soon as it was cool enough to handle with bare hands I took it out of the goop. I immediately knew it was not 5160 because of the appearance. Blades come out of the edge quench with a distinct color difference between the hard edge and soft back. Edge-quenching of 5160 results in very little difference in appearance between the soft and hard parts of the blade. This blade had an absolutely clear visible line, as distinct as I have ever seen and the edge portion was extremely hard.

After the clean-up grinding prior to tempering it showed a sharp and distinct temper-line. The color of the steel had a slight yellow tint to it, that's different than 5160. It took a higher than normal temper to get it what I thought was right for a Bowie

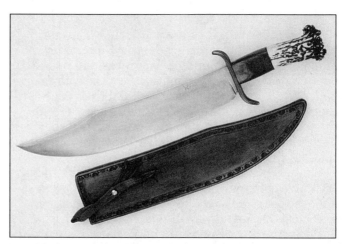

Bowie knife by the author with 15-inch blade of 6150 chromium-vanadium spring steel. Ironwood and deer antler handle, wrought iron guard.

style. It was somewhat difficult to finish, compared to 5160. I was now totally convinced that the blade was something other than 5160.

I finished that Bowie Knife with a Scagle style handle and wrought iron guard. I had it at the SOFA (Southern Ohio Forge and Anvil) Blacksmith Conference in the fall of 1998. I told the participants at my demonstration the whole story of working the steel. I told them that I was not sure what the steel was because it was different than anything I had ever worked. One of the participants explained that he had experience with heavy truck springs and to him my steel sounded like 6150.

W-2 is more difficult to work than W-1 and the only difference is a small percentage of vanadium. That same degree of difference is what I found with 6150 and its small percentage of vanadium when compared to 5160 which has only carbon and chromium as alloy content.

All of the following steels either have been or are still used for springs: 4161, 50B60, 5160, 6150, 8660 and 9260. To determine if what I have in the large spring is actually 6150 the next step in my steel detective project will be to purchase some 6150. I want to know what I'm working with and from it I'll make a couple of hunting size test knives and they will be compared to some made out of the remaining spring that the Bowie came out of.

See the table for a comparison between 5160 Chromium Steel and 6150 Chromium Vanadium Steel.

It is a much different thing with commercially manufactured knives. Few manufacturers state exactly what type of steel is in any particular model. Some even advertise exclusive steel, which seems silly to me. I guess they figure that the competition isn't smart enough to have a $50 chemical test done in order to find out what the steel is.

It is interesting to look at the way a lot of factory-made knives are advertised by mail order firms. One could form the opinion that they either don't know exactly what the steel is or don't care to share this information with the potential customer. I made a list of how the stainless steels were described in some of the most recent mail order cutlery catalogs to come in my mail. By the time I was finished with two catalogs it was clear to me that it was not a priority with these folks to inform the reader with accurate information on the steel types used. My observations and opinions follow.

The first steel listed was Sandvik 12C27, the catalog stated exactly what the steel was and I appreciate that. This is a very excellent stainless steel made in Sweden. (For the composition of most of the steels listed please refer to the chart that follows).

The rest of the stainless steels are described, in order as found, as follows: Strong stainless steel, 440-C, mirror-polished stainless steel, 440-C high carbon steel. Many were just listed as stainless steel, 440, high carbon martenstic, 440 stainless,

STEEL TYPES THAT EITHER HAVE BEEN OR STILL ARE BEING USED FOR SPRINGS							
Abbreviation	C	Mn	Si	Cr	Ni	Mo	V
STEEL TYPE							
4161 Chromium- molybdenum	.50	.80	.30	1.00	/	.20	/
50B60 Boron Steel 0.0005 minimum boron	.60	.90	.30	.80	/	/	/
5160 Low chromium	.60	.80	/	.80	/	/	/
6150 chromium-vanadium	.50	.80	/	.90	/	/	.18
8660 Nickel-chromium- molybdenum	.60	.80	.30	.60	.60	.20	/
9260 Silicon-manganese	.60	.80	2.00	/	/	/	/

STAINLESS STEEL USED FOR KNIVES

Identifying the steel used in handmade knives is more cut and dried than for commercial knives. Most makers of handmade knives know what their steel is inasmuch as they can tell you a number or name that the steel manufacturer calls it. Furthermore, the maker usually knows exactly what the alloy content is and can explain the advantages of why he or she used this particular steel for a certain application.

Stainless Steel									
Chromium is the element that makes stainless steel highly resistant to pitting and staining. The folks who make steel decided that 13 percent chromium is necessary to make steel stainless in what they call "normal use". Stainless steel does not become "stainless" until it is properly heat teated.									
	C	Mn	Si	Cr	Ni	Mo	Co	V	W
STEEL TYPE									
440-C	1.20	1.00	1.00	18.00	/	.75	/	/	/
425 Modified	.54	.35	.35	13.5	/	1.00	/	/	/
CPM 420-V	2.20	/	/	13.00	/	1.0	/	9.00	/
CPM 440-V	2.20	.50	.50	17.5	/	.50	/	5.75	/
440-XH Stainless D-2	1.60	.50	.40	16.00	.35	.80	/	.45	/
ATS-34	1.03	.25	.41	13.75	/	3.56	/	/	/
ATS-55	1.00	.50	.40	14.00	/	.60	.40	/	/
BG-42	1.15	.50	.30	14.50	/	4.00	/	1.20	/
CRB-7® Alloy	1.10	0.40	0.30	14.00	/	2.00	/	1.00	/
Elmax Uddeholm	1.70	.03	.08	18.00	/	.75	/	3.00	/
RS-30	1.12	.50	1.0	14.0	/	.55	/	.25	/
RS-30	1.12	.50	1.0	14.0	/	.55	/	.25	/
MBS-26	1.00	.40	.65	15.0	/	.25	/	/	/
G-2	.90	.37	.60	15.50	/	.30	/	/	/
12C27	.58	.35	/	14.00	/	/	/	/	/
AEB-L	.65	.65	.4	12.8	/	/	/	/	/
AUS-6	.65	1.00	1.00	14.5	.49	/	/	.25	/
AUS-8	.75	1.00	1.00	14.5	.49	.3	/	.25	/
D-2 (Almost stainless)	1.50	.40	/	12.00	/	.80	/	.90	/

I've included D-2 to show how close to being stainless it is. A few brands of D-2 have more chromium that the 12 percent listed on the chart. When properly heat treated and given a nice finish it will not stain in normal use.

440-B, 440-B modified, 440-A, T80, ATS-34, G-2 and AUS-6

Let's do some guesswork.... Strong stainless steel could mean that they do not know what it is, but they have tested it and it is strong! Perhaps the mirror-polished isn't as strong and the best thing they could say about it was that it was mirror-polished! 440-C is always high carbon and always martensistic, (that means it is hardenable). The one listed 440 could be 440A, 440B or 440C, but which is it?

The ones listed as 420, 440-A and 440-B, are cut and dried. The one referred to as "Surgical Steel" is probably 420, high carbon, martensistic, strong and mirror-polished steel. XT80 is a new one to me and I haven't a clue as to what is in it. ATS-34 is an old standard.

A-2 OR D-2 WHICH SHALL IT BE?

Eric Shaver of, Moscow, Idaho writes: For a fighting knife which is better, A-2 or D-2?

Answer: A-2 versus D-2, that's a tough one because they are such very different materials from the perspective of alloy content and common usage in industry. For example, there is a time when I want to eat an apple. At a different time I want to eat an orange. It's not that one is better than another is, just different.

If I only had a choice of A-2 or D-2 to use for a fighting knife, I would choose D-2. When it is properly heat treated it has more potential for strength and edge-holding ability. D-2 is resistant to corrosion to a degree that I consider it to be "nearly" stainless. I have used D-2 for my small to medium-sized personal working knives for many years.

However, I would prefer a selectively hardened blade of 5160 for a larger knife such as a camp knife or self-defense knife. I require that a large knife should be unbreakable. The strength factor with selectively hardened 5160 makes it my choice over either A-2 or D-2.

	C	Mn	Si	Cr	Ni	Mo	Co	V	W
A-2	1.0	/	/	5.00	/	1.00	/	/	/
D-2	1.50	.40	/	12.00	/	.80	/	.90	/

An alloy comparison of tool steels A-2 and D-2.

MYSTERY AIRCRAFT STEEL

Keith A. Steen, Cabot, Arkansas writes: Enclosed please find two bearings, both are from an aircraft. The silver one is a trunnion support bearing, which the landing gear pivots on in transit from gear-up to down. The other is a rear turbine support bearing from a jet engine. I have a supply of these and would like to use them for small knife blades; the problem is I have not been able to get these steels soft enough to cut

threads, drill etc. I have cooled them from various temperatures (1,500 to 2,000 degrees) as slow as I can. (About 5 hours to reach 200 degrees) after this the steels are still so hard a good hit with a hammer will snap them clean. My questions are: Do you have any idea what kind of steels these might be, they are not stainless as they rust readily. Is it possible some steel will not anneal to the point where it can be machined with common tools such as I have? And lastly I would very much appreciate it if you have time, to try to work one of these into a blade, and let me know what you think of it, most of all if I am just wasting my time trying to work with this material. Thank you for any help you can give."

Answer: Thanks for the fun project; I enjoyed playing "Steel Detective" with the two parts. First, I ground into them with an abrasive cut-off saw in order to study the sparks. The silver-colored one sparked like stainless. The brown-colored one sparked more like carbon alloy steel. I then ground a flat area on each one and applied a drop of cold blue solution. The brown-colored one blued immediately, that usually indicates non-stainless steel. The silver colored one did not blue at all, that usually means it would be one of the common stainless steel types. I then finished the abrasive cut through one side of the brown one and put it in my home made gas forge. As it was heating it formed almost no scale (an indication of high alloy content). When it was approximately 1,900 degrees F I attempted to straighten it by putting one side in a vise and pulling on the other. This was one tough piece of material; it did not want to move. (Bearing races of 52100 are easily straightened this way.) It took three heats to get it straight on the anvil with a 4-pound hammer. I thought I would forge it to shape but it did not want to move under the hammer so I put it back in the furnace and after it came up to temperature I turned off the gas and air for a slow cool. After cooling it was so hard that a file would only take off a little of the light scale. Another spark test was done and the sparks were close to a sample of A-2 that I have, however I do not think that A-2 would be used for this type of part.

It would seem that the trunnion support bearing is some type of stainless steel, possibly 154-CM, BG-42 or 440BM. The rear turbine support bearing is some type of air-hardening, high-alloy steel with not quite enough chromium to pass my stainless test. (That does not mean it is not some type of stainless steel that I am not familiar with.)

I see no point of forging stainless so I will keep the shiny one in my collection of metallurgical memorabilia.

Either one would probably make a good knife, if time was taken to learn how to heat treat them. I would rather use the labor involved to get them flat and annealed to do something more productive. Then I could afford to purchase four or more times the amount of known material that was already in the form of a bar. I'm all for recycling materials and I do it a lot, but I draw the line when the labor involved in working the material gets more expensive than the cost of new materials.

To answer your question if all steels can be annealed, yes. However, these type steels require a long soak time and then a long, slow cool to anneal. A-2 requires a soak of two hours at 1,550 to 1,600 F, then cool to 1,200 F at a rate of 50 F per hour, then air cool. This would be required after forging and before rehardening. 154-CM requires a soak of six hours at 1,650 F followed by a furnace cool. To anneal BG-42 it requires a soak of 5 hours at 1,625 to 1,650 F, then cool at 50 F per hour to 1,100 F, furnace cool to 800 F, then air cool to room temperature.

Update: I answered that question in August, 1997 *Blade*. After seeing my answer, *Blade* reader Jerry Glaser sent me some information sheets on M-50 high-speed steel. The printed information included a note: "Most American-made ball and roller bearings for high-temperature applications are made of M-50 HSS."

I hadn't considered a high-speed steel type for use as a bearing. The difficulty that I had in trying to straighten and forge it is easily explained by it being made of high-speed steel. Thanks, Jerry.

See the steel alloy table.

Abbreviation	C	Mn	Si	Cr	Ni	Mo	Co	V	W
STEEL TYPE									
M-50	.83	.25	.30	4.00	/	4.00	/	1.00	/
A-2	1.0	/	/	5.00	/	1.00	/	/	/
BG-42	1.15	.50	.30	14.50	/	4.00	/	1.20	/

An alloy comparison of tool steels M-50, A-2 and BG-42.

Randy Mc Ghee of Missoula, Montana writes:

I have been making knives for about five years. I started out buying blades from Bob Englath (Blades 'n' Stuff). Lately I have been making my own blades out of ATS-34 and saw blades. I have also used planer blades and whatever I can get. Recently I came across several bars of steel that are marked Rex-95. Someone had tried to work this material before but had given up. I understood why when It took me a little over 1-1/2 hours of persistent grinding with a 5-inch grinder to rough it in.

Answer: Rex 95 is a type of tungsten high-speed steel made by Crucible Specialty Metals. It is "T-8" (Tungsten HSS) in the tool steel classification system. Tungsten high-speed steels have high red hardness (ability to resist softening at high temperatures) and wear resistance. Lathe tool bits, reamers, drill bits, taps, milling cutters, punches and dies are typical uses. This material is available in the hardened condition and it sounds like this is what you have. A working hardness of 64 RC is not unusual.

I have made knives out of T-1, M-2 and M-4 HSS. I use these steels for light use knives such as small using knives, leather knives and paper cutting knives. The edge-holding ability is superior.

Because of the high alloy content HSS steels have some degree of stain resistance, but when used around salt water they will pit.

WHAT STEEL FOR A SWORD?

Scott Kaine, Las Vegas, Nevada writes:

I am building a sword, (handle and tsuba). Could you please tell me the difference between 440 and 440C? Would that be a good choice for a strong piece of steel that will be able to take a good beating?

Answer: When a blade is advertised as "440" it is usually not 440C. It is more likely 440A or 440B. 440C is the highest quality of the 400 series and if the manufacturer were using it, I would think that he would be proud enough to advertise it as such.

When it comes to the type of flexible strength that a sword needs, stainless would not be the best choice. I would recommend 5160, either stock removal or forged. It has what is required for taking a "good beating." Blade-quality stainless steel does not stand up to this type of treatment when compared to 5160 chromium steel.

When enough chromium is put in steel to make it stainless there is a subsequent weakening of the grain boundaries. As a blade is flexed the inside of the bend is put under compression while the outside curve is under tension. On the molecular level, the grain boundaries are trying to pull apart. The more a blade is stressed, the weaker the boundaries become. Microscopic cracks start across the grains and grow with the flexing. When enough of the cracks line up the blade will break.

Ron Flax of Boulder, Colorado writes:

I am interested in purchasing a Katana and I have been having some difficulty in gathering information. Many different sources discuss the composition and properties of the steels that were used in Japan in the past. Some sources discuss steels that are used today in the attempt to most accurately re-create the materials that were used in the past. But I have yet to find anything that discusses what is being used (or could be used) to create the best (sharpest and most durable) sword using state-of-the-art materials. I would appreciate any assistance you can give me in my search.

Answer: My choice of steel would naturally be based on my own test procedures of what I call the combat-quality blade. I would use 5160 chromium spring steel to forge a sword that I would have confidence to put up against any and all other materials. It is not the forging or the steel, but the combination of the two, and then giving the blade the optimum heat treatment for a sword blade.

The real secret to the success of the Japanese sword was in the selective heat treatment. In the best swords, the steel was very pure and refined; however, the heat treatment had to be just right to turn that superior steel into a combat-quality blade. The best

Japanese sword blades were of a composite construction, then selectively hardened. The edge was very hard and brittle with a carbon content that was ultra-high by today's standards. The back was a medium carbon steel and was soft, the center was springy.

In my opinion, any sword that is the same hardness all the way through will break at some point of deflection. (I was assuming that it had enough hardness to be an effective cutting tool.) A blade could be made with a spring temper all the way through that would be very tough and unbreakable. Regardless of the strength, it would have poor cutting ability.

The properly done blade of 5160 with a hard edge and a soft back will flex 90 degrees without the edge cracking. The blade should return to around a 10-20 degree bend, which can be straightened without the edge cracking. My students and myself consistently make such blades. The 5160 will give up some edge-holding ability to the higher carbon blades, but the extra strength is worth it. These opinions are based on knife-sized blades but I believe they translate well enough to apply to sword blades.

THE OLD FAVORITE, D-2

I call D-2 "The Old Favorite" because it has been around for a long time. I can't find the reference to it but I remember reading somewhere that it was developed during World War I in an attempt to find an alternative to High Speed Steel.

When properly heat treated, D-2 will make about as good a knife as could be wanted. A quick survey of the steels used by makers listed in "Knives '99" shows approximately 40 percent of the makers listed as using D-2 for at least part of their production. (The survey counted only those who list what steels they use.)

The "D" series tool steels are classed as Cold Work Tool Steels—high carbon, high chromium type. All D-2 is not created equal; my 1969 "Guide To Tooling Materials" shows 51 versions. In 1969, some steel makers put a little nickel and cobalt in their D-2. Others left out the silicon but added to the molybdenum. D-2 is made in a free-machining grade with the addition of sulfur. The free-machining grade does not polish well and hence is not as suitable for knives as the standard grade.

From the standpoint of the alloy content, D-2 looks a lot like 154-CM/ATS-34. (See the D-2 Spec. Sheet.)

It would seem that D-2 with it's higher carbon content and .90 vanadium would have better edge-holding ability when compared to ATS-34 and 154-CM. My comparisons, which were done at a hardness of 60-61 Rc, indicate that there is not enough difference to notice.

Thirteen percent chromium is considered to make a steel type stainless by industry standards. D-2, which can have from 11 percent to 13 percent chromium when properly hardened and given a good finish, is very stain-resistant. D-2, as well as all hardenable grades of stainless steel, loses stain resistance when not fully hardened. In normal use, I have not found it to rust or stain.

	C	Mn	Si	Cr	Ni	Mo	Co	V	W
Standard D-2	1.50	.40	/	12.00	/	.80	/	.90	/
D-2 Planer Blade from test below.	1.88	.51	.43	12.75	/	.90	/	1.16	/

* Elements not listed are in quantities too small to be considered as an alloy, they are "trace elements."

```
ACT NAME : LOAL TIME : 23-DEC-88  07:57
10
          I.S.    C      MN     SI     P      S      CR     NI
EXP# 1   14955   1.919  .5154  .4343  .0288  .0058  12.77  .1052
EXP# 2   15221   1.876  .5153  .4343  .0293  .0056  12.75  .1055
AVERAGE  15088   1.898  .5154  .4343  .0290  .0057  12.76  .1054

          MO      CU     CO     V      AL     W
EXP# 1   .9106   .0164  .0309  1.184  .0228  .0232
EXP# 2   .8978   .0164  .0308  1.158  .0206  .0231
AVERAGE  .9042   .0164  .0308  1.171  .0217  .0232
```

Actual chemical test results compared to the textbook formula.

I use Ohio Knife Co. D-2 planer blades to make hunting knives. (See the chemical test results) Note the additional carbon and vanadium, plus the nickel and tungsten which are not in most D-2 steels. I had been using OK-6 (Ohio Knife Co. D-2) for over 20 years not knowing that it had the extra goodies in it.

With my brass-rod edge-deflection test, D-2 shows more strength at the working hardness of 60 Rc than 154-CM/ATS-34. I attribute this to the lesser amount of chromium and the addition of the vanadium. The 154-CM and ATS-34 have a lot more molybdenum, which theoretically should give it more strength and toughness. The bottom line: When comparing the grain size, D-2 has a much finer grain, and a fine grain always means more strength.

One disadvantage of working D-2, at least my planer blades, is that it does not take a shiny finish easily. It has a distinct orange-peel texture when overworked on soft buffs. I usually put a shiny satin finish on a working knife and call it good.

For many years it was puzzling to me why some makers and writers did not like D-2. The question was solved when I determined that their conclusions were reached using knives that were defectively heat treated. The hardening temperature of 1,825 to 1,875 degrees F is critical. When overheated, the blade will not be as hard as it should. It does require a 20-minute soak time at the hardening temperature prior to air cooling.

I had a customer who did not like D-2 and I could never figure out exactly why. His favorite steel was 154-CM. When he asked me to develop a prototype design in a hurry and had not specified the steel type. I made it from the D-2 planer blade stock. He liked the way it performed and was very surprised when told it was D-2.

I needed a quick knife for the free-hanging rope cutting contest at the 1999 Oregon Knife Show. I used a large, new, Spear and Jackson (Sheffield steel) D-2 planer blade and ground out a straight-edged blade. The size limit of the blade for the contest was 12 inches by 2 inches so I made my blade to the limit. It was as thin at the edge as any hunting knife I ever made. We started out with one at a time and worked our way up. I was able to complete a cut on six at a time which was good for third place. This knife is too thin to cut anything harder than rope so I am regrinding it with a thicker edge and will reshape it into a camp knife.

D-2 has an honorable history and should be with us for a long time to come.

D-2 Specification Sheet

Tool steel type D-2 has been around forever (at least since WW1) and from recent questions about heat treating and forging it, there may be a resurgence in usage. It is one of my favorite steels for making hard working, stock removal knives. There are a lot of scrap planer blades around and these can be utilized in the hard stage, which is how I work them. They can be forged or annealed and worked with normal stock removal methods. D-2 is available from many steel manufacturers and most knifemaker supply companies.

	C	Mn	Si	Cr	Ni	Mo	Co	V	W
O-1	.90	1.60	/	.50	/	/	/	/	.50
A-2	1.0	/	/	5.00	/	1.00	/	/	/
D-2	1.50	.40	/	12.00	/	.80	/	.90	/
ATS-34	1.03	.25	.41	13.75	/	3.56	/	/	/

Preheat Temp	Austenitizing Temperature	Hold Time	Quench	Freeze Treatment	Tempering Temperature
1400-1475 Preheating is recommended to decrease the possibility of cracking or warping.	1825-1875	15-45 min	Air	-250 F 4-8 hours	Two hours two times 300 61-63 Rc 400 60-62 Rc 500 59-60 Rc 600 58-60 Rc 700 57-59 Rc 800-900 57-59 Rc

Annealing: Hold for two hours at 1600-1650 cool in the furnace at 50 F per hour below 1200 F then air cool.
HOLD TIME: Most of the useful alloy content of tool steels exists as microscopic carbide particles in the soft matrix of the annealed steel. These carbide particles must be at least partially dissolved into the matrix of the steel during the hold time at the austenitizing or hardening temperature.
CRYOGENIC TREATMENT: D2 is likely to have retained austenite after quenching. By cooling the steel to sub-zero temperatures, retained austenite may be transformed to martensite. In the past, freeze treatments were done between tempering cycles. Recent experimentation indicates that continual cooling from the austenitizing temperature to -250 f does the best job of transforming any austenite. New martensite is similar to the as-quenched martensite, and must be tempered to relieve the stresses created during it's formation.
TEMPERING: D-2 should be tempered at least 2 times for a minimum of 2 hours for each temper. All tool steels should be allowed to cool completely to room temperature between tempers.
FORGING: Heat slowly and uniformly to 2,000-2,100 F
Do not forge below 1700 F
Cool slowly from the forging temperature. (this does not anneal it)
D-2 must be annealed as per the instructions above for correct hardening results.

STEEL FOR STEAK KNIVES

Charles Williams of Raleigh, North Carolina writes:

I recently hand-forged a couple of knives to be used as steak knives. I made them of 5160 steel, heat treated them with an acetylene torch to a non-magnetic state, quenched them in transmission fluid and annealing in a natural gas oven at 400 degrees F for one hour. After their first steak the blades turned a very light shade of blue. What caused this, and how can I prevent it from happening again? Also, could you recommend some books that discuss in detail the handle-making process? I have found this part of knife-making more difficult and time-consuming than the

forging and polishing of the blades. Specifically the installation of guards, bolsters and butt caps.

Answer: 5160 does not have the quality of being stain resistant. I've seen it in print that because it is a chromium steel it will have more stain resistance than simple carbon steel. That statement must have been written on a theoretical level and not on a practical level. To be stainless in normal use a steel type must have a minimum of 13 percent chromium as an alloy element. The people who make steel established this percentage by making comparisons. With its .80 chromium, 5160 has no resistance to rust or staining from the type of use that stains all non-stainless knives. Most lovers of non-stainless knives value the patina that builds up on a knife. It becomes a protective layer and, after a certain point, it does not seem to get any worse. The non-stainless knife should be washed and dried after use, which will keep it from pitting and rusting.

One solution would to be blue the blades with a good cold blue like Super Blue made by Birchwood Casey. I use this on a lot of my forged camp knives and it does protect the blade to a great extent. It is available at most sporting goods stores and don't settle for any thing else, it's the best I have found. For good results you must follow the directions on the bottle very closely.

Another solution is to make steak knives out of a stainless steel like 440-C or ATS-34.

They don't need to be forged, just grind them out and send them off to a good heat treater that does freeze treating as part of the process.

You're right about handles, guards and butt caps being the hard part of knifemaking. The specific treatment given to the back end of a knife can double or triple the amount of labor needed to complete the project. In my opinion the best all-around book on knifemaking is *How To Make Knives* by Richard Barney and Bob Loveless. It is available from Krause Publications by calling 1-800-258-0929. A variety of methods are shown. The style of knife that you want to make will determine which of the methods to use.

The style of knife that I have come to like the best is the narrow tang, which I do two different ways. I use an inletting process to make ultra-lightweight knives. The handle is made of two pieces, half the shape of the tang is carved in each half, and then it is glued and pinned. When it is carefully done the blade looks like it grew out of the handle.

For heavy-use knives I use a pierced guard, narrow tang and screwed on pommel cap. In my experience this is the strongest and most foolproof handle. When the application is not quite so heavy duty I may leave off the pommel cap.

WHAT STEEL FOR A HOG BONE CLEAVER?

William Valera of Hawaii writes:

What steel would you use to make a hog-bone-chopping cleaver, and how would you temper it?

Answer: The only work I have done on cleavers is to sharpen and rework chipped ones. I do have some ideas about what steel to use and the temper to start with. My first choice would be to use the heaviest circular saw steel material that I could find. This will make a very tough blade. Second choice would be 5160 or any old truck spring. The cross section of a cleaver needs to be more like an ax than a knife. Start out on the thick side, it can always be thinned down later if it does not cut well. Harden and then triple temper the blade at 450 degrees F. If the edge chips out in use, re-temper it 25 degrees higher. Always start out on the low end of the tempering temperature. This way you will be able to ease up on the right hardness. If the blade is tempered too soft at the start it will have to be annealed and re-hardened.

Experiment with the geometry of the cross section and the tempering temperature until you find the best possible combination. Making comparisons is the only way that I found to work out a problem like this.

Good luck, and let us know how the cleaver comes out.

WHAT IS CARBON V STEEL

Vern D. from Salem, Oregon writes:

I have been using a Cold Steel Kukri to carry while hunting in the Oregon woods. I am wondering about fashioning one for myself. Can you think of any compiled information or treatise on edge hardened or differential tempered blades? What is Carbon V? Is it another chromium spring steel? Where can I obtain the analysis of this steel?

Answer: The closest thing to Carbon V would be known as chrome-vanadium cutlery steel. The chromium spring steels have no vanadium, just carbon and chromium. There is a chromium vanadium spring steel that is classed as 6150.

I had one of the original Trailmaster Bowies tested and the alloy was as per specifications in the chart. (See Chart)

See the chapter on heat treating for methods of selective hardening and tempering.

KNIVES FROM O-1 AND FILES

James Yats of Coleman, Michigan writes:

I am a hobby knifemaker and have made knives from files. I know they are brittle, I've been told they range from 72-84 Rockwell C. A knife is not a screwdriver or a pry bar and if used properly they will give good service. I have also used O-1, oil hardening gauge stock, hardened and drawn back to 58 Rc.

	C	Mn	Si	Cr	Ni	Mo	Co	V	W
O-1	.90	1.60	/	.50	/	/	/	/	.50
W-2	1.00	.35	.35	/	/	/	/	.20	/
L-6	.70	/	/	.75	1.50	.25	/	/	/
52100	1.10	.35	.35	1.5	/	/	/	/	/
50100-B	1.10	.45	/	.45	/	/	/	.20	/
0170-6 (Sharon)	.95	.40	.25	.45	/	/	/	.20	/
Carbon V Chemical Test	.95	.46	.16	.48	/	/	/	.19	/
L-3 (BB)	1.00	/	/	1.5	/	/	/	.20	/
0170-6	.96	.40	.25	.45	/	/	/	.20	/

```
ACT NAME : LOAL TIME : 03-FEB-89  12:57

           I.S.    C      MN     SI      P      S      CR     NI
EXP# 1    18147  .9603  .4588  .1615  .0094  .0051  .4785  .0540
EXP# 2    17425  .9612  .4686  .1640  .0102  .0073  .4851  .0546
AVERAGE   17786  .9607  .4637  .1627  .0098  .0062  .4818  .0543


ACT NAME : LOAL TIME : 03-FEB-89  12:57

           MO     CU     CO      V      AL     W
EXP# 1    .0385  .0635  .0044  .1875  .0002  .0017
EXP# 2    .0402  .0842  .0045  .2040  .0035  .0018
AVERAGE   .0394  .0738  .0045  .1957  .0018  .0017
```

This is what the computer read-out of a chemical test looks like. The elements circled are the ones that count, the other elements are in such small quanities that they should be considered trace elements.

A comparison of steels with chromium and vanadium as alloy elements.

Can you tell me the metallurgical difference in these steels? Is O-1 as brittle if hardened and not tempered? Also, what type of grinding stones and belts are best for fast cutting of hardened steels such as files?

Answer: Most files are simple carbon steel of .095 – 1.00 percent carbon. Twenty-year-old Nicholsen Black Diamond files that I had tested are 1.25 percent carbon steel. (Carbon steel has only Manganese as an alloy element.) O-1 has quite a lot of alloy in it; .090 Carbon, 1.60 Manganese, .50 Chromium and .50 Tungsten. As-quenched hardness of 1.00 carbon steel and O-1 is 67-68 Rc.

The alloy elements in O-1 make it tougher than the simple carbon steels at any hardness; it would be very brittle if not tempered at all. Your O-1 blades at 58 Rc should perform very well. Files make excellent knives when properly worked. The following chart shows the as-quenched hardness of some common tool steels and the expected hardness with a 475-degree F draw.

STEEL TYPE	AS QUENCHED HARDNESS	475 DEGREE DRAW
D-2	64	58
O-1	66	60
W-1 (most files)	68	60
L-6	65	57
A-2	64	58

Several years ago I ran into a new maker who was selling O-1 knives that he told me were 62 Rc. His heat treater told him that this was a good hardness for O-1. I explained that In my opinion that is too hard. I showed him how a knife of 58 Rc would not be harmed by dropping it point first onto a cement floor. One of his 62 Rc blades of O-1 broke into several pieces when tested in a like manner.

When I use grinding wheels for roughing knife blades I use NORTON 36-grit Norizon wheels designed for saw making. My favorite rough grinding belts are the 3-M Regaloy belts, 36- and 60-grit. I use the 36-grit belts for roughing stag, micarta and wood, when they slow down just a bit I start using them on steel.

WORKING WITH FILES AND SAW STEEL

Gary Purvis of Springfield, Missouri writes:

I have a large supply of files (200) and sawmill blades. What steel is in them? How do I anneal and heat-treat these materials? At what temperature and for how long should I temper them?

Answer: Most modern flat files are 1.00 percent simple carbon steel. I have a large supply of older files marked Nicholson/Black Diamond. These files tested out at 1.25-percent carbon and make excellent knives. To gain superior strength, it is necessary to grind away the teeth from the edges, corners and sides that will make the edge. This eliminates stress risers that can cause cracking in the quenching process, or unexpected failure while in use. Some rasps and files are not suitable for knives because they are made of a low-carbon steel that has been case hardened.

It is easy to determine if a file or rasp is made of high carbon-steel. Simply bring it up to the hardening temperature, quench it in warm oil and then see if it breaks like glass. If it stays springy, it is usually case hardened and not suitable for knifemaking. The exception is to layer it up with high carbon steel in a Damascus billet. A good rule to follow whenever you are working any new type of steel is to do a quench test before putting any labor in it.

While on the subject of knives made from files, recently there was an article in another publication where the author made some statements that directly contradict what I teach about removing most of the teeth from a file before forging. I got some questions about it, so I'll try to answer them.

In no uncertain terms, the author stated, "Even with teeth forged in all over both sides, they (knives made from files) are virtually unbreakable if properly heat treated." The author also said he had used knives made from files, including a throwing knife, for years on end, and never had a problem. The author went on to say, "It is a good idea to get all the tooth tracks off if you are forging a spring from file steel, which is where this mistaken interpretation originated."

I haven't made any springs from files. However, with a spring, since it is much softer than a knife, it would seem that the issue of stress risers causing cracks would not be as important. The author of the article has had better luck than I with knives forged from files when the teeth are forged into the surface. I've seen old and new knives made from files that were broken, and the breaks were always running through a stress riser where a file tooth was not removed prior to quenching. Often you will notice a dark area at one side of the break that is exactly where the crack started when it was quenched. The elimination of stress risers applies to all types of steel. My experience with the strength of blades is always dependent on the absence of stress risers, and that means removing most or all of the teeth from the surface of a file.

I decided to do a new forging experiment with a file to see if I was wrong about grinding some of the teeth off a file before forging on it. I forged a 4-inch-long blade on the end of one of my favorite Nicholson/Black Diamond files. When the forged-to-shape blade was finished, the teeth were almost untouched along most of the spine and the sides within half an inch of the back. The teeth remnants decreased in the areas where the sides were forged to create the wedge shape of the blade. Enough teeth were left at the edge so that it needed to be ground to a depth of approximately .015 of an inch to clean them up. This is within the range of normal grinding to clean up after forging. With a little more grinding as security and with a correct heat treat, the blade would make a good knife. The only problem areas on my experimental blade were along the spine and on the sides of the blade. These are still stress risers and should be eliminated to make a first-class blade.

My experiment convinced me that it is necessary to grind the teeth off the corners, edges and most of the sides that will make the edge. They're going to have to be ground off after forging anyway. Why take a chance on a tooth that can't be seen from being forged into the edge? Great care should be taken to eliminate every possible factor that might cause the blade to fail.

I have made several thousand knives from band and circle saw steel. (I just happened to be working for a saw manufacturer when I started making knives.) Saw blades are made from a variety of steel types. However, most are of the Special Purpose "L" classification. "L" steels make some of the strongest knives I have tested. The carbon content will vary from medium to high and with varying percentages of alloy elements.

Most saw steel is usually fairly high in nickel content (1.50 to 2.75 percent). (See chart.) In order to make good knives of saw blades, it is necessary to work out by trial and error a hardening and tempering method for each individual blade. If you have a large saw, it is

	C	Mn	Si	Cr	Ni	Mo	Co	V	W
STEEL TYPE									
L-6	.70	/	/	.75	1.50	.25	/	/	/
Sharon 0186-5 (saw steel)	.75	.60	.35	.50	1.00	.10	/	/	/
Sandvik Bandsaw	.75	.25	.35	/	2.00	/	/	/	/
Udeholm Round Saw	.80	.30	.25	.20	2.20	/	/	/	/

A comparison of different types of saw steel with L-6.

wise to use it up before you start on another. If you mix and match heat-treat batches from different saws, you might not get consistent results. When an effective formula for heat treating is worked out and you start with a good, quality saw blade; the results can be excellent. I passed my Journeyman Smith Requirements for the ABS with a blade made from a circular saw. It didn't crack and returned to nearly straight from the 90-degree flex test.

I use a magnet to judge the hardening and annealing temperature of files and saws. Heat the blade slowly and uniformly, occasionally touching it with the magnet. When the blade becomes nonmagnetic, it is an indication of the low end of the critical temperature. Let the blade climb another 50 degrees F and quench in warm oil. To anneal files or saws, heat to nonmagnetic and place them, while still hot, into a container of vermiculite for a slow cool.

Vermiculite is available at garden supply stores and places that sell firebricks and other refractory materials. Wood ashes, if kept dry and warm, will work for annealing.

I like to recycle materials as much as the next person, however, I teach my students to buy new bar stock and learn to work with one steel until it is mastered. Steel like 1084 and 5160 will run less than a dollar per knife. You will usually have to buy a whole bar and that will run $25 to $45 depending on the thickness and width. It is the labor that makes knives cost what they do. Steel is cheap, buy good stuff.

KNIVES FROM HORSESHOE RASPS

J.W. Booher of Richmond, Texas writes:

I am making myself a knife out of an old horseshoe rasp and would like to know the best way to heat treat and temper the blade. I am a beginner in the knife-making trade and need all the help I can get.

Answer: Some horseshoe rasps are case hardened and as such will not make good knives. The first thing you should do is a quench test to see if it is made out of high carbon steel. Heat up one end of the rasp to approximately red-orange (nonmagnetic) and quench in water. Put the very tip in a vise and then flex to see if it breaks clean. If it breaks like glass it is has the right stuff in it to make a good knife.

SAFETY NOTE: ALWAYS WEAR SAFETY GLASSES AND HEAVY LEATHER GLOVES WHEN FLEXING KNIFE BLADES.

After shaping the blade, heat treat as follows: Judge the hardening temperature with a magnet. Heat slowly and uniformly to where the magnet no longer is attracted by the blade. Let the temperature climb just a little bit more, then quench in oil that has been warmed to 140 degrees F. Remove the blade from the oil when it has cooled enough to handle with the bare hands. Clean the blade down to bare metal by sanding. Place in an oven

that has been heated to 400 degrees. Leave for at least an hour and a half, then remove the blade but keep the oven on. When the blade reaches room temperature place it back in the oven for another temper of the same time as the first. Then repeat the process for a total of three tempers. The blade is then ready for finishing.

Woodson Gannaway writes:

Please check the composition of 9260 and S-7, in the books it is not comparable. When you compared 5160 and S-7 you wrote, "You would have great strength with Bearcat, Bethlehem Steel's S-7, though you would lose even more edge-holding than with 5160. 9260 is comparable to S-7. S-7 doesn't get that hard; it's made to be tough." Were you speaking from experience? I am skeptical that S-7 will suffer in comparison.

Answer: When I said that S-7 and 9260 were comparable, that was my opinion of edge-holding ability based in part on my own experience and reports from others. Here is another opinion. The carbon and chromium are the only alloys that we need to consider in a theoretical discussion of the edge-holding potential of these four steel types. (See the chart.) I threw in 52100 because in studying the relationship of it to 5160 in actual tests, it will give us a good picture of the effect of the carbon and chromium content on a specific steel type.

52100 has nearly two times the carbon and chromium as 5160. This gives it more potential to make a superior blade. My results of comparing the edge-holding ability of 5160 and 52100 indicates that the 52100 will cut two to three times longer than the best 5160. Since the earliest days of tool steel development it has been understood that it was primarily the carbon content that gives steel abrasive resistance. It is my understanding that vanadium and chromium when alloyed with carbon make harder carbides. Therefore, steel types with these alloy elements will be expected to give better abrasive resistance, but only if they are hard. From personal experience I know that chromium, when added to .60 carbon steel in the amount of .80 percent, increased greatly the edge-holding ability and strength. (Actual tests with 5160 and .60 simple carbon steel) 5160 has .80 Manganese which, in my opinion, is there for strength and will have little or no effect on abrasive resistance.

I made some knives out of 9260 and couldn't get them to cut that well. At least three other bladesmiths have had the same experience. I have not tested S-7,

Abbreviation	C	Mn	Si	Cr	Ni	Mo	Co	V	W
STEEL TYPE									
S-7	.50	.70	.30	3.25	/	/	/	/	/
9260	.60	.80	2.00	/	/	/	/	/	/
5160	.60	.80	/	.80	/	/	/	/	/
52100	1.10	.35	.35	1.5	/	/	/	/	/

Shock-resisting steels compared to 52100 (ball bearing steel).

but have talked to others who have; their experience was similar to mine with 9260. It is my opinion that the 3.25 chromium will not offset the relatively low carbon content of .50.

A POSSIBLE HOT NEW
STEEL TYPE FOR KNIVES

While surfing the WWW one evening looking for things that have to do with steel, I found Carpenter Steel's on-line catalog. Looking it over I found a steel type I hadn't known about. They call it CRB-7®. It is described as "Corrosion-resistant, wear-resistant, and secondary-hardening, high-temperature bearing steel with high-heat-treated hardness. Maintains high hardness levels at elevated temperatures."

It looks like a compromise between BG-42 and ATS-34. With vanadium content at 1.00 (which ATS-34 does not have) it should make a knife with great edge-holding ability. The extra Molybdenum serves to make CRB-7 more heat resistant but would do little to improve it as knife steel.

(See the alloy comparison chart.)

STEEL TYPE	C	Mn	Si	Cr	Ni	Mo	Co	V	W
CRB-7® Alloy	1.10	0.40	0.30	14.00	/	2.00	/	1.00	/
BG-42	1.15	.50	.30	14.50	/	4.00	/	1.20	/
D-2	1.50	.40	/	12.00	/	.80	/	.90	/
ATS-34	1.03	.25	.41	13.75	/	3.56	/	/	/

A comparison of chromium-molybdenum-vanadium steels with ATS-34.

D-3 STEEL: IS IT FOR YOU?

Gil Jennings of Shelbyville, Kentucky writes:

I've never read about, or met, a maker who's used D-3 steel. Could it be that it's too tough to work by stock removal? Do you know of anyone who's tried forging it? I work by stock removal and, though D-3 can be murder on sanding belts and is tough to mirror-finish, it makes excellent blades. I've used quite a bit of it in the last 30-some years and, for a using knife, it's my favorite steel.

Answer: D-3 shouldn't be that much harder to work by grinding than D-2, at least not enough to discourage anyone. Forging would be another matter; steel with more than 1.8 percent carbon and with 12 percent chromium would be most difficult to forge.

There are two reasons why I've never worked or tested D-3. I've never had any and my customer's never asked for it. I've worked D-2 for nearly as long as you've worked D-3. I've found D-2 to be one of the best-balanced steels there is. By balanced I mean edge/blade strength in relation to hardness. D-3 may not be as balanced judging from its alloy content and hardness/toughness comparisons.

According to one steel maker's data sheet, D-3 is about 32 percent more wear-resistant than D-2 but its toughness is about 33 percent less. That's usually the way it is with steel; to gain in one attribute, there's often a loss in another. One industrial-application chart rates the wear-resistance between the two as equal, with the toughness nearly the same as above. No mention was made of the hardness of the test samples. I've seen times when results were given where the hardness was not the same. The machinability of D-3 is 28-percent less than that of D-2. That means it will be harder to grind, mill and drill.

I started working with D-2 because it was a free source of excellent material that came in the form of worn-out planer blades. The brand I used was Ohio Knife Co., and the blades were marked OK#6. I learned to work D-2 with grinding wheels while it was in the hard condition (60 Rc). The main advantage of using grinding wheels is that it is an efficient way to shape knife blades from hardened steel. I probably have more than 100 pounds of D-2 planer blades. They are a mixture of OK#6 and Spear and Jackson, which are English-made blades. I may go looking for D-3 when I run low on planer blades.

THE WELL-BALANCED BLADE

A knife of the very best steel may not perform any better than one of inferior steel unless it is heat treated to bring out the full potential of the alloy content. In the search for the ultimate knife, proper heat treating of the steel for the intended use of the knife is often overlooked.

The consumer gets shortchanged whenever performance drops off 20 percent or more when compared to a correctly heat treated blade. My tests show that 50 percent or more of today's handmade blades are not heat treated to get the maximum out of the steel. The blades that do not measure up in fair comparisons run from defective to just adequate.

I have tested forged stainless steel blades made and heat treated by three different makers. One blade was soft and wouldn't cut anything; one cut very well but failed in the strength test. The remaining blade was totally adequate—it had been heat treated correctly. Even if the first two blades were forged correctly it seems a waste of time because the forging was not followed up by the correct heat treatment. The best of this group was not any better than a correctly heat treated stock-removal blade of the same steel. The tired old argument of forged versus stock removal or stainless against carbon steel wasn't even in the picture. It came down to the fact that the single most important factor in determining blade performance is the proper heat treatment for the specific steel and the knife's intended use. That's one part of what I call balance.

The reasons for a maker to turn out incorrectly heat treated blades are too many to list. The most common reason is not having the correct heat treating specifications from the steel maker. It has recently been brought to my attention that you can't trust your steel supplier for the correct information to heat treat your blades. More than a few makers who do their own heat treating have been using faulty information for 154CM/ATS-34 and D-2. Ask your supplier who made your steel and get the technical sheets for that steel directly from the steel maker.

The best cutting ability comes from a blade that has been fully hardened then drawn back to the working hardness. Most of the inferior blades that I have tested were under hardened; that is, they never achieved full hardness in the quenching operation. Under hardening usually results from using the wrong hardening temperature, soak time, or, in the case of the secondary hardening steels like 154CM/ATS-34, the wrong tempering temperature.

The correct working hardness for any steel is the hardest condition that still gives adequate strength. That is the other part of balance. This should be worked out carefully by making test comparisons. It is a fine line to walk. If the blade is too hard, the edge will either chip out or break. Make it too soft and it will not stay sharp. (See chart.)

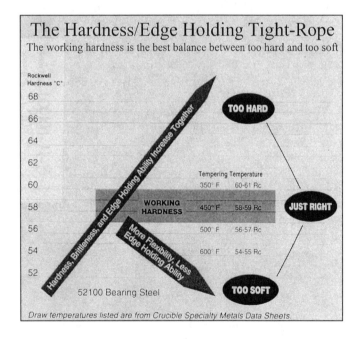

The Hardness/Edge Holding Tight-Rope
The working hardness is the best balance between too hard and too soft

Rockwell Hardness "C"

TOO HARD

Tempering Temperature	
350° F	60-61 Rc
450° F	58-59 Rc
500° F	56-57 Rc
600° F	54-55 Rc

WORKING HARDNESS

JUST RIGHT

Hardness, Brittleness, and Edge Holding Ability Increase Together

More Flexibility, Less Edge Holding Ability

52100 Bearing Steel

TOO SOFT

Draw temperatures listed are from Crucible Specialty Metals Data Sheets.

Pick a good steel type and be sure you have the correct heat-treating information and adequate equipment. Use the information to the best of your ability, and then compare the blades you heat treat to those done by a professional heat treater. The time spent doing rope-cutting and edge-holding test comparison is time well spent. Do it!

Do not trust others to give you accurate reports about the cutting ability of your knives. Learn it on your own! The confidence you gain is worth a million bucks.

WILL FORGING IN CHARCOAL ADD CARBON TO A BLADE?

Daniel Watson of Angel Sword Corporation, Driftwood, Texas writes:

We make our Living Steel (registered trademark) blades using hand carburization in a charcoal fire. Our experience shows this to produce a finer blade than by forging with coke or gas. Rather than present a group of statements that I cannot absolutely prove to be true, I thought it might be easier to present some of the questions that I have asked that have led me to my own theories as to why this works.

***Question #1.** At what temperature is trace sulfur released from the steel (if not reabsorbed at the same rate)?*

Answer: I don't have an answer about trace sulfur being released. There is sulfur in most coal; gas or charcoal is supposedly free of it. Steel at the forging temperature will absorb enough sulfur to be harmed by the coal fire that is made of high-sulfur coal. Sulfur weakens the steel. Smithing coal is supposed to be low in sulfur. I don't know how much time it would take to harm a blade.

***Question #2.** What is the difference in the purity of a charcoal fire versus that of a coke or gas fire?*

Answer: The purest is charcoal, next gas, the worst coal.

***Question #3.** At what temperature will the steel begin to absorb carbon from a reducing flame?*

Answer: What the bladesmith calls a reducing flame is probably not a true carburizing flame. Unless you are adding a carbon-rich compound to the surface of the hot blade, the process would more properly be called diffusion.

***Question #4.** How much carbon is absorbed into the surface of the steel with each heat (5 to 10 minutes)?*

Answer: The average carbon atom moves 0.06 inch in eight hours. That would be .0075 in one hour, (that's equivalent to the total thickness of two sheets of the paper I am writing on.) My opinion is that any gain in carbon caused by the forge fire is lost with the scale that forms as soon as the blade is brought out into the air. If there were any excess carbon left it would be ground away in the stock removal process necessary to clean up the blade.

***Question #5.** How much carbon is migrating deeper into the steel during the next heat and to what depth?*

Answer: The rule of 0.06 in eight hours would apply here, assuming that conditions were correct for true carburizing. I could theorize on this if I knew the type of steel, forge atmosphere, and the time/temperature factor. There are too many variables to try a guess.

Question #6. *Through repetition of this process, (20-60 times), can a gradient of carbon content be established throughout the steel, lowest in the center and highest where the steel is the thinnest?*

Answer: *Yes, if true carburization is taking place.*

None of my metallurgy books have information about carburization of steel in a forge fire. Just the opposite is true, they caution about the loss of carbon during the forging process. In order for the surface of the steel to absorb carbon there has to be an absence of oxygen. I believe that for a blade to absorb carbon at a rate that would actually increase the final carbon content it would have to be allowed to soak in the fire with almost no air blast. I can speak from experience that in the normal fire that the bladesmith uses the steel looses carbon rather than gains it.

Throughout history bladesmiths have used various organic compounds to "steel" the surface of the iron. Once steeled, the billet was often cut in pieces and then forge welded and drawn out. This might have been done several or many times to distribute the carbon throughout the blade. They judged their progress by the hardness of the bar when quenched in water.

References:

Elements of Physical Metallurgy, Albert G. Guy, Allison-Wesley publishing Co. 1959

Metallurgy Fundamentals, Daniel A Brant, Goodheart-Wilcox Co, 1992

Metals Handbook, The American Society For Metals, 1948

WHAT IS SURGICAL STEEL

Paul Trudel of Ontario, Canada writes:

I have three questions to ask: 1. What is meant by surgical steel? 2. I believe it is an alloy, of what metals? 3. Where can it be purchased?

Answer: To my knowledge, no steel company makes a specific steel that it calls surgical steel or even surgical stainless steel. In the past, I have seen at least four different steel types referred to as either surgical stainless or stainless surgical steel.

My collection of steel catalogs turned up two different steel types that have surgical and dental instruments listed as applications. The first is Crucible Specialty Metals 440-A. Other typical applications listed for it are bearings, cutlery, seaming rolls and valve parts. The second steel type is Armco 420; applications listed for it are cutlery, surgical and dental instruments, scissors, tapes and straight edges.

I went from my steel catalogs to the Worldwide Web and the search engine, Yahoo. Keywords searched were surgical steel and stainless steel. I found a strange and curious mix of products made of "Surgical Stainless." Even more interesting to me was that both heat-treated and non-heat-treatable stainless products were being made of surgical stainless. I found all of the following to be made of it: pots and pans, the genuine Ginsu® knives, kitchen utensils, handles for silverware, thermos bottles, miscellaneous jewelry items (including objects worn in pierced body parts), broadheads (steel arrowheads), and refrigerators. Most of the products I found were not identified by the type of stainless of which they were made. Those that were identified listed 304 as the stainless steel. I also found knives made of 420-J2 surgical stainless steel. One advertisement listed the alloy content of 420-J2 and it is identical to standard 420 as made by the steel suppliers from whom I have catalog sheets. I talked to Kit Rae at United Cutlery about 420-J2. He said that the J2 is a designation for the Japanese steel mill that produces it.

After my research was done I had worked myself into a circle and ended up back where I started with my collection of surgical stainless types. What I have to assume from this is that there seems to be no standard for surgical stainless.

As for alloy content, chromium and nickel are the elements that make steels stainless. Type 304 is an austenitic stainless and, among other things, that means it is nonmagnetic in the annealed condition and cannot be heat treated. The combination of 18 percent chromium and 8 percent nickel make it a very good form of stainless for anything used in food preparation or surgical trays and appliances. Type 304 is sometimes called 18-8, the numbers coming from the alloying elements.

440-A and 420 are martenistic stainless steels and that means they can be heat treated. They are the stainless steels of which real surgical cutting-type tools are made.

There is one more group of stainless steels known as ferritic. They are magnetic but not hardenable by heat treatment. They are used in high-temperature applications where strength is not the most important factor.

(See table of alloy content for the stainless steels mentioned.)

	TYPE	C	Mn	Si	P	S	Cr	Ni	Mo
★	304	0.08	2.00	1.00	/	/	19.00	10.00	/
	308	0.08	2.00	1.00	0.040	0.030	21.00	12.00	/
	316	0.10	2.00	1.00	0.040	0.030	18.00	14.00	3.00
	416	.15	1.25	1.00	/	/	14.00	/	/
★	420	0.20	1.00	1.00	13.00	/	/	/	/
	425 Modified	.54	.35	.35	13.5	/	1.00	/	/
★	440-A	.75	1.00	0.04	/	/	18.00	/	.75
	440-B	.95	1.00	0.04	/	/	18.00	/	.75
★	440-C	1.20	1.00	1.00	/	/	18.00	/	.75

Common Stainless Steels — Those with a star are used as "Surgical Steel".

THE STEEL OF BRAZIL

Geraldo Leão of Brazil writes:

Here in Brazil most of knifemakers I know use VC131 (D6 tool steel?). I had never heard about this type in knifemaking discussions or steel charts. Can you tell me anything about this steel? Can it be used to make good knives?

Answer: My three-hour search on the WWW for specifications for a steel type "VC131" came up dry. Even though I didn't find what I wanted it wasn't a waste of time because I did find a lot of information that will be useful in the future.

Whatever VC131 is, it must be good for knives if it is used by most of the knifemakers in your country. In order to speculate about it I have to assume that the D-6 used in Brazil is the same alloy content as AISI D-6 as we get it in the U.S. One thing that all the AISI "D" steels have in common is high carbon content and 12 percent chromium. The differences come in the varying alloy elements nickel, molybdenum, cobalt, vanadium and tungsten. I have used D-5 and it is excellent steel for knives. D-5 has molybdenum and cobalt and D-6 has none. (See chart)

	C	Mn	Si	Cr	Ni	Mo	Co	V	W
STEEL TYPE									
D-2	1.50	.40	/	12.00	/	.80	/	.90	/
D-3	2.35	.35	.30	12.00	.50	/	/	/	/
D-4	2.25	/	/	12.00	/	1.00	/	/	/
D-5	1.50	/	/	12.00	/	1.00	3.00	/	/
D-6	2.00	.80	.35	12.00	/	/	/	/	1.2
VC 161	2.10	/	/	11.5	/	/	/	.20	.70

AISI D-6 is not used much in the United States by industry and I've never heard of it used for knives. My opinion from looking at the alloy content of D-6 is that it is not enough better than D-2 for most applications to make using it advantageous. Carbon (C) makes the steel hard. The more carbon a steel type has, the harder it will become when quenched (the hardness giving it most of its ability to hold an edge). D-6 with its 2 percent carbon might balance out against the Molybdenum (Mo) and Vanadium (V) in D-2. The 1.2 percent Tungsten (W) in D-6 would give it wear resistance but, from a theoretical standpoint, I doubt that it would give it more edge-holding ability than the D-5 has. My old favorite, D-2, has .80 Molybdenum and .90 Vanadium and those two elements in combination might give it more theoretical edge-holding ability than D-6. Vanadium carbides are the hardest, and it looks like D-2 will have the most and that's why I think it has more-edge holding potential.

There is a saw steel used in WoodMizer blades that is called D6-A. (See chart.) With it's low carbon content I doubt that it would make knives that would hold a superior edge. Don't ask me how a saw steel ended up with a "look alike" name with an AISI steel type.

I feel another question coming so I'll answer it before it gets here. Why is the letter designation for tungsten "W"? If I remember right; when it was discovered it was called wolfram and the "W" stuck to it whenever they decided it was actually going to be called tungsten.

Update on VC-131

I've said this before; one of the best things about my job as Q&A person is that I have access to thousands of research assistants by way of the readers of *Blade Magazine*. I'm always glad when I receive an envelope from *Blade* reader Jerry Glaser because I know it will have some new information in it. Thanks to a couple of photocopies that Jerry sent, I now have the correct answer for VC-131. The information is from the ASM book *Woldman's Engineering Alloys*, 7th Edition. It's made by Villares, classed as cold work tool steel, DIN 1.2436 and similar to AISI D-6. See accompanying table of alloy content. Thanks, Jerry.

Chapter 3

HEAT TREATING: THE REAL SECRET TO BLADE PERFORMANCE

All blades are not created equal and it is usually variances in the heat treatment that causes discrepancies in performance. A blade that chips in normal use is not worth much as a working tool. The same is true if a blade does not have the full potential of edge-holding ability that is typical of that specific steel type. When a blade fails, the blame often falls on the steel. In my experience, I have found that it is usually the heat treatment that is at fault. I like to put it like this; poor steel with a superior heat treatment will make a much better knife than good steel with a poor heat treatment. To me, proper heat treating for the intended use of the knife is the most important part in the making of a knife.

I once read the following in a magazine article: I've had D-2 that stained like O-1, was too hard, was too soft, and in effect D-2 has shown me more variation than any steel I have worked with.

Why would an experienced knife user find this much variation in a steel type that I find to give absolutely consistent and superior results? My opinion is that the variances found was not the fault of the steel but could be traced to differences in heat treating of the individual knives. The one that stained like O-1 may not have been D-2 and that would not be the first time that a maker mixed up his steels.

Heat treating methods used by knifemakers vary quite a lot. From studying the performance of many blades produced by a variety of methods, I have come to believe that using a specific method is not as important as getting good results. In other words any method can be misapplied.

Ed Fowler's experiments with ball bearing steel and Al Pendray's search for the steel known as Wootz, point out the advantage of taking a steel type as far as is possible. Why settle for the common denominator when the ultimate is out there to be found?

In my opinion there is too much emphasis on specific steel types and not enough thought put into the effectiveness of the heat treating. A question I hear a lot is "What is the best steel?" My typical reply is that it will depend on the heat treatment. In the past I have made the statement that I believed a large percentage of the commercial and hand-made knives were not heat treated to their full potential. I'm happy to say that the quality of heat treating is improving. Many commercial companies are making blade performance a priority. Better steel with improved heat treatment is bringing commercial knives closer to the performance level of handmade knives. This is a nice change from the tendency of the commercial knifemakers to choose a steel type because it was easy to work.

In the simplest terms possible, heat treating proceeds like this for simple carbon and most carbon alloy steels. Each steel type has a unique time-temperature sequence of heating, then cooling and then heating again. The proper time and temperature sequence will result in a blade of great strength and cutting ability.

When the steel is heated to a certain point and then cooled rapidly by quenching in oil, it becomes very hard and brittle. When heated to a temperature of around 300 degrees F, the hard and brittle steel starts to soften. When heated to around 374 degrees to 425 degrees F, it becomes suitable for a knife. If heated to around 700 degrees F, it is then suitable for a spring. If cooled very slowly from the hardening temperature, the steel becomes soft and malleable. Industry as we know it could not exist without the certainty that steel can be heat treated to a specific and suitable hardness for specific applications.

THE METALLURGY OF KNIFE STEELS

Steel is useful not only because it is can be hard, but because it can also be soft or anywhere in between. When heated to a certain point and cooled sufficiently quickly it becomes very hard, brittle and full of stress. Tempering is heating the hardened steel to a lower temperature. There is a specific temperature for each steel type that makes it durable yet hard enough to hold an edge. Annealing is a heat treating process that results in steel being in the softest condition possible; then it can be more easily shaped by milling, turning, grinding, press forming and etc.

It is important to not only to have the correct degree of hardness, but in the case of a knife blade it is essential to have a fine grain structure. A knife blade that has a fine grain structure will always show superior strength to one of the same hardness that has a coarse grain. Blades fail because of poor quality heat treating; it's usually not the fault of the steel itself. Poor steel with good heat treating will make a superior blade when compared to one made of good steel with bad heat treating.

In my opinion there is too much emphasis put on steel types and not enough on proper heat treating practice. The proper heat treating for the intended use of the knife is the single most important characteristic of a quality knife. Proper temperature controls during the hardening and tempering operations insure that the blade will have a fine grain and the proper balance of not too hard or too soft. To accomplish this, it is necessary to know the temperatures required for the specific steel type as well as to be able to accurately regulate the heat source used for hardening and tempering.

Heat treating can be described as certain time-temperature treatments performed on a metal to gain specific strength, ductility or other properties. The practice of heat treatment applies not only to the steel used for blades, but also to the brass, nickel silver, aluminum and titanium alloys that are used as fittings for knives.

Throughout the ages the hardening and tempering methods for steel have been either kept secret or made to be seen as magic or mystical. The actual molecular and physical changes that take place during heat treatment have only been well understood in the last hundred years.

Sixteenth century writer Vannoccio Biringuccio advanced the following theory of the hardening of steel. "When the pores of the steel have been well dilated and softened by the strong fire, and the heat has been driven out of them by the violence of the coldness of the water, these pores shrink, and the steel is converted into a hard material which, because of the hardness, is brittle." A previous owner of the book where I found that had scribbled in the margin "GOOD GRIEF!" I agree, but even though we know how to make steel hard and we can identify the hard form under the microscope, to the best of my knowledge it is still not understood exactly why the steel is hard. There will be more about that as this lesson progresses.

It seems to me that most of the books on metallurgy are written on a theoretical level and I have difficulty understanding them. It was after I found several books that were written on a more practical level that I began to grasp the fundamentals. I hope to present only what theory is necessary to present simply and clearly the fundamentals of metallurgy, and heat treating theory as it applies to knives. In order to do this I have modified some of the standard charts and diagrams in order to make them more understandable.

There are three elements to any heat treating process, heating, cooling and time. A little difference in temperature can have a big effect on the results. The element of time is less important, but is always

the combination of time and temperature that is necessary to accomplish the transformations that give the desired results. Each steel type has it's own unique combination of time-temperature cycles that will result in a blade of superior strength and cutting ability. These cycles can be charted and shown in a graphical manner and as such are known as isothermal transformation diagrams.

The Iron-Carbon diagram is the starting point of for understanding the heat treating of steel. (See Diagram). It shows the relation of carbon content to the **TRANSFORMATION TEMPERATURE**. When steel is heated above the **TRANSFORMA-TION TEMPERATURE** it takes an internal form known as **AUSTENITE**. **AUSTENITE** is the non-magnetic form of iron and has the power to dissolve carbon and alloying elements.

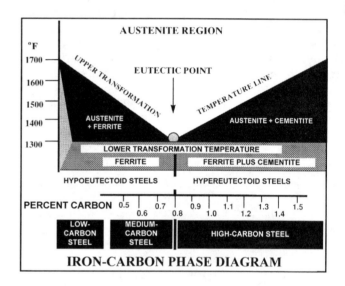

IRON-CARBON PHASE DIAGRAM

The **EUTECTOID POINT** is where the upper transformation temperature line, the lower transformation temperature line and the 0.8 percent carbon pearlitic lines meet.

The two triangular black areas on each side of the eutectoid point make up the **TEMPERATURE TRANSFER RANGE**. This is where the action is. On the rising heat the low temperature structure of **FER-RITE, PEARLITE, CEMENTITE** or **MARTEN-SITE** is transformed to **AUSTENITE**. On the falling heat, depending on the speed of cooling, **AUSTENITE** is transformed to **MARTENSITE, FERRITE, PEARLITE** or **CEMENTITE**.

MARTENSITE is the hardest of the transformation products of **AUSTENITE** and is formed only on cooling below a certain temperature known as the MS temperature (about 400 to 600 degrees F for carbon steels). Cooling to this temperature must be sufficiently rapid to prevent **AUSTENITE** from transforming to softer constituents at higher temperatures. **FERRITE** is practically pure iron (in plain carbon steels) existing below the lower transformation temperature. It is magnetic and has very slight solid solubility for carbon. **PEARLITE** is a mechanical mixture of **FERRITE** and **CEMENT-ITE**. **CEMENTITE** or **IRON CARBIDE** (Fe_3C) is a compound of iron and carbon.

Note the following on the iron-carbon phase diagram.

1. The **Lower Transformation Temperature** remains the same regardless of the carbon content.

2. The **Upper Transformation Temperature** changes with the carbon content.

3. Below the lower transformation line the structure of **Hypoeutectoid steel** is **Ferrite**.

4. Below the lower transformation line the structure of **Hypereutectoid** steel is a mixture of **Ferrite** and **Cementite**.

5. The crystal structure of ferrite is **Body-Centered Cubic** (BCC). The BCC crystal is a tightly packed arrangement of atoms.

6. The crystal structure of austenite is **Face-Centered Cubic** (FCC).

7. The mixtures of austenite + ferrite and austenite + cementite exist on the rising heat in the area between the lower and upper transformation temperatures.

As the Ferrite crystal is heated above the lower transformation temperature, (approximately 1,333 degrees) it opens up and begins the transformation to BCC. When carbon is present the carbon atoms slip between the iron atoms and form a solid solution of iron and carbon (**Austenite**). (See diagram.) When Austenite is cooled rapidly it transforms to **Martensite**. If austenite is cooled at a rate slower than necessary to form martensite, it transforms into a variety of structures dependent on the specific rate of cooling.

Carbon atoms trapped in the iron put strain on the lattice structure of the crystal. The stressed condition of the crystal is thought to cause the extreme hardness of martensite.

Proper heat treating for a stock-removal knife blade starts with the blade in the annealed condition. When annealed, the steel responds to the transformation temperatures in a consistent manner. Bar stock that is purchased for making stock-removal knives is usually HRA (Hot rolled and annealed) and as such is in the proper condition to go into the heat treating operations. Those who forge blades must normalize and anneal; or normalize only, to prepare their blades to get them ready to respond properly to the subsequent heat treatment.

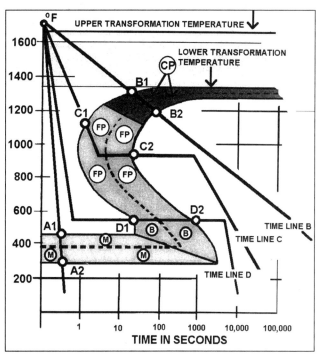

This time-temperature chart shows the effect of four different cooling rates as time lines A, B, C and D. Each steel type has it's own unique "nose" curve which is determined by quenching sample pieces of the steel type at different cooling rates. In order for steel to become fully hard it must be cooled fast enough to miss the nose of the curve as in time line A. This time line results in martensite which is the hardest transformation product of steel. Martensite has to be tempered to make a serviceable blade. Time line B is the slowest cooling and results in the soft structure coarse pearlite. Coarse pearlite is a combination of coarse pearlite, coarse ferrite and coarse cementite. Time line C causes the steel to have the structure fine pearlite. Time line D causes the steel to transform to banite. Banite is more ductile than martensite and is a good compromise between the softer structures ferrite, cementite, or pearlite and the hard and brittle martensite.

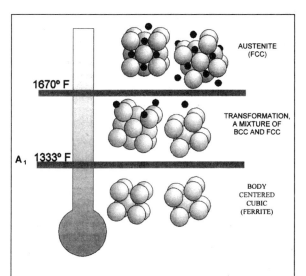

THE CRYSTALLINE NATURE OF STEEL

At temperatures below A_1 the structure of steel is body-centered cubic (BCC or ferrite) As the temperature increases above A_1 the structure begins to transform to face-centered cubic (FCC). The temperature where the transformation is complete is at, or above the critical temperature. The transformation to FCC is also the transformation to austenite. At this point the carbon atoms are in solution with the iron. (Remember that we are talking about simple carbon steels.) The large balls in the crystal represent the iron atoms, the little black balls represent the carbon atoms.

When quenched sufficiently fast the open FCC structure is instantaneously transformed to body-centered tetragonal (martensite). The carbon atoms, which are dissolved in the austenite are trapped, forming martensite. The hardness of martensite is thought to be caused by the strain on the crystal. There wasn't really enough room for the carbon atoms in the grain, thus the stressed condition.

The Crystalline Nature of Steel

As a metal cools from the liquid phase there is a point where one spot becomes cool enough to solidify and form one unit cell. As the metal continues to cool branches begin to form on the single cell. Eventually colonies of cells form and when completely cooled the colonies form boundaries which are visible with magnification. The individual colony of cells is called a grain. The term crystal usually refers to a colony but may be a single grain. A single grain or crystal of iron that is .10 inch in size contains 10^{18} iron atoms. A dendrite is a full-grown grain. (See drawing.)

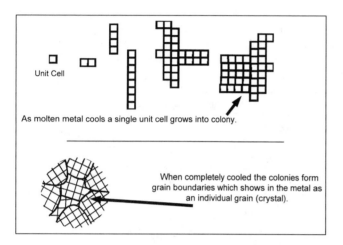

Unit Cell

As molten metal cools a single unit cell grows into colony.

When completely cooled the colonies form grain boundaries which shows in the metal as an individual grain (crystal).

It would be proper to think of the finished knife blade as a mosaic made up of innumerable crystals. When we do this it will, or should, give us more respect for the changes we are causing by the heat and pressure cycles we subject it to. If we abuse the blade material it can cause damage that will result in a blade that is defective. Even if the blade is not outright defective, it will be inadequate when compared to one treated with proper respect. Blade steel is becoming more like a living thing to me as I gain a better understanding about the internal structure and the processes it takes to make a superior blade. The most desirable property in a finished blade is that it is the proper working hardness for the intended purpose. But, at the same time we want a fine grain (crystal) structure and that assures us of a strong blade. This will be achieved only by proper heat treating.

Steel recrystallized many times during the processes of rolling and annealing that brought it to us in the finished state as bar stock. Those of us who heat our steel to the plastic stage and then hammer it into shape put it through the recrystallization process many times. The final crystal size is determined largely by the last time through the recrystallization process during the quench. To a lesser degree, the size and stressed condition of the crystal structure prior to heat treating has an effect on the finished grain size.

At temperatures below A_1 the structure of steel is body-centered cubic (BCC or ferrite) As the temperature increases above A_1 the structure begins to transform to face-centered cubic (FCC). The temperature where the transformation is complete is at, or above, the critical temperature. The transformation to FCC is also the transformation to austenite. At this point the carbon atoms are in solution with the iron. (Remember that we are talking about simple carbon steels.) The large balls in the crystal represent the iron atoms; the little black balls represent the carbon atoms. (See pg. 39 bottom left.)

When quenched sufficiently quickly, the open FCC structure is instantaneously transformed to body-centered tetragonal (martensite). The carbon atoms, which are dissolved in the austenite, are trapped, forming hard, brittle martensite. Once the martensite is properly tempered it will make a good knife blade.

Glossary of Metallurgical Terms
(With a translation in knife language.)

POLYMORPHISM is the ability of a material to exist in more than one crystallographic structure. Numerous metals change in crystallographic structure at transformation temperatures during heating or cooling. When the change is reversible, it is allotropy. Steel is allotropic. Translation: Depending on the heat treatment, steel can be brittle, relatively soft or anything in between.

CEMENTATION is a process of introducing elements into the outer layer of metal objects by means of diffusion at high temperatures. Translation: The process of carburization is cementation. Some bladesmiths believe they add carbon to the steel in the forging process, if so it would be an example of diffusion.

CEMENTITE or IRON CARBIDE is a compound of iron and carbon. Translation: That's what steel is, a compound of iron and carbon. Cementite can be hardened.

DIFFUSION is the movement of atoms within a solution. The net movement is usually from regions of high concentrations to regions of low concentration in order to achieve homogeneity of the solution. Translation: An example of diffusion in steel is commonly called carbon migration. This takes place in forge welded blades, for example; pattern welded, chain or wire Damascus. Each time the blade is heated carbon atoms move from the high carbon layers into the lower carbon layers. After three welding heats the carbon may be equally distributed throughout the blade. The blade will still show a distinctive pattern because of the difference in trace elements and other alloy elements that do not diffuse.

FERRITE is practically pure iron (in plain carbon steels) existing below the lower transformation temperature. It is magnetic and has very slight solid solubility for carbon. Translation: Ferrite is the form of steel where the carbon is not in solution in the iron.

AUSTENITE is the non-magnetic form of iron and has the power to dissolve carbon and alloying elements. Translation: At the hardening temperature the alloying elements are dissolved in the carbon and when cooled sufficiently quickly by the quench, the austenite transforms to martensite.

MARTENSITE is the hardest of the transformation products of austenite and is formed only on cooling below a certain temperature known as the MS temperature (about 400 to 600 degrees F for carbon steels). Cooling to this temperature must be sufficiently rapid to prevent austenite from transforming to softer constituents at higher temperatures. Translation: The formation of martensite is the purpose of the quench. Martensite as-quenched is too brittle to make a good blade. The successful tempering process softens the martensite to a degree sufficient to give the blade a correct balance of edge-holding ability and strength.

PEARLITE is a mechanical mixture of FERRITE and CEMENTITE. Translation: This is one of the components of steel when it is in the soft form.

The TRANSFORMATION TEMPERATURE RANGE is where steels undergo internal atomic changes that radically affect the properties of the material. Translation: Coarse grain recrystallizes to fine, body-centered cubic (ferrite) transforms to face-centered cubic (austenite) on the rising heat, then to body-centered tetragonal (martensite) upon rapid cooling.

LOWER TRANSFORMATION TEMPERATURE (A_1) Termed Ac_1 on heating, Ar_1 on cooling. Below Ac1 the structure ordinarily consists of ferrite and pearlite. On heating through A_1, these constituents begin to dissolve in each other to form non-magnetic austenite. This dissolving action continues on heating through the transformation range until the solid solution is complete at the upper transformation temperature.

UPPER TRANSFORMATION TEMPERATURE (A_3) Termed Ac_3, on heating, Ar_3 on cooling. Above this temperature the structure consists wholly of AUSTENITE which coarsens with increasing time and temperature. The upper transformation temperature is lowered as carbon increases to 0.85 percent (eutectoid point). Translation: This is the hardening temperature, sometimes called the quench temperature.

ANNEALING or FULL ANNEALING consists of heating steels to slightly above Ac_3, holding for austenite to form then slowly cooling in order to produce a small grain size, softness, good ductility and other desirable properties. On slow cooling the austenite transforms slowly to ferrite and pearlite. Translation: This is the desirable form for steel to be in to go into the hardening process.

NORMALIZING consists of heating steels to slightly above Ac_3, holding for austenite to form, then followed by cooling (in still air). On cooling, austenite transforms giving somewhat higher strength and hardness and slightly less ductility than in annealing. Translation: Forged blades need to be normalized to relieve the stresses created by the pressures and any uneven heating during the forging process. Normalizing puts the steel through the process of recrystallization, which causes a homogeneous structure.

FORGING RANGE: This temperature range extends to several hundred degrees above the upper transformation temperature. Translation: Steel in this temperature range is plastic enough to be shaped by hand-hammering, power hammer or press.

The BURNING RANGE: is above the forging range. Burned steel is ruined and cannot be cured except by remelting. Translation: The burning process has started when the steel is pulled from the fire and sparks are coming out of it. Burned steel has damaged grain boundaries and a loss of carbon. The weakened grain boundaries make it weak and the stuff that is left may not have enough carbon in it to make a good blade. The bladesmith needs to be especially careful in a coal fire as his steel is easily burnt with the high heat. The gas forge/furnace is usually not hot enough to burn the steel, which makes it a much safer heat source for forging and heat treating.

THE QUENCH

Oil Hardening

White, billowing, smelly clouds of smoke mixed with split tongues of flame swirl from a bubbling pot. There's no witch here with pointed hat, broom and black cat, but an old guy with a white beard wearing a dirty and wrinkled shop hat. He squints through the smoke and flame, watching for the boiling to subside. He's got something very hot on a wire hanging down into the bubbling oil.

He sticks a scarred, dirty and callused finger into the oil, gently feeling for the last of the heat to exit the blade. At last, he pulls the blade from the oil and attacks the edge with a file. This produces a loud noise, but has no effect on the glass-hard blade. A look of satisfaction spreads across the old guy's face as he unceremoniously dumps the blade in a box full of sawdust. He gives the blade a thorough rubdown with a stiff wire brush to remove excess oil and sawdust. Coarse abrasive paper is used to remove the dirty black scale and then the blade is put into a small oven for tempering to the exact degree of hardness.

The quench may not always be as exciting as the proceeding, but it is always the process that imparts life and usefulness to a fine blade.

The Quenchant

Most knife steels are hardened with oil and almost any kind of oil will work. I have used all of the following and they all work: Used motor oil, used and dirty automatic transmission fluid mixed with motor oil, cooking fat saved from the kitchen, old heat-treating oil, and many mixtures of the above.

I have used the old heat-treating oil for more than 30 years. I have hardened more than 2,000 blades in it and, although it stinks and smokes, it still works fine. It was made by Houghton and seems to be medium-speed oil. The place where I worked back then quenched saw blades in it. The oil was supposed to be worn out when I got it.

Quench oil is usually a mineral type with additives to give it desirable properties, and is generally rated as fast, medium or slow. The worst thing is to have an oil that is too fast for the steel type, which can cause cracked or broken blades during the quench. On the other hand, if the oil is too slow, the steel may not get as hard as it should. Two common quenchants used for knives are Texaco Type A and Brownells Tough Quench.

I do most of my quenching in a substance some folks call "Goddard's Goo." It is about one-third of each of the following: paraffin, cooking grease from the kitchen and dirty hydraulic fluid. It works great and everything quenched in it gets very hard. At room temperature it is a solid, and I like that. I developed it to have a quenchant that I could haul cross-country while teaching and demonstrating without worrying about spilling it. The only disadvantage is that it flames up, but I have learned to deal with that.

This is the appearance of a "goop" quenched blade . The light colored areas show the hard part.

I happened to come across an old recipe for a quenchant that sounds similar to Goddard's Goo. It is as follows: "For tools requiring a hard, tough edge, two-thirds tallow and one-third beeswax and a little saltpeter. Quench the edge and draw to a light straw color. This is a good thing. It improves the steel." I haven't tried the saltpeter, but can anyone guess why it helps the quench?

(Update, a *Blade* reader Thomas J. Janstrom wrote in and explained that it added nitrogen to the blade and that would make it harder and more flexible.) See "Fun with Quenchants."

The purpose of the quench is to get the blade as hard as possible. Blades will never perform up to their full potential if full hardness in not reached in the quench. Blades fresh out of the quench should be too hard to file and the appearance of the grain

when broken should be silky. The hardest blade can then be tempered back to exactly the correct working hardness.

Air-Hardening

Air-hardening steels usually contain 1 percent or more of both molybdenum and chromium. The combination of these alloy elements gives the steel such great hardenability that a fast quench in oil or water is not necessary for the formation of martensite. Most air-hardening steels are simply allowed to cool in still air, others are cooled in front of a fan to increase the hardness.

Water-Hardening

Water-hardening of steel parts the thickness of knife blades is risky business. The edge of a knife blade may warp or crack due to the severe shock of a water quench. A hot water quench at 180 degrees F will result in less strain, but will still crack some blades. My personal "Number One Rule" of heat treating is: "Never quench any blade in water unless it did not get fully hard in an oil quench." (See Quench Speed Table.)

TYPE OF QUENCH	"H" VALUE (cooling power)
Ideal	Infinity
Agitated Brine	5
Still Water	1
Still Oil	0.3
Cold Gas	0.1
Still Air	0.02
A comparison of the speed of different quenchants.	

I learned about water quenching the hard way in 1982 after I forge-welded my first blade made of wire rope. I assumed wrongly that the basic 1085 steel that the cable was made of would safely harden in water. (I had never quenched anything in water.) That beautiful hunting knife blade that I had welded up with much excitement and sweat broke into four pieces as soon as it hit the water. Overheating can also cause cracking of the quenched blade. Looking back on that experience I believe that that blade may have been overheated. At that time I had not yet learned that I could not judge the hardening temperature by eye. Testing taught me that. "The College Of Hard Knocks" and making comparisons between different steels and methods just happens to be the way I have learned almost everything I know about working steel into knife blades.

AFTER THE QUENCH, TEST IT.

ABS School student Bill Nease forgot to check his newly hardened test knife blade after he quenched it. One stroke with a dull file would have told him if it had gotten hard or not. He selectively tempered it, installed a temporary handle, sharpened the blade and made a successful cut on a free-hanging, 1-inch rope. The next test is to chop a 2-by-4 in half twice and the blade must still have the ability to shave hair. After chopping part way into the 2-by-4, the edge of Bill's test blade bent over. After some simple testing and detective work, I determined that the blade had been forged from mild steel. It was an honest mistake getting a piece of mild steel to forge a blade from. I did the same thing that same week, but caught my error when the material seemed too soft under the hammer.

Even in failure there is always some thing to be learned. Bill accidentally proved that the free-hang-ing rope cut is only a test of the sharpness of the blade and has nothing to do with the quality of the steel or heat treating.

BLADE-MAKING RULE #1: Test every blade you quench for hardness. The quench should be such that the blade achieves the maximum hardness possible. Moreover, the appearance of the grain when broken should be silky. Breaking a sample piece of quenched steel and comparing the grain size with known samples will show if the quench temperature was correct. Would you rather assume that it was heat treated properly or break a sample of the hardened steel and observe the grain size? When a blade is overheated going into the quench it will have a coarse grain. Coarse-grained steel will be hard enough to hold an edge but will be very weak.

The blade as-quenched is too hard to be durable. It must be tempered so that it is neither too hard nor too soft. That's what is known as the working hardness. When the blade is too hard, it may break in use. If it's too soft, it will not hold an edge. The hardness that is correct for a specific steel type and application is something that should be worked out by trial and error and not left up to chance.

The Concrete Floor Test

It was at the Oregon Knife Collectors Association Show about 15 years ago when I met a young maker who was working with O-1 steel. His knives looked real good and he told me his blades had been heat treated by a well-known heat treater of tool steels in the Portland, Oregon area. He said the heat treater told him that 64 Rc was a good hardness for knives. The heat treater probably arrived at that hardness by looking at the working hardness for O-1 as it applies to tools. A hardness of 64 Rc is much too hard for a knife blade and I told the young maker so. We talked about testing and then went to my table where I showed him the "concrete floor test." I dropped one of my knives point first onto the floor. A divot of cement was removed but there was no damage to the blade. The next day at the show the young maker showed up and announced, "I tested one of my knives this morning and it broke into four pieces." I believe he was going to have a talk with the heat treater.

The purpose of the quench is to get the blade as hard as possible. If the blade is not as hard as possible, it will not reach its full potential. A file test or Rockwell test is an essential part of the heat treating procedure. How accurate is a test with a file? I am convinced that I can consistently judge the hardness of a piece of steel to within one point on the Rockwell C scale by using a file. I have sample pieces of steel of different hardnesses and I compare the effect of the file on the just-quenched blade with the sample pieces. I use the triangular files used to sharpen saws. The files are quite hard (64 Rc). A dif-

A history-making rope cut.

ference in hardness of two points is quite obvious; one point is barely discernible.

Reality Check

I was tested on my skill with a file when I gave a talk and demonstration to a metallurgy class at a local community college. The students were very impressed with the ability of a blade to flex 90 degrees without breaking. I told them it was the selective hardening and tempering that resulted in a blade with a hard edge, springy center and a soft back. One of the students asked what the hardness difference was between the edge and the back. I told him that the edge was 60-61 Rc, the center was 54 Rc and the back was 48 Rc. The instructor suggested that we go to the lab and check the blade. (Time for a reality check!) The hardness tested out just as I had said in the different zones on the blade (within one point). I hadn't tested that blade before but it was a steel type that I had used a lot. I had my hardening-tempering formula worked out for that steel and I had tested enough blades to know what the results would be. That's the way it works.

When the blade comes out of the tempering furnace for the last time, the quality of the blade is pretty well set. Every time and temperature cycle that it experienced has had an effect, and the effect could be either good or bad. It is the maker's responsibility to determine if what he/she did was worthwhile. Testing blades will show very quickly where all weak spots are in the methods used for heat treating.

THE "GOOP" QUENCH

I was fortunate to spend time with old-time blacksmith Al Bart at the conferences of The Northwest Blacksmith Association. His wisdom came from years of practical experience added onto what had been passed down to him from generations of smiths. One of the things he told me was that he preferred to quench cutting tools in bacon grease. His opinion was that it made them good and hard and perhaps added some good qualities to the items quenched. Because bacon grease has salt in it, Al figured it was giving a faster quench than plain grease.

Cutting tools need to be made as hard as possible in the quench and then be tempered back for strength combined with edge-holding ability. If a quenchant cools the blade too slowly, something less than maximum hardness will be achieved.

I started my experiments with grease quenching in 1984. I saved up a lot of fat from the kitchen, put it in an old coffee urn and started using it for quenching. It worked great in getting everything hard. It was exciting to use because it made a great deal of smoke and fire. It got rancid in time, and it was a problem to keep the neighborhood animals out of it. I reasoned that if it were harder, then it

perhaps would not get rancid. About that time I bought a huge box of junk candles at a yard sale so I started mixing the grease with an equal part of candle wax. The candle wax was a mix of mostly paraffin with some beeswax in it. The improved goop didn't get rancid and the animals evidently didn't like the taste of it because they left it alone. I've improved the goop recipe by adding about 1/4 by volume of dirty hydraulic fluid. I like the way it works even better now and use it instead of oil for everything except double-edged blades, which require a tip down, straight-in quenchant container.

The goop stays semi-solid and that makes it very portable. It's difficult hauling oil around to demonstrations, so having a quench medium that will not spill works out well. My traveling outfit is a 2-inch by 9-inch by 14-inch cake pan; that's it in the photo. For traveling, it sets on its end in a 5-gallon bucket with a thin piece of plywood for a lid. I surround it with hammers, tongs and steel then I'm off for a day of fun. The one I use in the smithy is a stainless steel pan from a restaurant hot table; it's about 4 inches by 10 inches by 20 inches. It's just long enough to get a 12-inch blade, full tang, bowie or camp knife in by going corner to corner. I can do up to a 15-inch-long narrow-tang blade in the big pan.

The goop quench needs no preheating for an edge

The goop quench in action.

quench on small blades. The photo shows a 4-inch blade going into the solid goop. When doing blades 10 inches and longer I will heat a piece of scrap steel and quench it so as to create a groove of melted goop. The groove makes it possible to get the whole long blade cooled fast enough to completely harden. I usually have some small blades to do first, at those times it is not necessary to preheat a slot big enough for a long blade. The goop burns quite nicely when overheated so caution is needed. Keep a lid handy to smother any fire that starts.

(See photo above.) That's a forged blade made from a Honda car coil spring that has just entered the goop. It's getting an edge quench where just about half the width of the blade is hardened. It looks like goo, doesn't it? Bladesmith Ed Caffrey from Montana named the stuff "Goddard's Goo." It's more goopy than gooey, that's why I call it goop. The difference is determined by how much of a dent the end of a finger makes in it at room temperature.

After any quench, don't assume that a blade got hard; try every one with a file to make sure it got hard. I use the triangular files used for sharpening saws. When too dull to sharpen saws they are just right for hardness testing and you can usually get them free from a saw shop.

The goop quench makes a lot of smoke but my smithy is of the open-air type so it's not a problem. I would not recommend using it in an enclosed space without some major ventilation being available. The advantage of commercial heat treat oil is the low flash point and small amount of smoke compared to most types of oil.

HEAT TREATING WITH A TORCH

There are several things you can do to help get an even heat with an acetylene torch. First, the acetylene flame is more than 5,000 degrees F, and that's almost too much heat. You will have to experiment with it to get an even heat. The methods differ depending on whether you want to harden the whole blade or just the edge.

To harden the whole blade, I hang it on a wire and use a "heat trapper," which is simply a piece of channel steel 1 or 2 inches deep, 3 inches wide and about 12 inches high with a steel base to hold it up. I sit on a chair with the quenchant container and the heat trapper on the floor. With the torch in my left hand, I hold the wire on which the blade is hanging between the index finger and thumb of the right hand so that the blade can be turned frequently. I then move the torch over the length of the cutting edge, turn the wire and heat the other side of the blade. Pay extra attention to the tang area to keep the tip from over heating before the rest of the blade comes up to hardening temperature.

Attach a magnet to the heat trapper and every so often pass the blade by the magnet to see if it is still magnetic. When the blade is no longer magnetic, and if the heat color is even in the blade, allow the temperature to climb a little more and then quench. Quickly quench the blade straight down in the oil with no side-to-side movement. After about 20 seconds turn the wire to slowly move the blade around in the quench oil. Take the blade out when it reaches the temperature of the oil. This is determined by putting your fingers down in the oil. Quickly clean off the excess oil by wiping the blade off in a box of sawdust then brushing it quickly with a hard wire brush. Grind off the scale from at least one side for a "witness" of the temper color and then stick the blade in the preheated oven. When it goes into the oven the blade probably will be around 100

degrees F. It is important to temper immediately and to not cool the blade rapidly, such as setting it on a cold anvil or sticking it in water. The tempering temperature will vary with the type of steel and intended use of the knife, but 375 degrees F is a good place to start.

My current tempering oven is the convection type but any toaster or baking oven will work. Atop it is a board with a number of finishing nails driven into it. The nails are spaced to support a blade resting on its back with the edge up. After the blades have been in the oven for 90 minutes, take them out, place them in the rack and let them cool to room temperature. When they reach room temperature, put them back in the still-running oven for another 90 minutes. Temper all blades three times.

I've tried every method and the edge quench is the superior way to harden a forged or stock-removal carbon or carbon alloy steel blade. The critical thing in edge quenching is getting the depth of the regulator block at the correct point under the surface of the oil; too deep, and there is too much hard part of the blade. Too shallow, and not enough hard part. The proper depth for the regulator block will be different with each type of steel and will vary with the quench speed of the oil. Hold the blade with vise grips or tongs. When the whole blade or just the edge half gets up to hardening temperature, quench it edge down in the quench tank. If all goes well the edge will be hard and the back soft enough to give the blade great strength.

1. Heat the edge portion with an oxygen-acetylene torch then quench the whole blade. The whole blade is then tempered. This works pretty well on medium to wide blades, but gets difficult on very narrow blades, and it takes a lot of practice with the torch to get an even heat on just the edge portion of the blade.

2. Heat the whole blade to the hardening temperature and quench the whole blade. Draw the temperature on the back by applying the flame from an oxygen-acetylene torch. The correctly done blade should have the color indications shown in the drawing. (See the drawing.) Hardness tests on several blades done with this formula showed a hardness of 48Rc at the back with an even increase to 60Rc at the cutting edge. Tempering is done in an oven.

3. Harden the whole blade and draw the temperature with a set of "heat tongs." (See photo.) This method puts more heat uniformly into the back of the blade than the torch method. This translates to more soft back area without increasing the heat to the edge portion. It works best on large blades. Be careful not to let too much heat get into the edge and make it too soft. The color of the edge should not be allowed to go past dark straw color.

Selective Hardening/Tempering Techniques

SOFT BACK DRAW

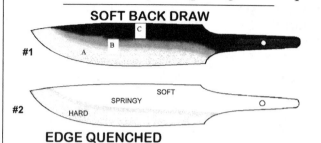

#1

#2

EDGE QUENCHED

Blade #1 above shows the relationship and proportion of the color bands visible from the soft-back draw. "A" would be straw color, "B" dark brown, "C" blue.

Blade #2 shows the approximate relationship of hard, springy and soft.

Blade #2 also shows the approximate line that the blade is inserted into the oil when edge-quenched. Both methods can be adjusted to give the same amount of hard edge. The edge-quenched blades will usually show more flexibility before the edge cracks

— FLAME→

When softening the back of a knife blade with the torch the angle of the flame should be as per the drawing of the blade cross-section.

COLOR	APPROXIMATE TEMPERATURE
YELLOW	420 F
STRAW	450 F
BROWN	480 F
PURPLE	550 F
DARK BLUE	590 F
GREENISH BLUE	630 F

As steel is heated a layer of oxide forms on the surface. The colors darken as the temperature is increased. The "temper color" is a fairly accurate indication of the temperature reached but only within one type of steel. Each steel type will show it's own colors. Test this by placing an assortment of steel types in an oven preheated to 500 F and observe the variety. Double and triple tempering will darken the color when compared to a single temper.

4. The edge quench hardens only the edge. I try for about a third the width of the blade. This method consistently gives me the strongest blades. It is the easiest to learn and most foolproof. The triple tempering is done in an electric oven.

Martin Yurman of Brooklyn, NY writes:

In a recent article a torch is used to remove the hardness from the tang and back of a knife. Is there a specific method used for this? Color? Time in heat? Quick water quench?

The heat tongs in action, the edge of the blade is kept in water to keep it from being over-tempered.

Answer: When a torch is used, the temperature is judged by the oxide color formed by the heat. I go for a dark blue for the back and tang. As to the time, I do the soft-back draw three times, whatever time that takes puts the steel at the temperature for an adequate period of time. I don't recommend water quenching from a temper heat because it puts unnecessary stress on the blade. I saw three test blades break one time in an ABS Journeyman Smith test. The maker had water quenched the blades after the soft-back draw. One blade was reforged, hardened and tempered without cooling in water and it flexed 90 degrees without breaking. The only difference was an air cool from the soft-back draw.

All of my forged blades are edge quenched. With the methods I use of normalizing, annealing, edge quenching, followed by a triple oven quench; the torch method of soft-back draw is unnecessary. The soft-back draw is extra insurance against the edge-quenched blade breaking in a flex test.

FURNACE OR TORCH HARDENING BLADES?

Robert Rogers Jr. of Acworth, Georgia writes:

In your columns you sometimes mention using a torch in the heat treating process. From what little I know about heat treating, it would appear that a furnace would give a more precise and even heat throughout the blade. Maybe I am missing something, but I cannot understand how. Using a torch you could have some spots hotter (or colder) than others. There is probably not another method that you could use to get a hard edge and soft back and tang, but this still seems like a makeshift way to heat treat. I don't mean to be controversial, maybe I am missing something. I do not understand what forging and differential hardening is all about, or why you need to do it this way. Forging a blade and heat treating it with a torch just seems to be more gadgetry than practical.

I use ATS-34, heat treated by Paul Bos. My blades will not bend 90 degrees without breaking. At 60 Rc, I seriously doubt if they would bend at all, but they still make a very good cutting tool. And a cutting tool is what my knives are.

Answer: You are wise in your decision to use ATS-34 heat treated by Paul Bos. You chose a fine steel and you can be assured that because of proper heat treatment your blades will give your customers the full potential that the steel is capable of.

Knives do not have to be made by forging and they do not need to be selectively heat treated. Selective heat treatments are only necessary if a nearly indestructible blade is needed. I made stock-removal knives for 19 years before I knew a knife could be made that would flex 90 degrees and not break. Like you, I made cutting tools and making a knife that would not break was not on my list of things to do. I still use the stock removal method to make 10 or 15 percent of my knives of ATS-34, CPM 440V, CPM

420V and D-2. My stock removal production consists of hunting and utility size knives that do not need the strength imparted by selective heat treatments.

Do I have to forge and selectively harden blades? The answer is no. I could probably sell everything I could make by the stock-removal method.

Damascus blades have to be forged from the billet, or forged into bar stock and then worked by stock removal methods. I forge because it gives me the ability to make Damascus steel, develop the pattern, forge it to shape, make an integral by forging and then selective heat treat my blades makes me a more versatile maker.

In my opinion it's not the forging but the selective heat treating that gives a blade the ability to flex 90 degrees. Why 90 degrees? It's proof that the maker has mastered the process of selective hardening. (See Photo.)

I have been hardening blades with an oxygen/acetylene torch since 1964. I can assure you that such a method is capable of making very excellent knives. I use and teach the method with full confidence for use on many carbon and carbon alloy steels. However, I would not recommend torch treatments of stainless and most high alloy steel types. Smaller blades up through hunting size blades are quite easy to do with a torch. When blades get over 8 inches it gets progressively harder to get an even heat with a torch.

Hardening with a torch takes a lot of practice to master. Any method is part art and requires much practice. Heat treating simply cannot be reduced to formulas and theories; it must be carefully worked out with the equipment a maker has to work with.

Electric furnaces do not always heat uniformly, especially when the blade is nearly as long as the furnace. If the temperature is 50 degrees off from one end to the other it may cause uneven hardening in many high alloy steels. No furnace hardening of high alloy steels should be done without hardness testing of both ends and the center of the blade.

TEMPERING KNIFE BLADES

The quenching operation was a success if the blade reached maximum hardness. At this degree of hardness the blade is brittle and full of stress. Tempering will relieve the stress and soften it enough to give it a correct balance of hardness and toughness. Tempering consists of heating the hardened blade to a temperature of between 350 and 900 degrees F for about one hour. Percentages of carbon and other alloying elements in a steel type determine the temperature that will give a specific hardness. Each steel type has a unique and appropriate tempering procedure.

Newly hardened blades are hard because they have a high percentage of martensite. Martensite is the structure that determines the hard form of steel. Tempering causes a decomposition of the martensite. A blade at its proper working hardness has an internal structure that is tempered martensite. The combination of temperature and time at a certain temperature determines the degree to which the martensite decomposes. The carbon atoms in martensite are dispersed throughout it. During the tempering process, by the phenomenon of precipitation, the carbon atoms become particles of increasing size. With enough time and temperature the martensite will revert to the room temperature form of unhardened steel which is known as ferrite.

There are numerous ways to temper blades. The tempering process chosen will depend somewhat on the type of quench. Here are some of the common methods:

Full Hardening And Tempering

The whole blade is hardened and tempered which leaves the back, edge and tang all the same hardness. Probably 99 percent of stock-removal blades are done this way. That makes it the most common type of heat treatment for knife blades. Multiple tempers and freeze treating are used on some steel types.

Audra and Mike Draper are smiling because their blades have passed the ABS 90-degree flex test. Audra with a Damascus blade for her Master Smith requirement and Mike with his Journeyman Smith blade.

Selective Hardening

There are three common methods: (Note! Selective hardening is usually not adaptable to stainless and air-hardening steel.)

1. **Edge Quench**. This is the method that I feel consistently gives the strongest blades. The whole blade is heated to the hardening temperature. The blade is quenched edge first with only approximately one third of the blade going into the quenchant. The edge portion gets hard while the back stays soft. The whole blade is then tempered which leaves the edge tough; the soft back is unchanged.

2. **Clay-Coated Back**. Heat-resistant clay is applied to the back of the blade. The whole blade is heated and fully quenched. The coating on the back of the blade slows the cooling rate so that the coated area does not harden. For this method to be successful it is imperative to bring the edge up to the hardening temperature sufficiently fast so that the clay coated area does not have a chance to come up to the hardening temperature.

When I first tried to harden a blade with clay coating on the back the whole blade got hard. It was a long tanto blade that I forged from 1095 bar stock. I was working in a real slow and mellow hard coke fire. Because the fire was not hot enough it took me too long to bring the blade up to the hardening temperature. The clay coating came up to the hardening temperature at the same time as the edge. Quite naturally, the whole blade got hard. After being annealed, the back of the blade was once again coated with fire clay. It was put back in a very hot fire and successfully hardened and tempered. It showed a nice temper line with a soft back.

3. **Heating only the edge.** (See Photo.) The oxygen/acetylene torch is used to quickly bring only the edge portion of the blade up to the hardening temperature. When the flame is too small or too cool it will make it difficult to heat just the edge without the whole blade coming up to the hardening temperature.

Selective Tempering, (soft-back draw)

The whole blade is quenched and then the back is given a blue color temper with the oxygen / acetylene torch. With practice it is possible to get an even selective temper down to the desired straw color at the edge. It is always wise to give the whole blade a one-hour oven temper. Steels like O-1 and 52100 need an hour at the tempering temperature.

The effectiveness of these methods will depend somewhat on the condition of the grain structure going into the quench. It was assumed that proper thermal treatments brought the blade up to and through the quenching operation with a fine grain size. Steel is interesting to study because it keeps an internal record of its treatment, both good and bad. I have never seen a broken test blade that had a fine grain in the back portion of the blade. Some blades that break do not have a real coarse grain but are what I would describe as questionable. I define questionable grain size as, "other than fine." Questionable and large grain structure in the back portion of a blade is usually the result of improper normalizing and annealing of forged blades. A coarse grain in the edge portion of the blade is usually caused by overheating of the blade for the quench.

A superior blade is the result of doing everything right, never from doing most of it right. It comes down to knowing the material on an intimate basis. This knowledge can only be learned from having worked out by trial and error every little detail in the heat treating process.

WHAT HARDNESS IS BEST FOR A KNIFE?

I was selling cutlery door-to-door in 1959 when I met an old-time blacksmith who told me something like the following. "You can make a pretty good knife out of a lathe rasp. First, draw some of the

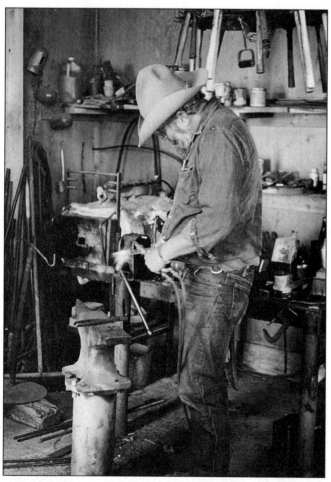

"Master of The Torch" Ed Fowler heating the edge of a blade. I'll bet it's made of ball bearing steel and will be edge-quenched.

hardness out of it by tempering it in an oven to a straw color, then just grind it out real careful so as not to get it hot enough to change the color of the steel." It took me a few years to find a worn out lathe rasp. I tempered it in the kitchen oven to a dark straw color and then ground it carefully to shape. I finished it up with a steel guard and a Myrtlewood handle. It didn't take a lot of knowledge about metallurgy or heat treating to get me started.

The year was 1963 and that was the start of my career as a knifemaker. It was a good knife, I used it to dress and skin several deer that I shot with a muzzleloader. I still have it and I like looking at it once in a while to help me remember how far I've traveled on my journey.

I went to work for a saw manufacturer at the same time I was finishing up that first knife. There were piles of scrap saw steel available, so I started using it. Those saw steel knife blades were heated to the hardening temperature in the large salt "pot" that was used to harden the saws we made. The pot, as we called it, was 3 feet in diameter and 3 feet deep; the molten salt in it ran at 1,475 degrees F. The saws to be hardened were suspended on hook-type hangers and lowered into the orange-hot salt. At that temperature the salt was transparent enough so that the room temperature steel, when put into the pot, was visible until it reached the temperature of the salt. After sufficient soak time in the molten salt the saw blades were quenched in oil, cleaned up and then tempered to a hardness of around 44 Rc. If I remember right the tempering temperature was 750 degrees F.

I had no idea what the correct hardness for a hunting knife should be. I borrowed all the knives I could get from friends and the people who were in the two different gun clubs that I belonged to. With the knives I had a list of which knives they liked or disliked and why. It was a mixture of knives of all ages and quality. I did Rockwell tests on all the knives and compared the hardness with the list of likes and dislikes. The hardness of the knives that were best liked for edge-holding ability and strength were 56-57 Rc. From this I formed an opinion that the correct hardness for carbon alloy steel hunting knives should be 56-58 Rc. This was in the days before I ever dreamed about using stainless steel for knives. Because of the alloy content and with proper heat treating stainless knives of ATS-34 can have adequate strength at 60 Rc.

Edge-holding ability is almost entirely dependent on a relatively high hardness.

I would estimate that 95 percent of handmade knives are between 56-61 Rc. The specific alloy elements in some types of steel will allow them to have more strength than other types at the same hardness. The intended use for the knife will determine the maximum hardness that will be acceptable.

Hunting-size knife blades will have adequate strength at 59-60 Rc when made of D-2 or 154CM/ATS-34. 440C is brittle at 60 Rc, so it is usually given a hardness of 56-57 Rc. When D-2 or 154CM/ATS-34 are drawn back to 56 Rc, neither will cut any longer than 440C at the same hardness. A knife with a hardness of 52 Rc will have almost no cutting ability, but it will be extremely strong.

Each steel type will have a hardness where adequate strength and edge-holding ability are at the optimum. This hardness is referred to as the "working hardness." Steel types that can be differentially hardened and tempered can have a hardness of 60-61 Rc at the edge, 54 Rc at the mid-point and 47 Rc or less at the back.

My tests show a decrease of up to 20 percent in edge-holding ability when the hardness is decreased by two points. When tested at the same hardness, there is very little difference in the edge-holding ability of the majority of steels being used for knives. Certain alloying elements will allow one steel to have a higher working hardness than another will. Most of the gain in edge-holding ability is dependent on the higher hardness, which was possible because of the gain in strength due to the specific alloys. The alloys themselves do not usually cause the increase in edge-holding ability.

HEAT TREATING OF ATS-34

Alva May, Hot Springs Nat. Park, Arkansas, writes:

Is there an optimum hardness for ATS-34, which would be suitable for a working knife that will be abused? What might be the highest and lowest hardness for such a knife, even if it is theoretical?

Answer: Good question! Many of the blades that I test are not the optimum hardness for their size and intended purpose. A knife is supposed to cut, and cut for a goodly amount of time. No matter what the steel type and alloy content, it has to have a certain amount of hardness or it will not do much cutting before it gets dull. In order to have great edge-holding ability a blade must be as hard as it can be and still have adequate strength for the intended purpose. This is what is known as the "working hardness."

The optimum hardness for a hunting-type knife of ATS-34 is 59-60Rc. In my opinion, it is a waste of good material to make knives out of this material with blades softer than 59 Rc. When the hardness is decreased by two points, my endurance cutting tests show a decrease of 15 to 20 percent. ATS-34 is an excellent steel and has a very good reputation at hardness levels of around 59 to 60 Rc. The alloy content allows it to have good strength at this hardness.

There are those who believe the high temperature temper cycle used by Paul Bos results in less strength. I don't agree with that. Paul has done my heat treating of ATS-34 for many years and I find no fault with it. All theory aside, his blades speak for themselves.

I have presented the two methods so that you can make a comparison and form your own conclusions. Let me know your test results if you get a chance to try both methods.

(See instruction sheet.)

Paul Bos Heat Treating for ATS-34	
Preheat	Loaded into 1400 F oven.
Hardening Temperature and soak time	1975°F 40 minute soak at temperature
Quenching medium	Argon or rapid air
Hardness as quenched	1900°F 62Rc 1950°F 60Rc 2000°F 54Rc * see footnote
Tempering Temperature and Freeze treatment sequence.	Freeze after quench -220° for 6-8 hours followed by two tempers of two hours @ 950°
Spring temper hardness	50Rc 1050° F
Working hardness	58-60Rc
Annealing	For maximum softness, soak at 1650°F for six hours, followed by a slow furnace cool. Cycle anneal by heating to 1600°F, hold for two hours, cool to 1300°F, hold for four hours. Then cool in air

*Although ATS-34 and 154-CM are nearly identical in composition they do not always respond equally to the same heat treatments.
Both have secondary hardening characteristics. This means: (depending on the hardening temperature), they may gain hardness during the tempering and freeze treatments.

Low Temperature Tempering for Heat Treating ATS-34	
Preheat	None
Hardening Temperature and soak time	1935°F
Quenching medium	Gas fan cool
Tempering Temperature and Freeze treatment sequence.	-300 F LN2, over night. 350-400 F, 1 hour, gas fan cool. 350-400 F, 1 hour, gas fan cool. 350-400 F, 1 hour, gas fan cool.

A QUESTION ABOUT HEAT TREATING 440-C

William Myers of Parkersburg, West Virginia writes:

I have been heat treating my 440-C blades for quite a while and I have a couple of questions that I have never heard anyone mention before. I bring my blades up to temperature and check them with a Tempilstik™ to make sure they are hot enough. They are then air cooled. After they have cooled I check them with a file and the file will just barely cut them. After 24 to 48 hours they are hard enough that a file won't touch them. Some blades were tempered at 450 degrees for one hour and some were not and I can't tell a bit of difference in them.

Should 440-C be tempered after heat treating? If so, what temperature and how long and what hardness should I expect? Also, why does it take so long for the blades to get hard after heat treating? Is this normal? If you could give me some heat treating suggestions for 440-C I would appreciate it very much. Making knives is a retirement hobby for me and I want to learn all I can and do it right. Thanks for any help you can give me.

Answer: Quench-hardened parts should always be tempered to relieve stresses set up by the quench.

Quenched and untempered parts can develop cracks that will cause failure at some future time. Knife blades are tempered to give them the required hardness to be serviceable; stress-relieving comes for free with the tempering process. The general rule is to temper as soon as possible. I'd guess that a double temper for two hours each time would be good. A six- to eight-hour freeze between the temper cycles will give you an improvement in edge-holding ability and perhaps one point of hardness. The retained austenite will be transformed by the temper and freeze cycles. Your blades are gaining hardness as retained austenite transforms to martensite, but this is not the way to do it. As the retained austenite transforms it is untempered martensite and as such full of stresses that have to be relieved by the subsequent temper cycle. A good working hardness for 440-C is 56-58. Your tempering temperature of 450 degrees F would get you on the low side for hardness.

The finished hardness at any specific tempering temperature will depend on the as-quenched hardness. I don't heat treat stainless steel, so I have to go to the books or follow what Paul Bos recommends. Crucible Specialty Metals data sheets gives the following tempering temperatures and the expected hardness for 440-C.

As-Quenched	59 Rc
212 degrees F	59 Rc
400 degrees F	56 Rc
600 degrees F	54 Rc

FUN WITH THE QUENCH

Thomas J. Janstrom of Townsville, Australia writes:

In response to your question as to the purpose of the saltpetre, in the December 1996 Blade, in the quenchant the saltpeter is included to add nitrogen to the blade steel. Nitrogen in steel, which is hardened and tempered increases the hardness achieved and the overall flexibility of the finished blade, it also adds a certain amount of corrosion resistance to the steel. (Some information courtesy of the Australian Broadcasting Corporation program Quantum.)

In the early period of the Viking age, the Vikings quenched their swords and other cutlery in stale cattle urine. This produced some of the best blades Europe had seen at the time. I'm not sure as to how or why this is so, but only that it is. So as you can see it is a piece of old knowledge, one that has been around for at least a millennium. This topic is of great interest to me as I am both a knifemaker and of Danish descent. I hope the information on nitrogen in steel is of some use to you.

Answer: Thank you for sharing that information with us, I always enjoy hearing from *Blade* readers and especially from one so far away. It is often hard to separate the true value of a process from a myth that might not work. It is always interesting to me when I find an actual reason for some of the things done in old times. In the book Shaka Zulu the process that the blacksmith used to make Shaka's custom made heavy assegai blade is described. During the forging process at just below a red heat the blacksmith rubs "various human remains" over the blade. These are reputed to be human fat, liver and heart tissue. Shall we speculate on whether this is a grain-refining, time/temperature cycle or whether it actually adds some alloy element to the blade?

Follow-up on quenching mediums

William Hartling sent the following information:

In the July '96 Q & A you mention some "unusual" blade quenching mediums. They were stale cattle urine and human remains. I read somewhere long ago that one culture used to plunge blades into living slaves for tempering. Life sure was rough in those days.

All gory details aside, these quenching mediums all share these things; first, they all contain salt. Some types of steel alloys benefit from a brine quench vs. plain water. Second is that most of them were warm when used, this could be the equivalent of heating the quenching medium. Finally, some of the mediums contained fat so you could actually say that it was the first form of oil quench.

Another practice was to forge special blades by the light of the full moon. It has been theorized that full moon light will show a forging color better. It might prove to be interesting if someone were to try it.

Answer: Thanks for the interesting letter. I've heard the slave story two ways. One said the steel should be heated to the color of the sunrise, the other the color of the sunset before quenching in the slave. There are two reasons why I think this story may have no basis in fact.

1. During most of recorded history slaves would have been much too expensive to waste in this way.
2. I doubt that the cooling rate would be fast enough to give adequate hardness to a blade. It might have been possible to accomplish some sort of a marquench that would leave a blade spring tempered.

Thirty-five years ago I was told about a blacksmith in the Dexter, Oregon area who became quite famous for the temper in his blades during the 1930s. He always kept his method a secret but his neighbors became convinced that he quenched his blades in live chickens. Be it a result of his quenching method or pure coincidence, his family always ate chicken on the days following the hardening of his blades.

As to judging the hardening temperature by the light of the full moon, it is possible to learn the correct color judgment in any light condition. In several accounts I have read where old-time blacksmiths would close all the doors and block out all outside light when hardening steel. My experience in judging the hardening temperature by eye taught me that uniform light conditions

from one time to the next is more important than a specific type or degree of light.

Fun with the quench?

THE TOASTER OVEN FOR TEMPERING BLADES

Philip Chase of Port Jarvis, New York writes:

Your articles on methods of hardening and tempering are great but at least twice you've dropped a clue to a tempering method without an explanation. Quit teasing, Wayne, how about a complete fill-in on ... "and temper the blades in a modified toaster oven." I'd really appreciate a drawing on how to make one and how it's used."

Answer: A toaster-oven in the knife shop will help keep peace in the family. I tempered knives in the kitchen oven for almost 20 years. It was hard to get all the oil off of the blades and there was usually some smell of smoke in the house during tempering. I finally figured out I could do it in a toaster oven kept in the shop.

Hotpoint made the toaster oven I mentioned. The internal chamber measures approximately 8 by 12 inches. I bought it at an as-is thrift store for less than a dollar. It worked fine, but was very dirty. Some cook figured it was easier to give it away than clean it up. The gunk makes it just right for knife work. It's real nice not to have to worry about messing up your shop oven. Any oven that will give a uniform temperature over the range from 325 to 500 degrees F will work.

There are four modifications to the toaster oven:

1. I added a thin plate of stainless sheet that works as a deflector or diffuser. The bottom element is quite close to the one rack when it is in the middle of the oven. The stainless plate is under the blades and evens out the radiant heat from the element. The diffuser plate is also bent up at a right angle at the front, which will prevent round items from rolling off onto the element. (I occasionally temper drills, counterbores, punches and chisels that I have made.)

2. A good quality oven thermometer is mounted to the rack as a visual indicator of the temperature. (They are $3 new, mine was 25 cents at a yard sale.)

3. A wrap of fiberglass insulation is wrapped around the top, back and bottom. I got the insulation out of an old water heater that I scrapped out. The insulation keeps the heat in and thus the oven does not cycle as much. This is not necessary on some of the newer toaster ovens.

4. In order to make it possible to do larger blades than would fit completely inside the oven, I cut a slot in one end that will accept the tangs of two or three knives. (See drawing.) The slot is placed as near as possible to the front so as to give the most room to get a long blade in the oven.

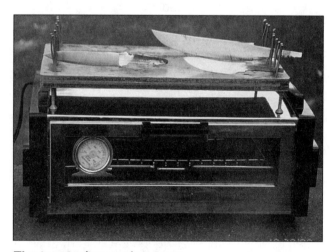

The toaster/tempering oven

A. Jay Bigler, Anna, Illinois writes:

In the May Issue of Blade, *you had an article on using a toaster oven to heat treat a blade. But how long would a 440 stainless blade have to be in to temper?*

Answer: The toaster oven is used only for tempering carbon alloy and Damascus blades. I do not heat treat stainless steels; therefore I haven't tried the toaster oven for tempering them. I send my stainless blades to Paul Bos because I don't believe it is time-

and dollar-efficient to do it myself. I expect 100 percent of the potential performance of the blade, and I get it with the blades Paul heat treats for me. That includes the proper sub-zero freeze treatments I believe are essential for stainless blades. When the as-quenched hardness of 440-C is 59Rc, a 212 degree F temper will result in a hardness of 59Rc. This is a stress-relief-without-softening temper. Tempering at 400 degrees F will give a hardness of 56Rc. (Information from Crucible Metals Spec. Sheets) The usual hardness of 440C knife blades is in the range of 56-58 Rc.

UPDATE

I'm now using a Farberware Convection oven for tempering carbon and carbon alloy steels. (That is anything up to 550 degrees F.) Like it's predecessor, it is also from a thrift store and cost me $5. It has a larger capacity and since the heat source is outside the chamber the heat is very uniform.

HOW TO ANNEAL AIR-HARDENING STEELS

Joe W. from Texas writes:

I forged a blade out of CPM T440-V and it is too hard to drill a hole in. I annealed it in vermiculite, but it is still hard. How can I anneal it, and should it be normalized?

Answer: Crucible Steel Data Sheets for CPM T440-V give the following for annealing. Soak at 1,625 to 1,650 degrees F (885-899C) for two hours followed by a furnace cool at a rate of 35 degrees F (14C) per hour to 1,200 degrees F (649C), then air cool. When properly annealed, the blade will not need to be normalized.

The only way to get a true anneal on an air-hardening steel is to use the formula that the steel maker has worked out for each specific steel type. Vermiculite, which works well for most steel, will not cool air-hardening steels slowly enough. I have used wood ashes that have been preheated with a heat lamp. I've also inserted orange hot iron bars into either vermiculite or wood ashes and then put the blade to be annealed in with it. The ashes, when used very hot, seem to cool the blades much more slowly than vermiculite. It has to do with thermal mass, not insulating value of the material.

This question has been asked several times concerning different steels, information for 440C, D-2 and A-2 follows:

Crucible Data sheets for 440C give the following: Annealing, Soak at 1,650 degrees F for six hours followed by a furnace cool. Cycle annealing, heat to 1,600 degrees F, hold for two hours, cool to 1,300 degrees F hold for four hours, then the steel may be cooled in air.

Here is how I "sort of" anneal D-2. I clamp four or five pieces together, bring them up to approximately 1,800 degrees F in a gas forge, then put them in the hot ashes.

I use this method to soften the handle area when I make knives from the hard planer blades. They will not be dead soft, but soft enough to drill and file easily.

A-2 should be annealed as follows. Heat slowly to 1,500 to 1,600 F, cool not faster than 50 degrees F per hour in the range of 1,450 down to 1,300 degrees F.

Heat Treating Specifications for A-2 Tool Steel	
Hardening Temperature	Preheat 1450° Harden at 1700°-1800°
Quenching medium	Air
Hardness as quenched	63-65 Rc
Working hardness	58-62 Rc
Forging Temperature	1800° -2000°
Normalize (air cool in still air)	Do Not Normalize after forging.
Annealing temperature	1550° -1600° cool at 40° per hour
Tempering Temperature	300° -1,000°

ANNEALING O-1 STEEL

An unnamed *Blade* reader writes

I forge my blades using 3/16-inch, O-1 flat stock. I cannot achieve a truly annealed state after forging. I've ruined numerous cobalt drills trying to drill tang and guard holes. I even ruined a logo stamp trying to stamp the steel while cold. I've tried heating to both the high and low end of the critical temperature, then slow cooling in warmed vermiculite, ashes and also lime with no noticeable difference in the hardness. I've also buried blades in the coals after shutting down the forge for the night and let them cool overnight. I had the same results: too hard to drill.

I can use carbide drills which drill the O-1 with no problem and I can stamp my logo by first heating the blade to a dull cherry color. Should this be necessary? What can I do differently to end up with blades that I can drill?

Answer: I have the same problem with ball-bearing steel (52100). Those two steels are very similar in composition. O-1 is a very excellent steel for non stainless knives, probably as good as 52100. It requires a cooling rate of 40 degrees per hour from 1,400-1,450 degrees F for to be fully annealed. I think you should be able to get the blades soft enough to drill without so much trouble, but you will probably need to keep stamping your logo in while hot.

From what you said I believe you may be overheating for the annealing temperature. If you go to 1,450 or above you have reached the critical temperature and there will be some degree of hardening. Do some test pieces and use a magnet to judge the temperature. With the first test piece heat slowly and uniformly to just where the magnet won't be attracted and then cool as slowly as possible. Do a second piece and heat it to just below the temperature where you cooled the first sample. When the sample pieces have reached room temperature try to drill them and see what you have. If they still are too hard to drill you should heat the hardest one to a blue color starting to go into silver and allow a slow cool. You should be able to drill the sample after this spring tempering. Never water cool a knife blade or other cutting tool from a tempering temperature as it can cause unnecessary stress in the blade.

Heat Treating Specifications for O-1 Tool Steel	
Hardening Temperature	Preheat at 1200° Harden at 1450°-1500°
Quenching medium	Oil
Hardness as quenched Rc	64-65
Working hardness	58-62
Forging Temperature	1700° -1900°
Normalize (air cool in still air)	1600°
Annealing temperature	1400°- 1500°
Tempering Temperature	300° -475°

SELECTIVE HARDENING TECHNIQUES

A *Blade* reader writes:

Explain what is meant by the term "soft-back draw."

Answer: The soft-back draw is used to soften the back of a blade while leaving the edge hard. When properly done it gives a blade the optimum in edge-holding ability (good hardness) and, at the same time, very good total blade strength.

Here's how it works: The whole blade is hardened, then the back is quickly heated in order to draw the hardness of the back down, yet leaving the edge at nearly the full as-quenched hardness.

This is done by heating the back of the blade either with a torch or with special tongs that have been heated. The quick heating of the back is necessary so that the edge does not have time to become heated enough to soften it.

Another method used to gain strength in the blade is edge quenching. The whole blade is heated and then quenched edge down in a pan of oil. A block of steel or aluminum is placed in the pan to regulate the depth that the edge will penetrate into the oil. This effectively regulates the amount of the blade to be hardened. I learned this method when I saw Bill Moran demonstrate it at an American Bladesmith Society Hammer-In. After comparing both methods, I have come to prefer edge quenching for the majority of blades that I make. It works especially well on thin, narrow blades. Edge quenching eliminates some of the variables that cause problems when heating the back of the blade with a torch.

Can stainless steel blades be selectively hardened or tempered?

Terry Primos from Shreveport, Louisiana writes:

I soften the spine and ricasso area on all my carbon steel blades. I've heard this referred to as differential or selective tempering. Can this be done with air-hardening steels such as 440C?

440C is listed as an air/oil-quench steel. I have seen information that says oil quench is the preferred method. Is this true, and if so, what are the benefits of an oil quench with this steel?

Answer: It would be difficult or impossible to harden the edge only on 440C because it is an air-hardening steel. In an edge quench, the back would probably not cool slowly enough to not get hard to some degree. As for softening the back with a torch, the temperature and time involved to soften the back would cause a softening of the edge. Several years ago one of my customers sent me two stainless knives for testing that were supposedly selectively hardened or tempered. The edges on these knives were not much more than spring temper. It seemed to me that they would be quite strong because they were so soft. The only problem with the two knives is that they wouldn't cut anything.

Crucible Specialty Metals Data Sheet says: Crucible 440C can be hardened for maximum hardness by oil quenching or air cooling from 1,850 to 1,900 degrees F.

It does not say one quench is any better than the other is. Some oil/air hardening steels will be harder if oil quenched, but evidently that is not the case with 440C. Let's go with the air cool, it's not so messy and unlike quench oil, you don't have to buy it.

David Olson of Lindsborg, Kansas sent instructions for two methods of selective hardening/tempering:

1. Harden the entire blade. Mask off (protect) the cutting edge with a piece of raw potato and use a propane torch to temper the back. Unplug the fire alarm.

2. I use Grant-Wilson Furnace and Retort Cement to cover the spine of the blade and harden the edge only. This stuff stays on through three quenches and doesn't need wire reinforcing like the pottery type of clays. It is available at local hardware stores.

Edge Quenching

Matthew Butterly of Australia writes:

I'm forging my blades from 5160 steel. I edge quench them and was curious about a few things. Why is it that you only quench the edge if just the edge is heated (as per ABS master smith Ed Fowler)? Why not just submerge the whole blade? Fowler's blades look beautiful. Do you know how he brings out the hardening lines?

Answer: It's clear from your questions that you've been doing your homework and then thinking through the information that may seem confusing. That's very good because, to be successful at making quality blades, you need to study the different heat-treating methods and adopt the procedures that work for you. The type of steel, the speed of the quench oil and as-tempered hardness you want all help determine your final methods.

Regarding edge hardening, it sounds as if you've watched Fowler's how-to video because it shows him heating just the edge portion of his blades with an oxygen/acetylene torch. Both on the video and in real life, the heat often goes up farther on the blade than it appears from the color. When this happens and the whole blade is quenched, there's a loss in flexible strength from it having too much hard edge. The edge-quench, properly done to the right depth, guarantees great strength in the finished blade.

After Ed polishes his blades, he gives them a quick etch in ferric chloride mixed with water to bring out the patterns that are a result of the triple quenches.

Knifemakers rarely get the same results with the same steel type. My "goop" or oil-quench oil may be slower- or faster-acting and used at a different temperature than another maker using the same steel. This can result in the as-quenched hardness of my blades being slightly dissimilar, which requires a different tempering time and temperature.

There are dissimilarities in steel, too. Different melts of the same type won't react exactly the same to identical heat treatment. A few years ago the formula I used for 5160 at home wouldn't work at the ABS School with 5160 from a different source.

I do most of the heating for quenching a blade in a specially built gas furnace. (See Photo.) I usually get more than just the edge hot and that's exactly why the edge-quench works best for me. When I use a torch to heat for the quench I can get just the edge hot, and then I quench the entire blade. I do it that way because it works best for me, with my equipment.

This picture shows the heating and quenching department in my smithy. The little "Dragon Breath" forge was specially constructed to run at hardening and forging temperatures. The goop quench is located close by. Under the quenchant tray is a container of wood ashes that are occasionally heated and used for annealing. A box of vermiculite, which is normally used for annealing, is at the left of the quenchant tray.

WARPED BLADES

Fred Sherron, from Texas writes:

I am having a problem with very thin forged blades of 5160 warping when I harden them. I have not had this problem before because I have not made knives this thin. What would you suggest?

Answer: Some blades just want to warp and especially the thin ones. It's their nature. Overheating of the steel going into the quenchant can cause warping. I had a lot more warped and cracked blades in the days when I was judging the hardening temperature by eye, and it was from overheating. Using a quenchant that is too fast-acting can also cause warping.

Blades that have been edge-quenched and have a true spring temper in the back can be straightened by using a three-point set up in a vise. (See drawing.)

An old blacksmith book told of a method where long thin blades were sandwiched between two plates of heavier steel, heated to the hardening temperature and quenched. I haven't tried it, but I am sure it will work for you. Let me know if you try it, and of course, if it worked.

Follow up: A few months later I received the following letter from Fred and thought it was worth passing on. I've also heard from several others who have used this method with good results.

Following your advice, I fabricated two plates of 1/16-inch thick 440C steel about an 1-1/4 inch wide by 7 inches long. I then placed the blade between the two plates and then laid a 1/4-inch by 1/4-inch by 6-inch piece of 440C on each side. I then placed this sandwich in the vise and used "baling" wire to make several ties about 1-1/2 inches apart. The total composite was then placed in the forge and the outside plates brought up to the proper heat. There was a problem in trying to determine if the blade inside was at proper temperature. As the outside plates reached color, the blade could be seen as a dark outline. I continued to soak until the silhouette began to fade, which indicated that the blade was reaching the same temperature as the outside plates. The bundle was then quenched in oil and allowed to cool. Wal-aah! The blade was very straight and the hardness was about right. I then drew the blade using a torch. The result was excellent.

While there may be a better way, at least this does work and will allow me to complete my order. Thanks again for your help. I do appreciate it.

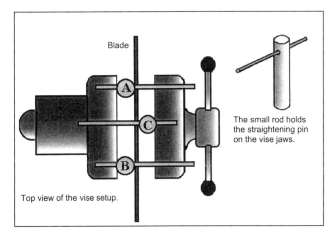

Three-point vise jig for straightening blades. The rods A, B, & C, are 5/8-inch or more in diameter; brass, copper or Micarta® will work. They are held in position by 3/16-inch cross rods. The blade is crinked into straightness by the pressure exerted by the vise screw. Use a good straightedge to check the blade. This operation is done with the blade at the tempering temperature. Ease into it with the pressure, going too far will cause extra work. You may break a blade occasionally.

DOES EDGE-QUENCHING MAKE A BLADE WIMPY?

Matthew Butterly, writes:

ABS master smith Robyn Hudson wrote an article on differential tempering ("The Best Method Of Differential Tempering," January 97 Blade*) and stated that edge quenching produces a wimpy blade. Your thoughts? I have noticed your preference for the edge-quench. I was wondering how the width is kept even, especially on curved blades?*

Answer: The following is what I require of an edge-quenched blade that's 10 inches long: It must undergo a 90-degree flex test without cracking. The appearance of the blade when viewed from the back should be as in Figure A (see illustration). Results such as in Figures B and C would be considered "wimpy" and not serviceable because they could be bent in normal use.

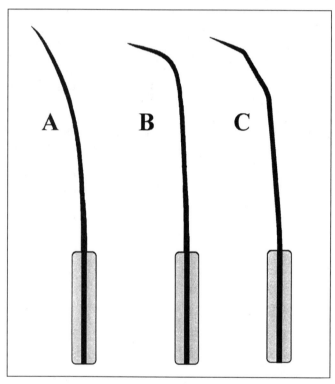

Three knife blades have been flexed 90 degrees. The drawing shows a view from the back of the blade, which shows the condition after the flex. "A" is a strong and stiff blade. This is about as good as it gets. "B" and "C" are wimpy. Blade "B" didn't have enough hard part and "C" was not tempered evenly. The areas where the sharp bends are show the areas that are softer than the rest.

Any method of selective hardening/tempering can result in a wimpy blade if not enough of the blade is hard. The way I do my selective hardening/tempering is so that the blade will return to less than a 15-degree bow from a 90-degree flex test. That's not wimpy.

Most makers who use the edge-quench have a regulator block, which is adjusted so that it is at the correct distance under the surface of the oil. The block makes the depth of quench nearly automatic. The distance the block is under the surface depends on the maker and width of blade. I want one-third to one-half of the blade hard on wide-blade camp and bowie knives. Hunting-size knives will get half or more hardened.

The curvature of the blade needs to be accounted for by rocking the blade on the regulator block. Usually the blade is put in tip first and then rocked down to quench the rest of the edge. This has to be done quickly with no hesitation.

I no longer use a regulator block but trust my judgment to get the desired amount of hard part in the blade. The edge quench is something that needs to be practiced before you attempt it on a real blade. Practice on an unheated blade until you have confidence in the method you chose. If the first blade you harden comes out uneven, just anneal it and do it again.

FREEZE TREATING

Cryogenics is the study of the properties of matter at low temperatures. The temperatures required for the full benefit of cryogenic treatment range from -200 to -300 degrees F. For example, the freeze treatment used by professional heat treater Paul Bos on ATS-34 is –220 degrees F for six to eight hours.

Steel that has chromium as an alloy element does not always harden with 100 percent martensite. Certain cryogenic treatments will complete the transformation of austenite to martensite. The first thing I learned when my testing program started 25 years ago was that freeze-treated blades always out cut the non-freeze-treated blades. Those first test comparisons were made between 154-CM and 440C by making slicing cuts on the single strands out of 1-inch rope.

Rifle barrels treated with a cryogenic process shoot tighter groups and have a longer life expectancy. An information sheet published by 300 Below Inc. explains the procedure the company uses on rifle barrels thus: "The new machine which processes rifle barrels uses controlled dry thermal treatment. Controlled simply states that the process is performed according to a precise and prescribed timetable. A 486 computer acts as a process controller to operate the descent, soak and ascent modes. The material is cooled slowly with a complex program to -310º degrees F, held for a day, then raised to +310 degrees F, and slowly returned to room temperature. The computer can be programmed to duplicate the optimal cooling curve within 1/10 of 1 degree F, so the mass descends at an even, slow rate. The control is extremely accurate and repeatable, time after time after time. The 'dry' process prevents the barrel from being subjected to liquid nitrogen and eliminates the risk of thermal shock.

"In one study there were three times more carbides observed in the steel after deep cryogenic processing. The internal stress in martensite is reduced, which minimizes the susceptibility to micro cracking. Carbide fillers are the particles that fill open spaces in the matrix. It is believed these particles are largely responsible for the great gains in wear resistance. Freeze-treated blades actually have a denser structure and a resulting larger surface area of contact."

Keep in mind that the above is from advertising literature. Ed Fowler and Phil Wilson had knife blades that were treated with liquid nitrogen and tested for stress cracks. None have been found so it seems that the stress in the relatively thin cross section of a knife blade is not sufficient to cause a problem.

As reported to me several years ago by knife-maker Steve Mullin, ATS-34 blades that he had hardened gained two points in hardness with an overnight freeze in a home-type freezer. This would not have been confirmed without a hardness tester. (It is essential to have a hardness tester if you are going to heat treat your own high-alloy blades.)

Several people have told me that because the temperature reached in a home-type freezer was not close to –300 degrees F, that the transformation would be somewhat reversible. I have not been able to confirm this, but it makes sense. The cryogenic industry would not be spending big money to make things real cold if it could be done with home freezer temperatures.

I like a good mystery because it gives me something to work on in my spare time. When I finally solve the mystery, I usually end up learning something new.

There was a mystery about the difference of opinions concerning the edge-holding ability of the two most popular steels of the 1970s — 154-CM and 440C. This mystery kept me going for the better part of 10 years. The solution to that mystery had everything to do with freeze treating.

As stated above, one of the first things I learned when I started comparing the edge-holding ability of blades was that freeze treating made an improvement. It made sense to me because in 1965 I had read a magazine article about cryogenic treatments done to a variety of materials. Every type of metal part that was treated would show an improvement of some type after freeze treating. The researchers had even noticed an improvement in the strength of nylon stockings after freeze treating them.

Back to the mystery from the 70s. I had a better opinion of the edge-holding ability of 154-CM than some makers who were using it did. There was also a general consensus among knifemakers that there was not enough difference between 154-CM and 440C to argue about. It shouldn't have taken me so long to figure out that they were right because the 154-CM knives they were using were not freeze treated. The mystery was solved. It was logical that there was not that much difference. That was a good lesson for me because it taught me to look past a disagreement to find the basis for the opposing opinions. I often get so excited about being right that I forget that I am sometimes playing with different rules than my adversary.

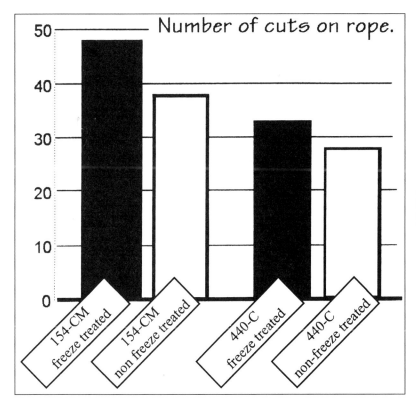

A comparison in edge-holding ability between freeze-treated and non-freeze-treated blades.

The following all have an effect on the freeze treated blade: Alloy content, microstructure of the steel after quenching, rate of cooling, maximum temperature below zero reached and the time at the freeze temperature. If the purpose of heat treating knife blades is to impart optimal strength and cutting ability, it is important that the heat treatment be done correctly. This means that the blade should have as much hardness as possible and still have sufficient toughness. Steel with the highest alloy content will not have superior edge-holding ability if it does not have a relatively high degree of hardness. The hardness of steel is a result of the percentage of martensite in the finished blade. Blades gain hardness when freeze treated. In many steels, freeze treating is necessary to complete a heat treatment that will bring out the full potential of the steel. With simple steels the correct hardening heat and the heat of the tempering process is adequate to produce the optimal amount of tempered martensite in the finished blade.

As alloys are added to steel, the heat-treating time and temperature cycles are often drastically changed. Longer soak times at just under and at the critical temperature are often necessary to get the alloy elements into solution. The tempering temperature is often higher, as well as being more critical. Longer tempering times and multiple temper cycles are sometimes necessary. The transformation of austenite to martensite is often not 100 percent completed by the quench when the alloy content is high. Freeze treating will cause the retained austenite to transform to martensite. This makes freeze treating essential for the proper heat treatment of stainless and other high-alloy steels.

The following is also from 300 Below Inc. advertising material.

Says a research metallurgist at the National Bureau of Standards: "The wide distribution of very hard, fine carbides from deep cryogenic treatment also increases wear resistance." The study concludes: "Fine carbides and resultant tight lattice structures are precipitated from cryogenic treatment. These particles are responsible for the exceptional wear characteristics imparted by the process, due to a denser structure and resulting larger surface area of contact, reducing friction, heat and wear."

To freeze or not to freeze, that is the question. I recommend it as long as some type of comparison is made with non-freeze treated blades.

Eliminating Stress Risers

A knife blade ready for the quench should be free of stress risers. A stress riser on a blade would be any sharp change in contour, a surface defect or even a coarse grinding mark on the surface. The classic stress riser that has caused many knives to break is a square corner where the tang meets the blade. The knife breaks at the junction of tang and blade where the two lines meet at 90 degrees. (See the drawing.) The break started with a small crack that was caused by the stress of the quench. This junction should have a nice smooth radius which will spread out the stress created in the quench.

I see many knives were made from files and rasps that have marks showing where there are remnants of the teeth left. So-called "buckskinner" knives are often made that have hammer marks left on the surface. The hammer marks usually show remnants of scale that was hammered into the surface. These defects and irregularities are all stress risers where microscopic cracks can form during the quench. These stress risers may lead to failure of an otherwise good blade.

When a blade fails because of a stress riser there is almost always a discolored area visible that shows where the crack started in the quench. At a recent demonstration -- teaching day at Fort Vancouver one of the participants brought a drawknife that he had forged and heat treated. It had warped quite badly in the quench and I thought I would straighten it for him. I gave it a soft back temper using heat tongs and proceeded to try to straighten it. It broke in half with very little pressure. The break crossed a medium sized hammer mark that had fire scale in the bottom. There was a dark line spreading out from the bottom of the dent, proof positive that the crack that caused the blade to break started in the quench. The break showed a nice fine grain and such a blade will usually not fail when given a soft back temper.

The blade had been quenched back first into the oil. This puts the back under compression and the edge in tension. In my opinion this is exactly backwards to gain the maximum strength in a blade.

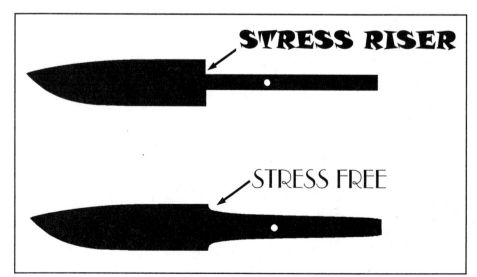

STRESS RISER

STRESS FREE

Heat Treatment of D-2	
Preheat	No preheat
Hardening Temperature and soak time	1800-1875F soak 20 minutes DON'T OVERHEAT
Quenching medium	Air
Hardness as quenched	63-64
Tempering Temperature and Freeze treatment sequence.	450° F 59Rc
Spring temper hardness	50Rc
Working hardness	59-61Rc
Annealing	Heat uniformly to 1550-1660F and cool slowly at a rate of not more than 20F per hour until the furnace is black. Turn off furnace and let cool naturally.

Heat Treatment of 440-C	
Preheat	Not necessary for blade size pieces
Hardening Temperature and soak time	1850°-1900° F
Quenching medium	Air or Oil
Hardness as quenched	59Rc
Tempering Temperature and Freeze treatment sequence.	212° F 59Rc 400° 56Rc
Spring temper hardness	1150° F 50Rc
Working hardness	56-58Rc
Annealing	For maximum softness soak at 1650°F for six hours followed by a furnace cool. Cycle anneal by heating to 1600°F, hold for two hours, cool to 1300°F, hold for four hours, then cool in air.

Heat treatment of CPM T440-V	
Preheat	1550º-1600ºF, then transfer to a furnace
Hardening Temperature and soak time	at 1850º-2050ºF Soak10-30 minutes depending on the section size and hardening temperature. (Lower temperatures require longer soak times.)
Quenching medium	Air or Oil
Hardness as quenched. The higher temperatures are used when abrasive resistance is desired. The lower temperatures are used when strength is required.	Air @ 2050ºF 61Rc Oil @ 2050ºF 63 Rc Air @ 1950ºF 59Rc Oil @ 1950ºF 60Rc Air @ 1850ºF 54Rc Oil @ 1850ºF 57Rc
Tempering Temperature and Freeze treatment sequence.	400-750 F Most makers use two 500F cycles of two hours. Freeze treating should be performed between the first and second tempers. Experiments are being done with continuous cooling from the hardening temperature right into the freeze treatment. More complete transformation of austenite is the desired result.
Spring temper hardness	50Rc 1100º F
Working hardness	58-60Rc
Annealing	Heat uniformly to 1625-1650ºF and hold for two hours, cool slowly with the furnace at a maximum rate of 25ºF per hour to at least 1200ºF, then air cool

Chapter 4

A LESSON IN PERSPECTIVE

There was a photo of a Scagle knife in a magazine and I wanted to make my version of it. The photo was about 3 inches long; the knife I wanted to make would be nearly 14 inches long. I took the magazine page to a copy shop and started making enlargements until I got the blade the size I wanted. At this point, the handle was nearly 7 inches long. That was about 15 to 20 percent longer than it should have been. It was then that I realized that the handle was closer to the camera than the blade. That put the perspective of the knife out of proportion to the real knife. In the small picture the perspective was not noticeable but it had to be reckoned with when enlarged to full size.

I surely can't see things from another's perspective because I haven't walked a mile in their shoes. I believe this causes many of the honest differences of opinion that are a part of life. I not only can't see an issue from the other side but my foolish pride will usually get me in an argument simply because I want to be right about my position. I'm so busy being right that I often don't hear the valid points that shoot down my argument. I once saw a sign that said: "What I said wasn't what I meant, and what you heard was not what I said." I've been there and done that. Most of us have filters that are quite efficient at blocking out things we do not to want to hear. We can't possibly have the whole picture on an issue when our filters are grinding away at it.

This applies to the methods and processes that are part of knifemaking. I don't always remember the exact instructions. I find it nearly impossible to do anything exactly the way I am told. I always think I can improve on it in some small way. That is why the things I present here may or may not work for another. Even if a method is followed exactly, differences in materials or equipment will give different results.

One of the more interesting things about knifemakers is that we do things in a lot of different ways and still get the job done. Many of the processes that are necessary to make a finished knife are quite complicated. If one step is omitted or done out of order the results may not be what was expected. When I say what works for me it doesn't mean that I am trying to get anyone to change the way they do it. What works for me is what works for me. I can't always defend my position other than to say it's just the way I do it.

Our shops, tools, and methods all have to evolve in their own time. It's like that with a good knife design. The real good ones have gone through an evolutionary process to get where they are; they didn't just jump off of a drawing board oneday.

My knifemaking journey has taken me a lot of different directions in 36 years of grinding and forging. I worked at several different specialties as I was developing my skills. I have tried lots of different ways of doing things. Some worked and others didn't, but I've always learned from the experience. I'm always changing the way I do things and what I end up with always works better than what I started with.

The Total Package

To start with, let me digress to an earlier time. The year was 1977. A knife had been sent to me for a minor repair and also to test the blade's edge-holding ability. It was a beautiful lock-blade folding knife with an ivory handle, filework and a Damascus blade. There were not a lot of Damascus knives at that time and Damascus folders were the rarest of all. It was a nice piece of work, but it would not cut anything!

When I tried to sharpen it, I could not get the blade sharp enough to make a single cut in the test rope. I could have concluded that the steel wasn't any good, but I didn't. The blade was much too thick at the cutting edge to be of any use as a cutting tool, a problem I refer to as "defective cross-section geometry." It was not possible to determine the edge-holding ability because of the thick edge.

From outward appearances and as a collector's item that knife may have been considered adequate by some, but as a useful knife it certainly was not. This started me thinking about knives as a total package, one that must be complete if the customer is to get full value for his money.

I teach my students a simplistic version of the total package concept, and that is that they should make knives that work, feel and look good. If one of these areas is lacking, the effort in making the knife is mostly wasted.

I understand that there is a market for fantasy and art knives, and as such it is not usually expected that they would ever do real work. Therefore, the exposition of my opinions that follows does not apply to such knives.

Deficiencies Often Found In Beautiful Knives And Possible Cures for Those Defects

1. Good steel, bad heat treatment. I am convinced that there is too much emphasis on the type of steel that is being used in knives. I get many skillfully crafted knives in for testing that will barely cut anything. In most cases the maker picked a good steel type but gave it an inferior heat treatment. Solution: Knifemakers interested in making real working knives should be doing some type of cutting comparisons with their knives. This is even more important for those who are doing their own heat treating. The number of heat treating furnaces in makers' shops is increasing. In my opinion, and especially concerning the high alloy steels like D2, ATS-34, 440C and the CPM steels, a hardness tester is essential. The performance of these steels depends on the tempered hardness being exactly right. Formulas for tempering and freeze treating are only good when the blade achieves full hardness in the hardening cycle.

2. Good steel, good heat treatment but bad cross-section geometry. At times the steel and heat treatment are good but the blade is too thick at the cutting edge to be of any real use as a cutting tool. Solution: Once more, if the maker was doing any comparisons, it would be evident that something needed to be changed.

3. The knife is not properly sharpened. When I did my cutting challenge at Knife Expo, the knives that were brought to the demonstration area for testing were either not sharp or had a wire-edge. These knives were on tables for sale at that show! None were capable of making a slicing cut on rope. Can it be that the maker who delivers a knife with an improperly sharpened blade has not cut many things with his knives? These knives were mostly well designed and were made of good quality steel. The total package was deficient because the blade would not do what it is supposed to do, and that is cut. Solution: To practice sharpening techniques and learn what type of edge gives the best results for each different kind of knife.

A VISIT WITH AN OLD-TIMER

I visited Rudy Ruana in 1969 and I don't remember seeing any belt grinders. There were several double-ended, pillow block arbors with large grinding wheels on them. The first thing I saw when I walked into the door was Rudy sitting on a stool in front of one of those grinding wheels. When he saw me he looked up and said he just wanted to finish this batch before he quit. So I just watched him work. There was a tray with about 10 knives in it on each side of the grinder. Rudy would take a knife out of the tray on the left, make several smooth movements at the

grinding wheel and place it in a tray on the right side. He was using the corner of a wheel to shape the inside curve on the cast aluminum pommel cap.

As he showed me around the shop I was amazed at how close to the finished shape his blades were when they came from the anvil. He said it took him only a couple of minutes on a grinding wheel to finish off a hunting-size blade. His knives were not real flat and shiny like most of what is done today but they were 100 percent adequate for the hard-working knives they were intended to be.

I owned two Ruana Bowie knives at the time of that visit and I had taken them with me in order to get a photo of Rudy holding them. (See photo.) When I showed them to Rudy he wanted us to go around to the back of the shop so he could show me how well he could "stick" (throw) them. Those Bowie knives had each cost me about two or three day's wages and I was not real excited about having them thrown. I told Rudy that even though I had heard that he was an expert knife thrower he didn't need to show me with my knives. Even though he assured me that it would not hurt them, he accepted the fact that I was protective of the knives. He had nothing in stock to throw and even seemed a bit disappointed that he could not demonstrate his knife throwing skills.

Rudy Ruana in front of his shop in Mill Town, Montana. The year was 1969 and he is holding two Ruana Bowie knives that belonged to the author.

The confidence he had in the strength of his knives was something I had not seen before and it gave me a worthy goal to work towards. It forever changed the way I was to think about what I was putting into my blades. I had only been making knives for about six years and it was a good time for me to be exposed to a high-performance, combat-quality blade.

THE COMBAT-QUALITY BLADE

Have you ever wondered what Jim Bowie or Davy Crockett would have thought of the knives in contemporary cutlery magazines? One such magazine was handy on my desk, so I opened it to see what I could find. I got to the Jantz Supply ad on page seven before I saw anything that Bowie or Crockett might recognize or find useful. Jantz will sell you a Russell, pioneer-style, sheep-skinner or buffalo-skinner blade. The two heroes of the Alamo would surely recognize those patterns.

As I continued my search through the magazine, I began to realize that there were not many pictures of down-to-earth, hard-working knives. I found myself categorizing the individual blades as being either real or make believe and that worked right into a discussion of what I call the Combat-Quality Knife (CQK).

Every knife enthusiast has an opinion as to what a bowie, camp, survival, tactical or combat piece should look like. It's not the precise shape of a knife but the cold, hard fact that it may be used as a weapon or as the primary tool in a survival situation that makes it a real knife.

When I make a "real" knife, it has to meet my CQK requirements. My specific standards for a CQK are based on the responsibility I feel toward my customers and myself. We must both have complete and total confidence in the overall strength and performance of my product. With these things in mind, I am limited to a rather narrow selection of steels, the type of heat treatment, handle construction and overall design criteria. I build the total CQK package with the goal of making it as fail safe as possible. I think Bowie and Crockett just might like the rough-use knives I put in that classification.

Of all the steels that I have worked with, 5160 chromium-steel has the best potential to make a blade that will have the proper balance of edge-holding ability and strength. The quality of the blade depends on the heat treatment and not so much on whether it is ground or forged to shape. I would rather forge a blade in my open-air smithy than grind inside my shop. There is less grinding time with a forged blade; I can make a big knife quicker by forging than I can with stock-removal. With forging, the whole blade-shaping process is more enjoyable for me.

What about Stainless Steel?

I am often asked to make a big, rough-use knife out of stainless steel but I don't do it. It's not that a good knife can't be made of stainless steel. It's my opinion that a rough-use knife should be unbreakable; at this point, I haven't mastered that in stainless steel.

Elements of the CQK Blade Design

Following are some of the things I have found to be true about a premium combat-quality knife: Blades with good distal taper will flex further without breaking than one that is parallel all the way to the tip. Thin blades have more ability to flex than thick ones. Cutting ability is how well the blade penetrates in chopping or slicing applications; it depends on the cross-section thickness of the blade. Edge-holding is the ability to stay sharp when compared to other blades and it depends on the alloy content and hardness. Selective hardening enables the blade to flex without breaking. The proportional amount of hard edge to blade width must be carefully worked out to give the blade adequate stiffness.

The Narrow-Tang Handle

Most of my early knives were full-tang; that's how I learned everything that can go wrong with full-tang knives. As I saw the results from rough use, abuse and even knives that had been lost and laid out in the weather for a season or two. This got me thinking about using narrow-tang construction. The exposed edges of a full tang are an open invitation for loosening, breaking or such. Properly done, the narrow-tang knife is superior because it is a sealed unit and there is less to go wrong with it on a rough-use knife.

I began to refine my full-tang construction techniques in 1982 when I got into making Damascus steel and forging most of my knives. I extend the tang with a piece of bolt or all thread. I use silver braze to attach the bolt section that goes all the way through the Micarta®. Only Micarta® will do for the CQK handle. I put the guard on first so that a bolt section can be used that is a larger diameter than the thickness of the blade which is rarely over 1/4 of an inch. I use a bolt size of 5/16 to 3/8-inch depending on the diameter of the handle. I silver braze a nut of the correct size to the inside of the pommel cap. It makes a very solid and perfectly sealed unit once the whole works is fitted up, filled with epoxy and the pommel cap is tightened. (See drawing.)

To test this type of construction, I hammered a narrow-blade Bowie through the cross-grain side of a 2-by-4. The knife had a forged blade, steel guard, Micarta® handle and steel pommel cap. The only damage was a slightly mushroomed and dented pommel cap. (See photo.)

The Combat Quality Knife that was driven through a 2 x 4. Wire damascus blade, steel guard and pommel cap, and a Micarta® handle.

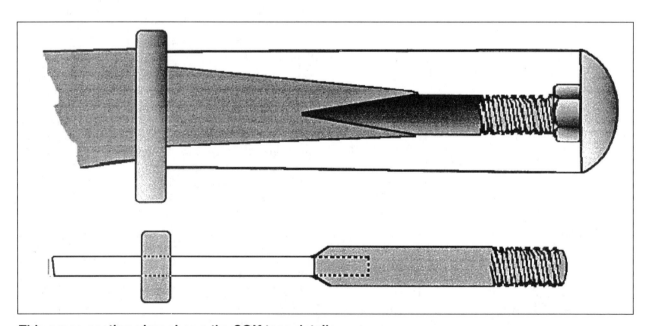

This cross-section view shows the CQK tang details.

CPM: THE STEEL OF TOMORROW?

by Wayne Goddard, ABS master smith
photos courtesy Crucible Specialty Metals

The advantages of CPM (Crucible Particle Metallurgy) steels as compared to their conventional counterparts would seem to make them a legitimate contender for front-runner status among knife steels. But what about other factors, such as cost and availability? Let's take a closer look at CPM and its predecessor, powder metallurgy (PM).

The traditional PM process uses the pressing of blended metal powders into a mold (compacting). The compacted part is then heated to just below the melting point (sintered). Sintering is similar to forge welding since the individual particles are bonded without melting down. Parts can be produced that contain elements that would not be possible to include in normal casting procedures. An example of this is the self-lubricating bearing used in power tools and electric motors. Porous metal parts can be made through the PM process, such as the filters used in gas and oil lines, as can metal-cutting-tool inserts of tungsten carbide and the ceramic inserts. Most PM parts are made to the finished dimensions required.

One of the first modern uses of PM dates back to 1909. The process for making tungsten wire had not yet been developed. The PM process was successfully used to make tungsten filament wire, which then made possible the economical manufacturing of the electric light bulb. This example shows one of the major advantages of the PM process, that is, it makes possible certain alloys, shapes and grain structures that otherwise would not be possible or commercially feasible.

According to Bill Owens of Crucible Specialty Metals with division offices in Syracuse, New York, his company took

the traditional PM process one step further when it introduced the Crucible Particle Metallurgy (CPM) process in 1970, and produced solid bar and plate stock from pre-alloyed tool-steel powders. The CPM process is different than the PM process in that it is used to make a large compact (billet), which is then forged or rolled into the desired bar shapes.

Crucible Specialty Metals' brochure describes the CPM process as follows: "Molten pre-alloyed steel is poured into a high pressure gas atomizer and sprayed out in fine particles of steel, each particle a micro-ingot containing the precise analysis of the molten steel. Because the particles are cooled instantly, carbide segregation is eliminated and each micro-ingot is a duplicate of all others in structure and composition. The atomized particles of steel are screened for a uniform and fine size to assure full density and uniformity in the finished steel. The screened

particles are poured into steel cans, which are evacuated of all gases, sealed, heated and lowered into the chamber of a gas autoclave (an airtight chamber). The filled and heated cans are isostatically pressed to produce a fully dense compact of steel. These compacts are then forged and rolled on conventional mill processing equipment to produce the variety of bar, rod, wire, sheet or plate product forms required by industry."

The hot part of this operation is very much like the forge welding of Damascus steel. If the temperature is not kept under the melting point, forge-welded Damascus steels and CPM steels would

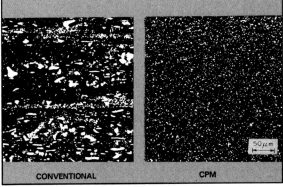

Large grain size and uneven distribution of the carbides are the disadvantages of conventional stainless-steel bar stock (left). The CPM steels (right) solve this problem.

not have their unique physical properties.

Large grain size and uneven distribution of the carbides are the disadvantages of conventional stainless-steel bar stock. The CPM steels solve this problem. The wear resistance and strength of CPM steels are always greater than the same alloys made in conventional methods; this is a direct result of the fine grain size and the even distribution of the alloy elements.

CPM 440V shows most promise as a

CPM Steels Vs. Common Knife Steels

Steel Type	Carbon	Manganese	Silicon	Chromium	Molybdenum	Vanadium
440C	1.20	1.00	1.00	18.00	.75	-
CPM 440V	2.20	.50	.50	17.5	.50	5.75
154CM	1.02	.60	.25	14.0	4.0	-
CPM 10V	2.45	.50	.90	5.23	1.3	9.75

(Left) Molten, pre-alloyed steel is poured into a high-pressure gas atomizer and sprayed out in fine particles of steel. Each particle is a micro-ingot containing the precise analysis of the molten steel. Because the particles are cooled instantly, carbide segregation is eliminated and each micro-ingot is a duplicate of all others in structure and composition.

in the toughness department.

(Editor's note: Bill Owens writes, "We do not dispute Wayne's test results comparing toughness between CPM 10V and CPM 440V, as we do not know the method that he used. However, our extensive research indicates that CPM 10V should have the same toughness at Rc 57-58, although most people harden it to Rc 60-62 for greater wear resistance.")

The very high carbon content of CPM 440V and CPM 10V, along with their high vanadium content, gives them superior edge-holding ability. The fine grain and even distribution of the alloy elements is advantageous in grinding and finishing. Crucible is making a strong attempt to make CPM 440V easily available and perhaps more economically priced than previously. If they succeed in this and the knifemakers give it a fair try, CPM 440V may become the most used steel of the '90s. —

Editor's note: Texas Knifemakers Supply stocks CPM 440V in several sizes for knifemaking. For more information contact it at 10649 Haddington, Ste. 180, attn: Ed Thuesen, Dept. BL, Houston, TX 77043 (713) 461-8632.

superior blade material for working-type stainless knives. My tests show it to have two-to-three times more edge-holding ability than 440C, both being tested at 57-58 Rc. The CPM steels that I have worked with are easier to grind and polish than conventional stainless. CPM 440V has more than adequate strength for hunting-size knives. CPM 10V, which is not stainless, has even more edge-holding ability than CPM 440V, but is not as good

(Left) The filled and heated cans are isostatically pressed to produce a fully dense compact (billet) of steel. (Right) These compacts are then forged and rolled on conventional mill processing equipment to produce the variety of bar, rod, wire, sheet or plate product forms required.

Tempil°
Basic Guide to Ferrous Metallurgy

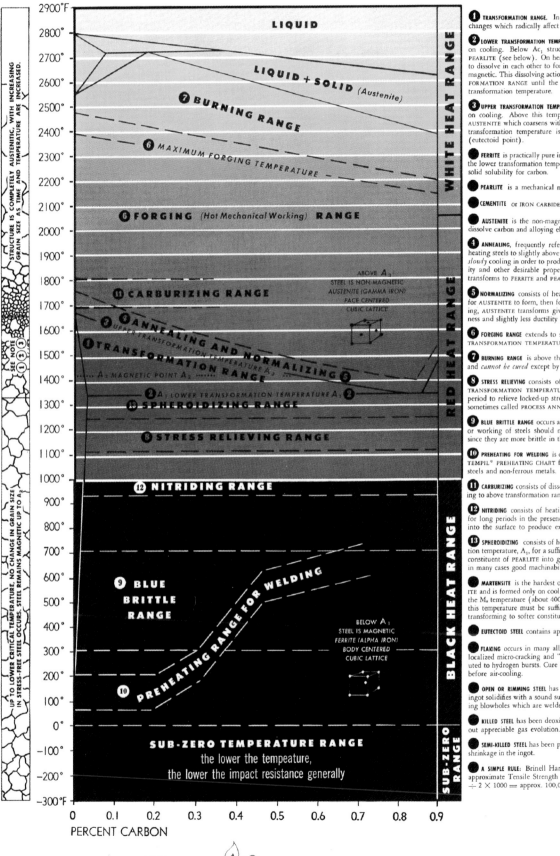

1 TRANSFORMATION RANGE. In this range steels undergo internal atomic changes which radically affect the properties of the material.

2 LOWER TRANSFORMATION TEMPERATURE (A_1). Termed Ac_1 on heating, Ar_1 on cooling. Below Ac_1 structure ordinarily consists of FERRITE and PEARLITE (see below). On heating through Ac_1 these constituents begin to dissolve in each other to form AUSTENITE (see below) which is non-magnetic. This dissolving action continues on heating through the TRANSFORMATION RANGE until the solid solution is complete at the upper transformation temperature.

3 UPPER TRANSFORMATION TEMPERATURE (A_3). Termed Ac_3 on heating, Ar_3 on cooling. Above this temperature the structure consists wholly of AUSTENITE which coarsens with increasing time and temperature. Upper transformation temperature is lowered as carbon increases to 0.85% (eutectoid point).

● FERRITE is practically pure iron (in plain carbon steels) existing below the lower transformation temperature. It is magnetic and has very slight solid solubility for carbon.

● PEARLITE is a mechanical mixture of FERRITE and CEMENTITE.

● CEMENTITE or IRON CARBIDE is a compound of iron and carbon, Fe_3C.

● AUSTENITE is the non-magnetic form of iron and has the power to dissolve carbon and alloying elements.

4 ANNEALING, frequently referred to as FULL ANNEALING, consists of heating steels to slightly above Ac_3, holding for AUSTENITE to form, then *slowly* cooling in order to produce small grain size, softness, good ductility and other desirable properties. On cooling slowly the AUSTENITE transforms to FERRITE and PEARLITE.

5 NORMALIZING consists of heating steels to slightly above Ac_3, holding for AUSTENITE to form, then followed by cooling (in still air). On cooling, AUSTENITE transforms giving somewhat higher strength and hardness and slightly less ductility than in annealing.

6 FORGING RANGE extends to several hundred degrees above the UPPER TRANSFORMATION TEMPERATURE.

7 BURNING RANGE is above the FORGING RANGE. Burned steel is ruined and *cannot be cured* except by remelting.

8 STRESS RELIEVING consists of heating to a point below the LOWER TRANSFORMATION TEMPERATURE, A_1, holding for a sufficiently long period to relieve locked-up stresses, then slowly cooling. This process is sometimes called PROCESS ANNEALING.

9 BLUE BRITTLE RANGE occurs approximately from 300° to 700° F. Peening or working of steels should not be done between these temperatures, since they are more brittle in this range than above or below it.

10 PREHEATING FOR WELDING is carried out to prevent crack formation. See TEMPIL° PREHEATING CHART for recommended temperature for various steels and non-ferrous metals.

11 CARBURIZING consists of dissolving carbon into surface of steel by heating to above transformation range in presence of carburizing compounds.

12 NITRIDING consists of heating certain *special steels* to about 1000° F for long periods in the presence of ammonia gas. Nitrogen is absorbed into the surface to produce extremely hard "skins".

13 SPHEROIDIZING consists of heating to just below the lower transformation temperature, A_1, for a sufficient length of time to put the CEMENTITE constituent of PEARLITE into globular form. This produces softness and in many cases good machinability.

● MARTENSITE is the hardest of the transformation products of AUSTENITE and is formed only on cooling below a certain temperature known as the M_s temperature (about 400° to 600° F for carbon steels). Cooling to this temperature must be sufficiently rapid to prevent AUSTENITE from transforming to softer constituents at higher temperatures.

● EUTECTOID STEEL contains approximately 0.85% carbon.

● FLAKING occurs in many alloy steels and is a defect characterized by localized micro-cracking and "flake-like" fracturing. It is usually attributed to hydrogen bursts. Cure consists of cycle cooling to at least 600° F before air-cooling.

● OPEN OR RIMMING STEEL has not been completely deoxidized and the ingot solidifies with a sound surface ("rim") and a core portion containing blowholes which are welded in subsequent hot rolling.

● KILLED STEEL has been deoxidized at least sufficiently to solidify without appreciable gas evolution.

● SEMI-KILLED STEEL has been partially deoxidized to reduce solidification shrinkage in the ingot.

● A SIMPLE RULE: Brinell Hardness divided by two, times 1000, equals approximate Tensile Strength in pounds per square inch. (200 Brinell ÷ 2 × 1000 = approx. 100,000 Tensile Strength, p.s.i.)

Tempil°
DIVISION, AIR LIQUIDE AMERICA CORP.

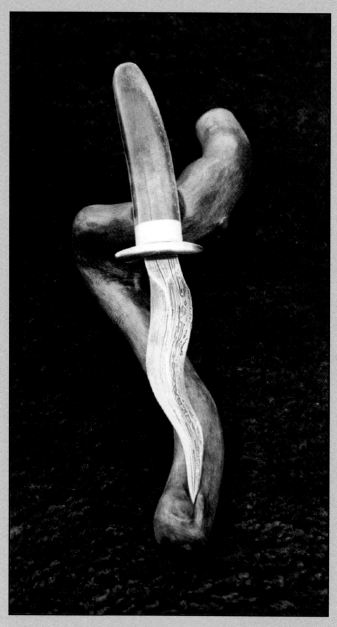

Wavy-blade dagger made of wire Damascus. The guard is copper-nickel, the handle of fossil ivory. The display base is a branch from a "corkscrew" willow tree.
(Goddard photo)

Folding knife group: At the top is a spring-back with a blade of ATS-34 and a handle of dyed and stabilized maple. In the center is spring-back with handle slabs of elk antler with a forged thong-holder. At the bottom is a friction folder with a forged blade and carved and sculptured handle of deer antler.
(Goddard photo)

Forged camp knife with a 12-inch blade of 5150, full/tapered tang with stag handle slabs.
(Goddard photo)

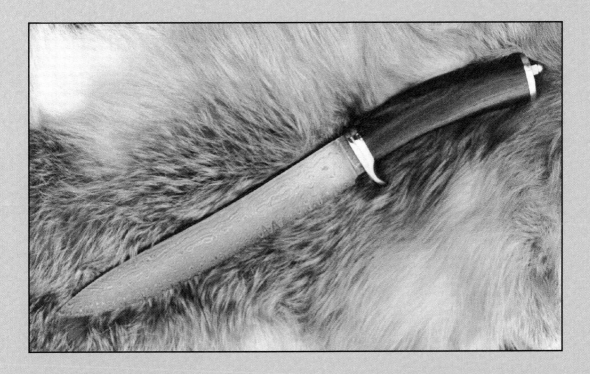

Pattern welded camp knife with bronze fittings and a desert ironwood handle.
(Goddard photo)

Stag-handled Bowie knife in a typical Goddard
hand-stitched sheath.
(Goddard photo)

A group of miniature knives. Top to bottom; pattern welded Bowie, guard-less skinner, pattern welded with fossil ivory handle, skinner with guard and fossil ivory handle, The two all steel miniatures at the bottom were forged from automobile valve springs. (Goddard photo)

Miniature "crown" folding knife that is 1-inch long when closed. The antler crown handle was carved crown from elk antler. It has a stainless blade and spring with file-work. The display base made out of a deer antler "button".
(Goddard photo)

A group of miniature knives that have pattern welded blades. All have fossil ivory handles except the one at the bottom of the picture, that one has a stag handle.
(Goddard photo)

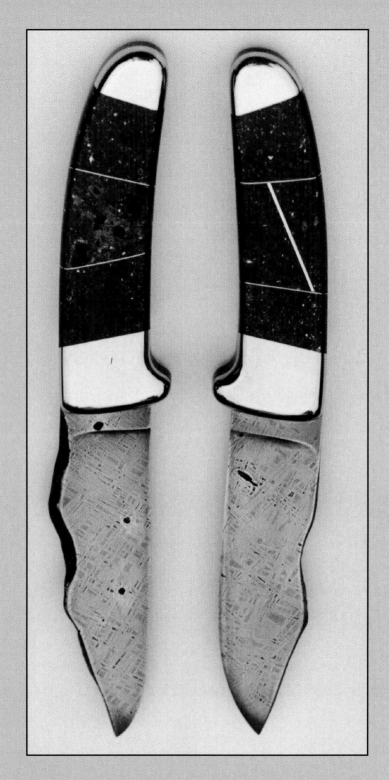

This pair of knives was a custom order where the customer furnished the materials. The blades are ground out of an iron meteorite slab; the handles are made of stony meteorite. The fittings are nickel silver. The shape of the back of the blade is the natural "thumb-print" pattern that is common on metallic meteorites.
(Goddard photo)

Group of four knives. At the right is a narrow bladed hunting knife with stag handle, nickel silver guard and pommel cap. The big knife is one of my Tribal series knives. It has a forged-in finger guard and pommel cap. The small knife is made of wire Damascus. It was constructed as follows. A square bar about 9 inches long was made by forge welding wire rope. The bar was then forged flat in the center section. The bar was then bent double and the two ends forge welded together to make the blade portion. It was then forged into the finished shape. These are simple looking knives but very challenging and time-consuming. The knife at the left is another in my Tribal series. The wavy blade was forged completely to shape with the only stock removal being the sharpening. The guard was forged and hot-punched to fit the tang. The handle is elk antler with a copper ferrule and pommel cap.
(Goddard photo)

Camp ax made of wire Damascus handle made to order for a horseback hunter. It takes a standard, tapered, "hawk" handle. The customer wanted this style handle so it could be taken down for carry in his saddlebags. The small hammerhead would be used to tighten or replace a horseshoe nail.
(Goddard photo)

This pair of forged knives both have integral guards. To get the double guard on the knife at the top, two "ears" were split off from the tang area and then forged to shape. The blade was then drawn out from the material ahead of the guard. It has a handle of snakewood with a steel guard. To make the single guard of the bottom knife, a short section of steel was split out from the bottom side of the tang, then forged and ground to shape. It has a full/tapered tang with slabs of desert ironwood. Both are made of 5160 round bar stock from a giant coil spring.
(Goddard photo)

Boot knife with a blade made of motorcycle chain. The guard is nickel silver; the handle made of green Micarta.
(Goddard photo)

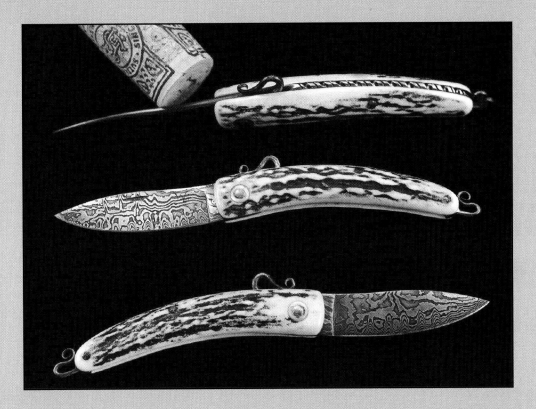

Friction folder with a 2-inch pattern welded blade, forged details and filework on the spacer.
(Barry Gallagher Photo)

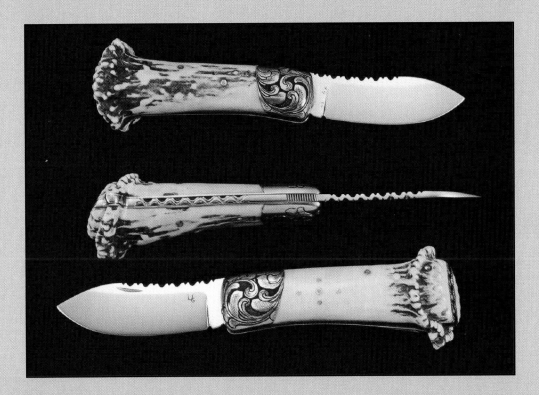

Crown folder from 1977. It has a stock-removal blade that is 3 1/2 inches long, filework and decorative pins to dress up the smooth area on the handle.
(Barry Gallagher Photo)

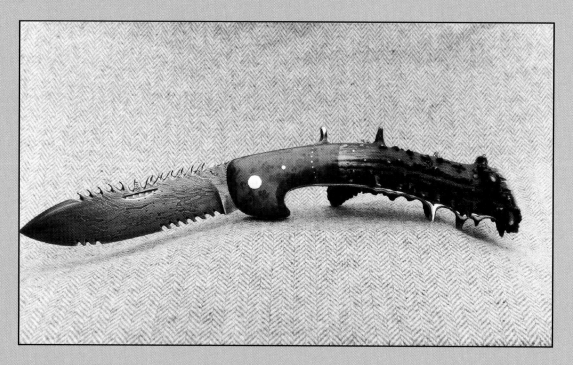

Large crown folder with a wire Damascus blade. The handle is deer antler with a bolster made of thuya burl decorated with pins.
(Goddard photo)

Crown folder with the button intact. This was accomplished by sawing out the back side handle piece. All the parts are made to work and then assembled to make it look like it grew that way. The rosewood bolsters have a decorative pattern made with pins.
(Barry Gallagher Photo)

Crown folder with a pattern-welded blade and rosewood bolsters.
(Goddard photo)

Forged hunting knife made to be in a movie. The knife and sheath were worked
to make them look old. The guard is steel, the handle is made of leather spacers
with a deer antler crown.

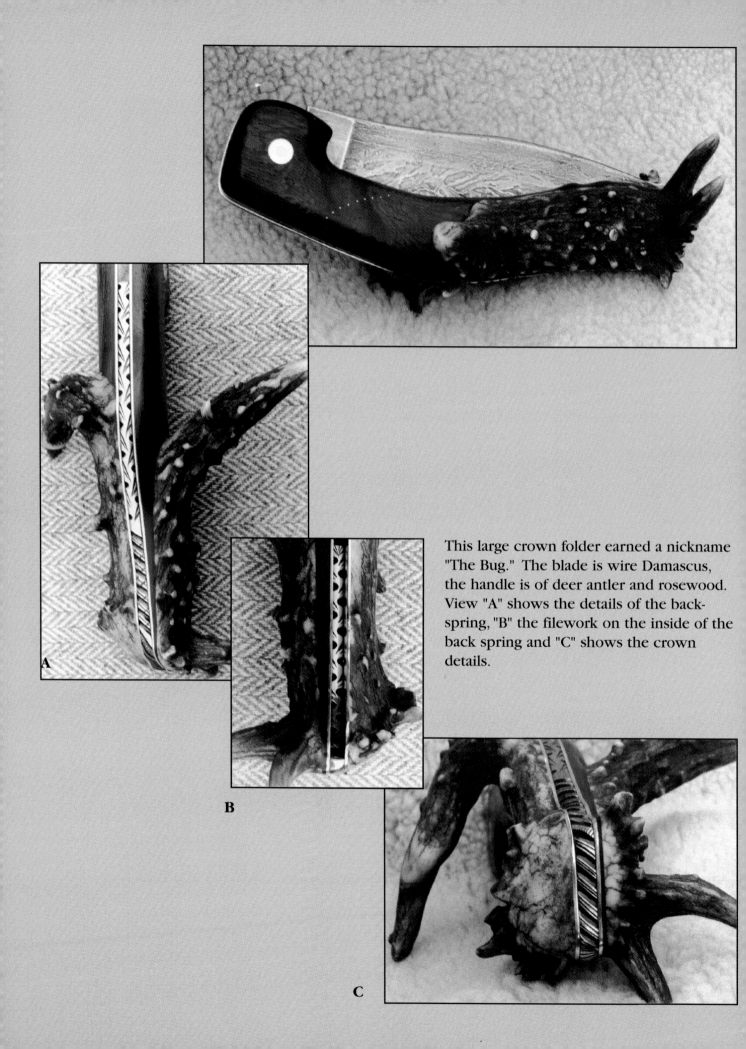

This large crown folder earned a nickname "The Bug." The blade is wire Damascus, the handle is of deer antler and rosewood. View "A" shows the details of the back-spring, "B" the filework on the inside of the back spring and "C" shows the crown details.

A

B

C

A group of three folding knives with Damascus blades. The friction folder at the top has a wire Damascus blade and a handle made of elk antler. The folder in the center is worn as a belt buckle. It has a wire Damascus blade, nickel silver fittings and a handle of weathered elk antler. The elegant little folder at the bottom has a pattern welded blade. The handle has nickel silver bolsters with pearl slabs. (Goddard photo)

Knife Jewelry. The knife in the bolo tie slide has a Damascus blade and a pearl handle. The slide is made from a brow spike from large deer antler; it has a snakewood top with a back made of ivory Micarta(r). The little folder in the center is worn as a pendant; it has a stainless blade, nickel silver fittings and pearl handle slabs. The miniature knife has a sheath that is hooked to a thong so that it can be worn around the neck. (Goddard photo)

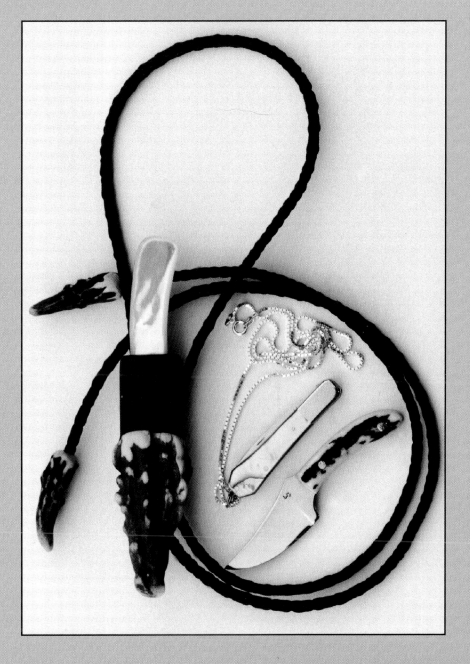

The bladesmith caught at work. The dirty hand is pulling the handle of an old-fashioned bellows at the reconstruction of Fort Vancouver in Washington State. That's honest sweat and I'm having fun teaching others what I can about forging knives.
(Photo courtesy of The National Park Service.)

Massive forged Bowie and sheath. The 15-inch blade is made of chromium vanadium steel (6150).
(Goddard photo)

Chapter 5

THE SMITHY

THE VILLAGE BLACKSMITH

Under a spreading chestnut-tree
The village smithy stands;
The smith, a mighty man is he,
With large and sinewy hands;
And the muscles of his brawny arms
Are strong as iron bands.
His hair is crisp, and black, and long,
His face is like the tan;
His brow is wet with honest sweat,
He earns whate'er he can,
And looks the whole world in the face,
For he owes not any man.
Week in, week out, from morn till night,
You can hear his bellows blow;
You can hear him swing his heavy sledge,
With measured beat and slow,
Like a sexton ringing the village bell,
When the evening sun is low.
And children coming home from school
Look in at the open door;
They love to see the flaming forge,
And hear the bellows roar,
And catch the burning sparks that fly
Like chaff from a threshing-floor.
He goes on Sunday to the church,
And sits among his boys;
He hears his daughter's voice,
And it makes his heart rejoice.
It sounds to him like her mother's voice,
Singing in Paradise!
He needs must think of her once more,
How in the grave she lies;
And with his hard, rough hand he wipes
A tear out of his eyes.
Toiling, -- rejoicing, -- sorrowing,
Onward through life he goes;
Each morning sees some task begin,
Each evening sees it close;
Something attempted, something done,
Has earned a night's repose.
Thanks, thanks to thee, my worthy friend,
For the lesson thou hast taught!
Thus at the flaming forge of life
Our fortunes must be wrought;
Thus on its sounding anvil shaped
Each burning deed and thought.

By Henry Wadsworth Longfellow

The Goddard Smithy

I didn't have a spreading chestnut tree so I built a lean-to on the back side of my shop. The floor space is about 9 feet by 15 feet and adequate for my needs. The climate in the Willamette Valley of Oregon is mild so I get by real well. I'm so used to the fresh air that I don't have nearly as much fun when I have to forge inside a building. The hydraulic press makes very little noise so I can do some heavy forging without shaking the neighborhood. I'm going to build an air hammer soon and I may have to put a building around it.

I'm outside the city limits but in a residential neighborhood. My neighbors are understanding and were surprised when they found out all that I was doing in my back yard. It's not like I'm hammering all day, every day. A three-hour forging party will keep me busy with finish work and heat treating for up to two weeks.

THE ANVIL: A BLADESMITH'S MOST IMPORTANT TOOL

The first anvil used by a metalsmith most likely was a large rock. I have a video that shows contemporary African ironsmiths making iron and forging tools. For rough forging, a large rock is used for an anvil and a smaller rock is used as a two-handed sledgehammer. I believe basalt would be adequate for an anvil and that is what I will look for someday when I decide to make a "mineral" anvil.

The anvil probably evolved from rock to cast iron and then steel. By the 1850s, the anvil reached perfection with a welded-up construction using two or

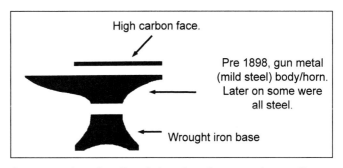

Construction details of the classic wrought anvil.

High carbon face.

Pre 1898, gun metal (mild steel) body/horn. Later on some were all steel.

Wrought iron base

three pieces of metal in what is called a London pattern anvil. (See illustration.)

The shape of an anvil is perhaps not as important as that it be hard and tough so as to withstand the blow of the hammer without denting or breaking. The anvil also needs to be heavy enough to absorb the blow of the hammer. (A heavy hammer requires a heavier anvil.) The horn that is typical of the blacksmith anvil is not necessary for forging knives. The Japanese sword maker uses an anvil that has no horn; it is instead a simple rectangle of steel. The Japanese have no need for a horn, and it is easier to forge blades on a short, rectangular anvil anyway.

As far as I am concerned, the anvil is the king of tools. A blacksmith who has mastered his craft can make virtually any object. All that is required is imagination, inspiration, a hammer, an anvil, a source of heat, and a good supply of iron and steel. A skillful smith can do good work on any heavy chunk of steel. A specific anvil shape only makes specialty work easier. A soft anvil will get dented up quickly and that makes it difficult to do good work. You have to work harder on a soft anvil because the hammer does not get the bounce it does off a hard anvil. If you plan to do much forging, it will be well worth the effort to find a first-class anvil.

The true value of an anvil with a hard face is not easy to understand until you have worked on both hard and soft ones. I would rather work on a small anvil with a good hard face than a big, but soft one. When I was getting started forging, I had a 150-pound Acme cast anvil in my indoor forge area. As anvils go it was quite soft but I used it for several years and got by just fine as long as I didn't know any better. I sold it and replaced it with an 85-pound Hay-Budden. That little anvil was as hard as any anvil I have ever seen. Only then did I realize how much easier it was to forge on a hard anvil. Because of its extremely hard face, the little Hay-Budden acted like a heavier anvil.

FINDING & SELECTING
AN ANVIL

In my experience, the best of the classic anvils are Hay-Budden, Trenton and Peter Wright. These brands were made using the welding process described above. Carry a 1-inch ball bearing with you when you go anvil shopping. Drop the ball onto the face from about 18 inches. The best anvils will bounce the ball back into your hand. Any bounce less than 60 percent should be considered fair. Less than 40 percent is poor. When one of the name-brand anvils has poor bounce it may have been through a fire. A quality anvil can be heat treated to bring it back to life. I recently hardened a 125-pound Peter Wright that was dead soft. The ball-bearing test only dented the face with little bounce. I will save the story of heat treating it for another time. Suffice it to say it took a lot of heat to get it hot

and a lot of water to cool it fast enough to get it hard. The results were very good and I now have a very serviceable anvil.

Judging from what I have seen, the average Hay-Budden has a harder face than most Peter Wrights do. I believe that is why I have seen more good-condition (those with less chipped corners) Peter Wright anvils. When a forged anvil has a hard face welded on it, the hard face is most often visible. The hard plate is usually about 1/2-inch thick on anvils in the 150-pound size range.

Square corners are not necessary for knife work so I do not let chipped edges bother me as long as I have a hard and somewhat flat face. I usually take an angle grinder and round off the chipped edges. I have a hardy tool with square edges for the rare times I want a sharp corner on which to forge. Chipped anvils can be built up by welding but that softens the rest of the hard face. I would rather have a hard anvil face with rounded corners than a soft surface with square corners.

Good work can be done on an anvil that is quite beat up. During the learning phase, the anvil is going to take some abuse from the hammer. It may actually be a good idea for a beginner not to forge on a new anvil. Unless you are a silversmith you don't need a virgin surface to work on. It is best to use an anvil for awhile and then consider what needs fixing on it. If you weld on an anvil to repair it you will usually soften it. (Not good!) Following is how I fix a dent on a soft anvil. Take a ball pein, (pein end) and work the area around the ding down even with it. Over a period of time the anvil gets better from the work hardening.

A question was asked about a hammer dent that was .035 deep, which is about 1/32 of an inch. I devised the "Divot Test" which goes like this. Heat a piece of steel to the forging temperature and place it on the anvil face directly over the divot. Give the hot steel some good hammer blows directly over and around the place where the divot is. Let the steel cool and inspect both sides of the forged piece. If your hammer dings are just as noticeable as the hump left by the divot, then no work should be done on the anvil. I do 99% of my forging in an area that is about 3 inches by 4 inches. If you have that much smooth area on a good hard anvil that's all you really need.

If you are buying from a knowledgeable tool dealer, you can expect to pay an average of $2 to $3 per pound for the aforementioned brands of anvils in good condition. You will pay around $4 per pound for a new anvil. A good source for new anvils, hammers and tongs is Centaur Forge at (800) 666-9175.

It is good to know how to tell a cast anvil from the ones with a forged body with welded-on faces (wrought anvils). Forged anvils have square holes at the waist and sometimes in the bottom, which is how they are held secure while being forged, ground and heat treated. Old cast anvils do not have the square recesses and are squat and chunky compared to forged anvils that are more slender and graceful.

THE ENGLISH SYSTEM FOR MARKING THE WEIGHT OF AN ANVIL

Most English anvils are stamped with the weight using three numbers. The numbers are usually in the waist area, with the first one at the far left, the second one in the center and the third one on the right. The first number equals 112 pounds (CWT or hundredweight); the middle number is quarters of 112 added to the first number; and the last number is the actual weight. Thus, a Peter Wright anvil, which is marked "1 1 16," is 112 pounds plus one quarter of 112 (28 pounds), plus 16 pounds, which equals 156 pounds.

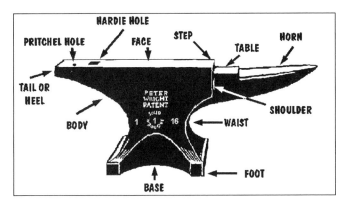

The classic Peter Wright with all the parts named.

Good luck in your search for an anvil. It is a fascinating tool and can turn up in the strangest places. Ask around. You may be surprised at how close to home you will find one. I went to look at a small coal forge that a plumber had used to melt lead. His widow had seen my sign, "WANTED TO BUY, BLACKSMITH TOOLS." I usually put the sign on my table when I have my knives for sale at a local show. I bought the small rivet-type forge and a lead pot. I asked about other tools and the lady told me that there was an anvil around somewhere on her place but she had not seen it for a long time. I looked around inside a falling-down shop building. Behind a door that had come off its hinges and half buried in the ground was the 150-pound Acme cast anvil that I wrote about earlier in this story. The lady put a fair price on it, so I lugged it off with the forge and lead pot.

I had a Henry Wright anvil once upon a time but that is another story...

The Henry Wright Anvil

(The rest of the story.)

We were coming home from some time off spent in Idaho. My favorite stop is a secondhand store in Burns, Oregon. A sign says, "I buy junk and sell antiques." I found some hammers, paid for them,

and was getting ready to leave. I would have missed the Henry Wright anvil but my wife Phyllis found it in a side room and called me over to see it. The price was right so I purchased it and we brought it home in back of our Camaro.

I fixed it up on a nice stacked particleboard base and it was in use for awhile by students who came to study with me. I took it with my portable outfit to the Northwest Safari Cutlery Rendezvous one year. I won the speed-forging contest using it. (See the photo.)

One day I got a call from a gentleman who wanted to buy one of my booklets on bladesmithing. I invited him out and as we were going through the booklet I decided it would be best to show him a homemade gas forge and what it would do. The real thing is always better than to just look at a drawing in a book.

We headed out to the smithy and I fired up my little dragon-breath forge. I stuck a piece of 1084 in it to get hot while we talked forges, hammers and anvils. When my steel was hot I forged a small blade to shape. I put another bar of steel in the forge

That's the little Henry Wright anvil. It only weighed 85 pounds and that's a bit light for me. Note the 30-pound steel plate between it and the base, this is exactly the same as having a heavier anvil. This is my portable outfit. The Work Mate® holds the forge, goop quench and a small Wilton vise. Note the plastic garbage can on the ground. That was a bright and sunny day so I put it there so I could stick the hot steel into the shade to see what color it really was. Note the square holes in the waist and base of the anvil. These holes show that it was a forged or wrought anvil.

and handed my visitor a spare hammer that I had fixed up for visitors to use. While the steel got hot I showed him some hammer techniques and talked about blade pre-forms. When the steel was hot he went to work and forged a blade.

The rest of the story is; he took home a booklet, some rough forged blades, a hammer and the Henry Wright anvil.

THE MAKESHIFT ANVIL

The lack of an anvil is the one thing that delays many people who would like to get into forging. A good quality anvil is a specially shaped, heavy chunk of steel with a hard surface. The hard surface makes the work easier but is not essential. Any heavy piece of steel will work, 100 pounds is a minimum size to start with. The weight is necessary to absorb the blow of the hammer. More weight is needed whenever the anvil and base are bouncing around under the hammer. The horn on a traditional shaped blacksmith anvil is rarely used by a bladesmith and ends up being an unnecessary attachment. Some bladesmiths use the horn for drawing out but it is not efficient for that. A rounded back corner on the face of the anvil works much better. (See photo.)

The $50 Knife Shop anvil. This anvil has an unusual shape and it makes the most unusual noise. It's kind of like "Whump" when you hit the work. It has a big hole through the center, I've thought about plugging it to see if that would make it sound more like a "real" anvil.

The side view of the 4-inch by 5-inch face of my post anvil. The edge at the left of the photo is rounded and is used as a drawing surface, it is at the back when the anvil is in use.

I made a makeshift anvil for "The $50 Knife Shop" series for *Blade Magazine*. (See photo.) All materials were obtained at no cost other than the labor and time to haul them home. The main body of the $50 Knife Shop anvil was one half of a coupling from a railroad car. I welded it to a base plate, added an upright support and then added steel plates to one side to make a 1-inch square opening for my hardy tools. There is a tapered concave surface on the top where I welded the plates to make the hardy hole. This works great for decorative or other work where a straight bar is bent into a curved section. The weight of the anvil, (135 pounds) plus the heavy particle board base makes it more than adequate for knife work. Note the spring fuller in the hardy hole.

Salvage yards sell steel chunks relatively cheap; it cost me $22 for a 125-pound rectangle that will be the body for my dream anvil. Don't wait to get started because you don't have a real anvil. Rocks were, and still are, used for anvils in places more primitive than our part of planet Earth.

THE WORST ANVIL I EVER WORKED ON

A number of years ago I went out to my friend Bruce's shop to teach him about forging knife blades. He had made a coal forge from plans found in *The Mother Earth News* and had a piece of rail-road rail for an anvil. The forge was made out of a 55 gallon drum and even though it was a terrible design it did work just well enough to heat a piece of coil spring to the forging temperature. The railroad rail "anvil" was mounted on a sawhorse. It was a rough evening, the anvil rang like a bell and it was interesting to chase it around the shop as it jumped and walked across the floor on its sawhorse base. The rail was not heavy enough to absorb the blow of the hammer and that makes the forging take longer because much of the blow is wasted. After that evening I formed a plan to someday make a good anvil out of a piece of rail.

THE RAILROAD RAIL ANVIL

I believed the three main problems with that rail-road rail anvil could be solved. First, as much weight should be added as is possible. Second, the waist of the rail should be boxed in with steel to eliminate the ringing. Third, the rounded edges at the top of the rail should be built up on two edges of the face to make a flat surface to work on. The off side should be left with the rounded edge of the rail intact so that the surface can be used for a bottom tool for stretching a blade blank.

It was at least three years after that awful experience when I finally found the time to do my experiment in making a rail anvil. I started with a 35-pound piece of rail that had been resting and rusting on my junk-pile for several years. Rail sizes are designated by the weight of the rail by the yard. Hundred-pound rail is 100 pounds to the yard. My rail must have been close to 120-pound. It was 6 1/2 inches high and 2-5/8 inches wide. While not the largest size, it would work for my experiment in anvil making. I read somewhere that 144-pound rail is the largest and it would be used where the traffic was heavy and fast.

I started by rough cutting the shape of a horn and tail with the oxygen/acetylene torch. An anvil for a

right-handed person will have the horn at the left side. Be sure to make the horn so that the most rounded edge of the top rail is away from you. This will give a nice rounded surface for drawing out. The horn was finished with a cup wheel on a disk grinder and then smoothed up with a disc sanding attachment. A 1/2-inch hole was drilled in the table that would accommodate a cut-off hardy made out of an old cold chisel.

I welded in plates made of 1/2-inch thick steel on each side, running it from the bottom of the top rail to the base. This was to add weight and hopefully quiet the bell noise created when forging on rail. This was followed by boxing in one end, filling the cavity formed with scrap steel and melted lead, then welding up the open end. The whole assembly was then welded to a 3/4-inch plate that was slightly larger than the base of the rail. The welds were then smoothed up with a disc grinder. The rounded edges of the rail were built up with Stoody #1105 buildup rod and then smoothed up with the disc grinder. The finished weight is around 125 pounds and is a good size to haul around to demonstrations. (See Photo.) If I were to consider my time as money it must have cost me around $400 to make the rail anvil.

That's my rail anvil at a hammer-in at Wendell Fox's smithy. Larry Milligan is holding and Shawn Vallotton is being the striker. The base that it is on is too light for doing serious forging but is nice when it comes time to haul it around the country.

After several years of using the rail anvil at demonstrations I decided it needed a 1-inch hardy hole. I wanted to be able to use the spring fullers and other anvil tools that fit my Peter Wright anvil. I obtained another piece of rail the same width and with the torch cut a 1-inch square out of one end. After cleaning up the square cut-out that would become the hardy hole, I butt welded it to the tail end of the anvil and then welded in heavy plates as braces on the sides and bottom.

The little rail anvil has seen a lot of hard use at hammer-ins and demonstrations and I still use it in my indoor forge area. The face is not as hard as it could be but it is hard enough to allow good forging. When the face gets a dent in it I simply pein the surface around it down to match. The peining process work-hardens the face and with time it will be only get better.

Any anvil needs to be fastened securely to a heavy base. If the anvil bounces around from the hammer blows it is not heavy enough. A heavier base will help the problem, or a thick chunk of steel can be placed between the anvil and base to boost the weight of the anvil. My favorite anvil bases are made of layers of particleboard, which are glued and nailed together. This type base is heavier than most wood and is always flat on the bottom and level on the top.

THE POST ANVIL

My latest makeshift anvil is a post anvil I put together for my primitive smithy. (I call it a post anvil because that's what it looks like; it's narrow and skinny.) The main member of the anvil is a 32-inch-long piece of forklift fork, which I'm told is steel type 4140 or 4150. I welded some railroad rail and heavy pieces of shaft along side the main member, it weighs about 220 pounds at present. After using the post anvil for awhile I am beginning to like it a lot. There is little noise or vibration from the heaviest blow. It is kind of hard to figure but I believe there is a harmonic characteristic to the blacksmith anvil that may be detrimental to the way they absorb energy. They are also top-heavy and that may contribute to the vibration. For whatever reason, I like the all-steel post anvil and will be doing more experiments with it.

THE "DREAM" ANVIL
FOR KNIFEMAKING

My hornless "dream" anvil will soon be a reality. The face will be 4 inches by 14 inches with a 1-inch hardy hole in the center. The hard face is 2-inch thick forklift fork welded onto a 125-pound rectangle of mild steel. Total weight with a heavy base plate will be around 180 pounds. All I need is some spare time to weld it together. It will have a 350-pound solid steel base made of junk steel. I believe

I'm told that during the Civil War it was the practice of those who captured an anvil to break off the horn and tail. I suppose this was thought to destroy the usefulness of the anvil. For the blacksmith perhaps; but an anvil in this condition makes it much like my "dream anvil". Those are the masterful hands of Don Fogg forging a Japanese-style blade at the Alabama Forge Council -- Bladesmiths Symposium in 1998.

that under the heaviest blow with my 4-pound forging hammer it will have enough total weight so that there won't be the slightest jiggle.

THE BLADESMITH'S HAMMER

I forged a blade once using a carpenter's claw hammer just to prove it could be done. It was a painful experience. There was lot of shock transmitted back into my hand and the weight of the hammer was inadequate to move the metal. A hammer with a good handle of the proper weight and shape will make forging a lot easier.

The most common mistake made by the beginner is to use a hammer that is too heavy. The heavy hammer can move too much material in the wrong direction. It becomes a battle of first pushing the hot metal one way, then back the other way. This causes an excessive amount of hammering and that leads to fatigue and wild hammer blows. Control is far more important than brute strength when forging knife blades. If you can get good control of the heavy hammer, you should use it, otherwise stick to a lighter hammer until your muscles and control develop. Every blade you forge will have one hammer mark that is deeper than all the rest. You'll have the blade ground out to the final shape and there will be one last hammer ding that looks like a gravel-pit on the nice clean surface. It can take a tremendous amount of grinding to clean these up so it's best to not make them in the first place.

I reshape the heads of my hammers so that the striking face is either roughly square or rectangular in cross section. The straight side of the hammer allows the knife edge to be forged right down thin without hitting the anvil face. When the hammer head is round in cross section there is always part of the face overhanging the edge portion of the blade. As the edge gets refined, the hammer is hitting the face of the anvil. The face is slightly rounded with a

small flat in the center. The corners are slightly rounded too. If the edges of a hammer are sharp and square it is easy to make a cold shut in a blade. A cold shut is formed when a hammer blow forces metal over onto the surface of a previous blow. If a cold shut is not ground out as soon as it is created it can be forged deep into the surface.

The shape of the hammer face will have a large effect on the direction that the metal is moved. When forging the bevel into a blade it will curve upwards, this curve will usually be more than is wanted. A hammer with a round striking surface will create even more curve than the rectangular type. (See the drawing, this illustrates the flow of the metal when struck with different shaped hammer faces.)

The photo shows one of my favorite hammers. I made it up with a shock-absorbing handle as per Bo

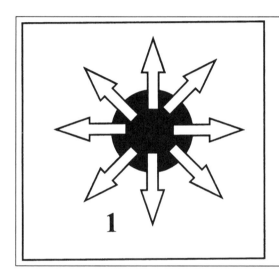 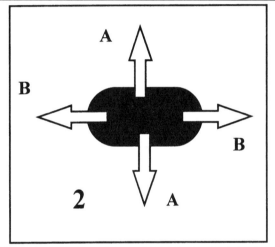

When the face of a hammer leaves a round impression on the work, the material is spread equally in all directions. (See figure 1.) When forging blades this will cause the edge profile to take much more curve than it really needs to have. A blow with a fullering style hammer leaves an impression on the work that is twice as long as it is wide. (See figure 2.) This blow moves the material twice as much in the "A" direction as it does in "B." The "A" direction would be the direction that the bevel in a blade is being forged. The result is much less curvature being developed in the blade. The blade gets beveled and wider much more quickly with less hammering.

The shock resisting hammer handle.

Hickory's instructions that appeared in several blacksmith association newsletters.

I'm bothered by nerve damage, carpal tunnel syndrome and arthritis. I wouldn't have believed the difference it made until I worked back and forth between the shock-absorbing handle and a solid one. Discovering this type of handle made longer hours of forging possible. The difference is amazing and I'll never use anything else for heavy work. It is just the thing to help my worn out wrist and elbow. I can't prove it but the modified hammer with the springy handle seems to move more metal with a given blow. Several old-timers have told me that a handle with spring in it would give a harder blow and I believe it now. The shock-absorbing handle is sensitive enough that when working on an anvil that is not secured to the anvil base, the rebound of the work/anvil can be felt with the hammer! Almost everyone who has used one of the hammers that I have modified has taken the time to modify their heavy hammers (2 pounds plus) the same way.

I've made the handle two different ways, depending on whether it was a hammer with a good handle in it, or on a new handle to be installed in a head. On a new handle, I cut in from the wedge end (approximately 4-1/2 inches) up to a drilled hole. The sides of the cut-out are sanded and smoothed up with a radius on the inside edge of the cut-out. A wood spacer is super glued into the space that the head will take up, and then the wedge slot is re-cut. Handle is installed as per usual.

On an existing handle, I drill a 3/16-inch hole up next to the head. Then I cut a slot with the band saw the whole length of the handle, right up to the drilled hole. After smoothing up the slot I then glue (epoxy) in a spacer of a dark wood to get the handle back to the beginning dimension. The dark wood gives the hammer a custom look. If you have a milling machine, the slot could be milled out with a 3/16-inch end mill or router bit.

Tips for "Never Loose" handles.

Pick out new handles very carefully, make sure that they are straight and have no flaws in them. The best handles have a straight grain with the growth rings running in the same direction as the hammer blow. Make sure the handle is dry by putting it in a warm and dry place for several weeks before installing. Make sure there are no sharp edges on the hole in the hammer head. Take a file or small grinding wheel and put a nice smooth radius on the side of the head that the handle goes into. If left sharp, it will keep cutting the wood rather than wedging in and the handle will keep working loose. Use a rasp to work the handle down to a tight fit on the head. The head should seat up tight on the handle before the wedge is hammered into place. With the head affixed tight onto the handle, the head and 4 or 5 inches of the handle should be placed in a con-

tainer of linseed oil. Let soak for three weeks, remove, wipe dry and go to work. The head will never come loose.

THE FORGE

Blades can be forged using charcoal, coal, commercial coke or gas. Charcoal is not practical, unless you want to make your own. I used commercial coke for several years until I learned about homemade gas forges. The local supply of foundry coke had gone dry by then, so switching to gas was a good thing.

The home-made coal forge and the rail anvil. A bucket for coal, one for water, a hammer and some scrap steel and you're ready to go to work forging your first blade.

A simple coal forge can be made for far less money than a gas forge. See the photo of the $20 forge shop. It was a project done to show that a forged blade can be made with simple, homemade tools. I made the forge from a rusted out barbecue. The disadvantage is that coal is messy and slow compared to gas. My smithy is in a residential neighborhood and I would have a difficult time trying to work with coal. I don't recommend setting up with coal as a general rule. I prefer gas because it is clean and efficient.

My forge/furnaces are all homemade. At present, each is a horizontal steel tube lined with ceramic fiber that is coated with refractory cement. The burner tube is made of iron pipefittings. Plans for half a dozen different gas forges are available on the Internet.

I'm currently making a prototype "upright" gas forge. Michael Bell, a sword maker from Oregon, has used one for years. I have used the one made by my friend Richard Veatch. I first saw the upright version of a gas forge at The Alabama Forge Council Bladesmith Symposium. Don Fogg was using it and I think he built it. (See photo.) The main advantage

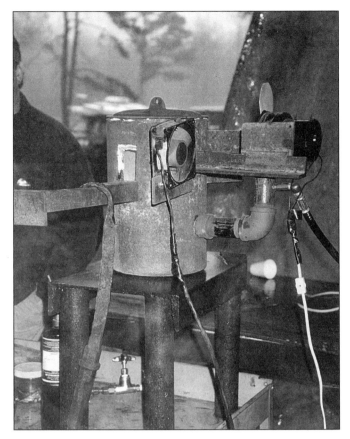

Don Fogg's upright gas forge. Note the cooling fan that keeps the bar stock cool where you will be handling it. Also note the crook tool hanging on the angle steel that supports the bar stock being forged. A long sword blade would tip up in the forge, the crook tool holds it down where it is supposed to be.

The oxygen/acetylene torch forge. Note the torch holder, this is a handy tool for many jobs.

is that the work is farther away from the flame. Combustion takes place in the bottom of the forge away from the work piece. Unburned oxygen is much less apt to reach the top where the work is. This makes it possible to achieve a more suitable atmosphere for forging and welding.

Make a depression in the ground and pipe an air supply into one side. Use charcoal or hardwood for fuel. To get more heat out of it, place a cover of fire-bricks over it to create a heat chamber. Once the bricks get hot the metal will heat much faster and the bonus is a larger work piece can be heated than on the open fire.

An oxygen/acetylene torch can furnish the heat for a heat chamber made from a steel tube lined with ceramic fiber. The one shown in the photo served me for a number of years inside my shop as a heat source for forging small blades and heat treating. (See photo.) This was during the time I burned coke or coal. Once I started making and using the homemade dragon-breath furnaces, the torch furnace got retired.

A stack of firebricks will also work as a small forge. Make the box with a brick on top with a hole in it and direct the torch flame into the hole just like the photo shows with the tube type.

POWER FOR FORGING

Foot-Powered Hammers

We live in a residential neighborhood and the smithy is in the back yard, the foot-power hammer and hydraulic press are the solution for noise. For 10 years I used one that I designed and built. It works on the principle that when you depress the foot pedal 6 inches with 35 pounds of pressure, the 55-pound hammer comes down 12 inches with a mighty blow. The two-to-one ratio of hammer travel to the foot lever gives a tremendous increase in power. A single blow from it has nearly the same power as a 50-pound Little Giant mechanical hammer. It has sped up my production of welded and straight forged blades considerably. The time spent shaping blades is reduced to 20 percent of doing it all with hand-hammering. Most of the heavy hand-hammering is eliminated. Blades come out straight and flat from under the flat dies. (See the drawing.)

The old-time blacksmith always had a helper who would swing a heavy two-handed sledgehammer when needed for drawing out heavy stock. The striker, as he was called, would also strike set tools that the smith would hold on the work for fullering, swaging, flatting, hot and cold cutting, punching, etc. The foot-powered hammer takes the place of a strong and willing helper, and doesn't cost anything to feed. It's not as efficient for drawing-out as a mechanical power hammer but is still a tool worth

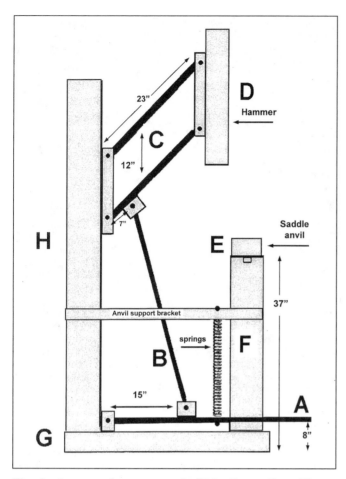

The foot-power hammer as built by the author. The hammer hits flat at one spot when the arms are parallel with the ground. The saddle anvil is necessary when working "flat to flat." It is taken off when the spring tools are used.

having. Once you get used to it, it is a hard tool to do without. (See photo.)

In November of 1996 I had two total knee replacements. The written material I received said activities that caused shock to the knees would not be allowed. If I expect my knee replacements to last 12 to 15 years that is anticipated, the foot-power hammer had to go. My knee joints have replaceable bearings but I'm not going to take any unnecessary chances with them.

Clay Spencer with his new and improved straight-blow foot-power hammer. The hammer guides are wheels from in-line skates.

An assortment of spring tools for the foot-power hammer.

There are some new foot-power hammers being built that have a straight drop on the hammer. That's a much better action than the swing-arms of the type I built. With a pulley or cam setup I believe a four-to-one ratio is possible with a straight drop hammer. With a spring-action / shock absorber built into the foot lever I believe I could operate one and not damage my metal and plastic knee joints. That may be a good wintertime project, but first I have a single-stroke air hammer to build. (See drawing.)

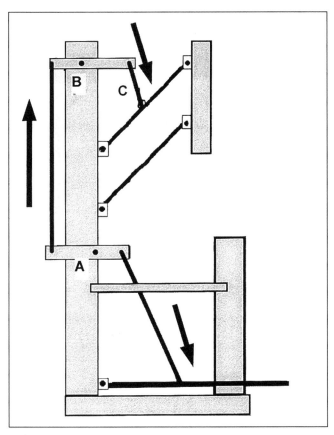

Here is an idea for a foot-power hammer that will impart to the hammer four times the weight that is put on the foot lever. Joints "A" and "B" each have a lift ratio of 1:1. Existing designs operate at a ratio of from 1:1 to 1:2. Perhaps the right kind of cam at point "A" that pulled a cable over point "B" would give a 1:3 or even a 1:4 ratio. The cable would lift the hammer and a spring would pull it down. The principle is the opposite of the original design. I want to experiment with this new idea but haven't had time to do anything with it.

Mechanical Hammers

Little Giant is the most common. The disadvantages of a mechanical hammer are numerous. They are expensive to purchase, and there are lots of parts to wear out. They are heavy to move and noisy, too. If you have one, use it, but before purchasing one check out the options listed below. I had a Little Giant power hammer set up at a friend's shop and got good use out of it in my early years as a smith. (See photo.)

As I got used to the foot-powered hammer and forging press I no longer used it and so I sold it to my friend whose shop it was in. (I retained visiting rights.)

Wade Colter demonstrates how to make damascus and look "cool" at the same time. Grant Sarver of Off Center Forge, Tacoma Washington, invented this unique air hammer. The guides for the hammer are twin air cylinders. The air is supplied through the hollow rams. This machine is compact and has more a more powerful blow for the size than anything I have ever seen. It has more than earned it's name of the "Kick-Ass Hammer". Photo by Barry Gallagher.

Wendell Fox forging damascus on the 50-pound Little Giant that used to belong to the author. Some of these machines are real old. This one was made in 1907 but was in near new condition when I found it in 1983.

Air Hammers

Commercial air hammers are the ultimate forging machines. They are even more expensive to find, move and set up than the smaller mechanical hammers. Unless you are going into a production operation I wouldn't recommend considering one.

A whole new generation of homemade air hammers has developed. I'm in the process of building one myself. It will be a single-blow type with a hammer weight of 75 pounds. I'm not using plans, just borrowing ideas from here and there. A search of the WWW will find plans and information available.

Hydraulic Forging Machines

Lately I use a hydraulic forging press for more of my forging and welding, and I've got a second one in the works. They are relatively simple and easy to build. The advantage is that they are quiet compared to the foot-powered hammer or a mechanical hammer.

Jeff Carlisle in Great Falls, Montana makes a dandy hydraulic forging press that is perfect for knife work. I've used it at hammer-ins put on by Rick Dunkerley and Ed Schempp. (See photo.)

That's the author putting the squeeze on a piece of 5160 round bar. This press was made for making coins and medallions. When I got it, the guided tooling had to removed and replaced with forging surfaces. I use many of the spring tools shown for the foot-power hammer on this press. The frame is one solid piece of 3-inch-thick T-1 structural steel. It will go to 85 tons but rarely takes more than 25 tons to do whatever I need it for. Photo by Barry Gallagher.

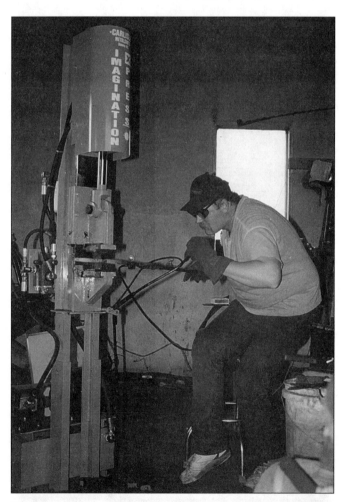

Rick Dunkerley making mosaic damascus with the Imagination X Press made by Jeff Carlisle. This is a very popular machine with damascus steel specialists. Photo by Barry Gallagher.

THE WORLDS SMALLEST FORGE

You'll need four firebricks; one soft and three hard. If you don't have any bricks lying around, you will find them in the yellow pages under "Refractories" or call a brick mason to find out where he gets firebricks. A hard brick will work for the little forge but it will be difficult to carve or drill; and it won't get as hot as a forge made with a soft brick. You'll need a propane torch; mine is an Ace Hardware Model AC-30. It is a push-button, self-lighting model. The heat tip rotates 360 degrees and that makes it easy to adjust the flame at a specific spot. The AC-30 is made for plumbing and puts out a nice three-pointed flame. The extra heat makes for quick heating of the chamber of the mini forge/furnace. The base and holding device for the 16-oz. propane bottle is a large juice can which is hooked to the wood holder with screws. Carve the 1-inch diameter heat chamber hole lengthwise completely through the brick with a junk knife blade or drill it out with an old drill bit. The 1-inch hole in the side is named the fire hole; it goes in only far enough to reach the heat hole. The heat hole goes all the way through the brick from end to end. Don't put the torch tip directly in the heat hole, keep it an inch or so from the opening. Experiment with your torch to see where the flame is aimed to get the most heat.

This little forge is not just a novelty item. I use mine almost every day for heat treating small parts or doing finishing forging on small blades. It is my heat source of choice for forging the rat-tails on my friction folder blades and also the thong holder on the end of a folder spring. (See photo.)

After using the mini-brick forge for awhile the brick started to crack and come apart. I repaired it by wrapping it with iron wire that is set down in a groove carved in the brick. The photo shows the mini forge sitting on the hard bricks. When I use it inside my shop it is surrounded on the back and top with hard bricks to support it.

Carve a notch in the side of a soft fire brick to make a cavity large enough for heating parts that are larger than the hole in the mini forge. This works for straightening out coil springs or other curved pieces. The part to be heated is held in the recess where the flame can wrap around it so that it is being heated from all sides.

I've made half a dozen different sizes of the mini forge in tin cans that were lined with Kaowool® brand ceramic fiber insulating material. The flame is directed into the can through a hole in the side. The goal is to direct the flame so that it rolls around the inside of the liner. As the liner heats up the heat radiating from the liner heats the work. The tin can forge is nothing but a miniature of the tube-type homemade gas forges that are so popular with bladesmiths.

A Mapp or oxygen/acetylene gas torch can be used in the same way. Either will give more heat than propane, which will make it possible to heat larger pieces. Be very careful when using oxygen/acetylene, the 5,000-degree F flame will destroy anything that gets too close.

The world's smallest forge?

Left to right: A friction folder with a forged rat-tail on the blade. Center, an antler-tip jack knife with forged thong holder. The little one-brick forge is perfect for forging these little details. At the left is a stock removal jack knife that has nothing to do with forging. It's the type of folder I started making back in 1974. I just can't seem to quit making them.

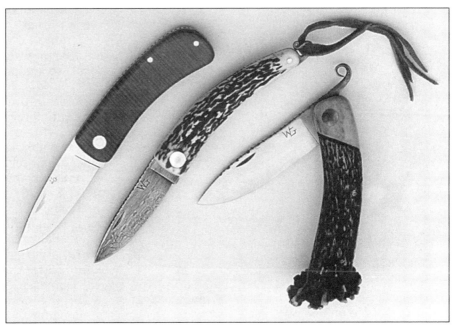

Chapter 6

THE FORGED BLADE

The new bar of steel was smooth and clean, straight as an arrow and had a nice fine grain. It is a terrible thing that I'm going to do to that bar of steel, but I'm a bladesmith and it has to be done. I will subject it to sufficient heat to get it a bright orange color, at that temperature the steel became "plastic." It's not really that soft but it is soft enough so that it can be shaped with a hammer. It may appear that I am taking my frustrations out on the steel but the hammer blows are carefully planned and struck. When finished, the bar of steel will have been transformed into the rough shape of a knife blade. The once-smooth surface of the steel bar is mutilated by hammer dents and dings, with an ugly layer of scale on the surface. It will most definitely

Brick box furnace for burning hard foundry coke. The air supply is a cross pipe in the bottom; made of cast iron with slots to spread out the air supply.

require a measure of stock removal before it will make a presentable blade.

There was a time when all blades were forged, but the machine age came in and changed that. The invention of man-made, high-speed grinding wheels and then, later, abrasive belts, made it feasible to shape the blade with what became known as the stock-removal method.

The hand-made knife world was running head-long towards being mostly stock-removal until Bill Moran came along and showed us the modern version of Damascus steel. I first saw it at the Knife-makers' Guild Show in 1974 and it changed my life. I wanted to learn to make it but it was nine years before I got started. If I had known sooner that I could do it in my backyard without a power hammer I certainly would have jumped into it much sooner.

There was a lot for me to learn and I did it the hard way by, trial and error. My first forge was a homemade coal-fire pot that I welded up from scrap steel. It worked pretty well, but I soon found an old Champion cast-iron fire pot and switched to it. I learned about foundry coke from my artist/black-smith friend David Thompson. I developed a brick box furnace to burn it. (See photo.) It worked all right but the source of good coke dried up and by then I was learning about gas furnaces from my friend Gene Chapman.

Those first brick-box gas forges we made were not very efficient, but they did work better than burning coal in a traditional forge. I learned the basic dragon-breath, tube-type; ceramic fiber lined forge design from Gene. I'm still using a refined version for all of my welding and a smaller and lower temperature version for forging and heat treating. (See photos.)

Bladesmithing today is more gas forges, hydraulic forging presses and homemade air hammers than anything else is. Some bladesmiths still burn coal, but more gas forges are being used all the time. The mechanical power hammer will always be with us, but the technology that they use is outdated and can't compete with current developments in air and hydraulic forging machines. If you're going to manufacture Damascus steel it's another story. You'll need the largest power hammer you can afford. My friend Devin Thomas just loves his 500-pound Little Giant for making his beautiful stainless Damascus. (See photo on page 96.)

Forging is one part of knifemaking that hasn't changed for thousands of years. It may be the low-

That's the author (front), knifemaker Bill Harsey (white cap) and stunt pilot and airplane builder Steve Wolf with the template. I took my welding furnace to the hanger where Steve builds airplanes and we heated two pieces of 3/4-inch thick by 6-inch wide 5160 to bend them to make landing gear for a stunt plane. At that time, Steve held the altitude record in a prop-driven airplane.

The basic Dragon Breath forge, this one is 8 inches in diameter and 10 inches long. It is used for forging and heat treating, temperature range: 1,300F to 2,000F. The welding furnace is 10 inches by 14 inches with a larger burner tube, it runs about 2,300+F.

Devin Thomas with his medium sized air hammer, just the thing for drawing out stainless damascus.

tech end of blade making, but it has one big advantage in the simplicity of tools required. Forging is not only the most basic metalworking process but a lot of us find it's great fun to heat a piece of steel, take hammer-in-hand and then coax the orange-hot steel bar into a new and exciting object.

Knifemaking can be accomplished with very simple tools when the blade is forged to shape. Forging the blade close to the final dimension eliminates the need for grinders and belt sanders to get the blade to the finished shape; files and hand stones are all that is necessary to finish it. There is no need for torches or electric furnaces, the heat source for forging is used to harden and temper the blade.

ARE FORGED
BLADES SUPERIOR?

Just because a blade is forged does not mean that it will have superior strength and cutting ability. The steel from which it is made must have a high carbon content, proper forging temperatures must not be exceeded and proper normalizing and/or annealing temperatures must be followed. This must be followed up with the best possible heat

treatment being given to the blade. Then, and only then, (assuming that it has good cross section geometry,) it just might make a superior blade.

The beginning bladesmith will have to do a lot of practicing to learn the accurate color judgments necessary for superior blade making. It's important to finish the blades at just the right degree of thickness, or what I call having good cross-section geometry. There is nothing quite like making knives and using them, to help get it all figured out.

It is wise to stick to one type of steel in the learning phase, and I recommend 1084 or 1086 carbon steel. It is reasonably priced, available in a variety of sizes, and makes very good knives. The most versatile size is 1/4-inch by 1-inch.

Once smaller knives are mastered it is time to make some camp knives and then later the king of all knives, the Bowie. I can recommend nothing other than 5160 for larger type knives.

FORGING TO SHAPE

In order to forge a specific blade shape, a pre-form of the blade must first be forged. Each different blade shape has it's own unique pre-form. If a rectangular bar of steel is forged to a point and beveled with no pre-form it makes a wild, crescent-shaped blade that I call a "Buffalo Skinner." This is the shape that almost everyone ends up with when they forge their first blade. Learning to make the correct pre-form for different blade shapes takes some of the mystery out of forging to shape.

To make the lesson easier to explain I've assigned "C" to the length, "B" to the width and "A" to the thickness of the bar stock. (Note the dimensions A, B, and C on the bar of steel in the drawing.)

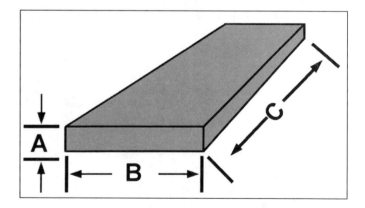

The pre-form is formed in the "B" dimension with no attempt at forging in the bevels. As the pre-form takes shape the thickness at "A" will increase. This should be continually worked down with the hammer as it forms. If the pre-form is correct, but the point is fat in the "A" dimension, the excess material, when forged out into the bevel, will make the shape of the point fat and rounded. As you are keeping the "A" dimension from getting too thick you can actually forge in a slight taper towards the point. This is known as distal taper.

(See the drawing.) The material at "A" will get hammered down to make the pre-form shape of the point. Note that the blade gets longer as the point is drawn out. The material at "B" gets drawn out to form the tang. Make a punch or chisel mark on the edge of a bar of steel at a distance of 3 inches from the end, then forge a blade on the end of the bar and

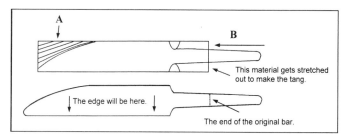

see if the tip of the blade isn't very close to 4 inches from the mark.

The finished pre-form looks like an upside-down blade. The hammer blows that form the bevel will cause the tip of the pre-form to move up towards the back line of the blade. (The hammer blows are indi-

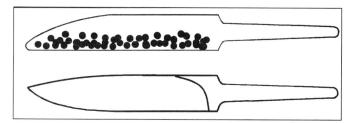

cated by the black spots on the pre-form in the drawing.)

The belly of the blade is formed (almost) automatically with very little hammer work on the profile. If the blade develops too much curvature in the belly it can be fixed at an orange heat by pushing the point back down with light hammer blows.

With practice, the point and blade shape can be forged exactly to shape. When starting out it is all right to do some stock removal on the profile.

The bevel is usually forged down to within approximately 20 percent of the finished thickness at the edge. If not left at least this thick, the blade is prone to warp or crack and might even get too thin during the finish grinding process.

USING A HOT-CUT PRE-FORM

Using a hot cutter to shape the pre-form of the point is a quicker way and also very traditional with blacksmith knifemakers. (See drawings below.) To make a "Clip" blade, the blade blank is cut off at an angle similar to "A." It can be removed with an abrasive saw, band saw, or hot cutter. The clip "B" and belly shape "C" forms almost automatically as the bevel is forged.

The American Bladesmith Society does not consider a blade made from a hot cut pre-form as being "forged to shape." Test blades must be forged to shape from the bar stock. However, that is the way many old-time smiths did it and probably for good reason. Much of the steel available at the time could not be pointed up in thin sections without coming

apart. I found the following in the 1876 book, "*American Blacksmithing, Toolsmiths and Steelworkers Manual*" by John Gustaf Holstrom and Henry I. Holford. "Never try to forge the point of the knife, but cut it to shape with a chisel." The book does not give the reason but I always assumed it was because the crucible cast steel that was common in that day was difficult to forge to shape without splitting.

I can find no difference in the quality of the finished blade between one that is pointed up with a hammer (forged to shape) and one that is forged from a hot-cut preform. That is why I teach both methods.

I have an "exercise" that I like to do when I teach or demonstrate. I start with a piece of 1/4-inch by 1-1/4 inches (1084) that I've hot cut to the pre-form shown as "A" in the drawing. I forge the bevel into the blank and in one heat end up with the finished shape very close to that shown in the drawing. Sometimes the point of the blade is even higher; it depends on how soon I run out of heat. You could call it a "clip point" blade shape, and I've always wondered if the name came because the smith "clipped" the bar of steel before forging the bevel. Not having to forge the pre-form into the bar is very fast and efficient.

To make a semi-skinner or butcher knife shape, two angle cuts are made as per "AA". The point shape "BB" forms itself as the bevel and some distal taper is forged in. Distal taper is that seen when looking down the spine of a blade. It gives the knife better balance and allows the blade to flex more before breaking. It's the same principle as the bow limb.

FORGING THE BEVELS

Always forge the blade uniformly on both sides, this keeps the stresses equal and the material flows into the desired shape in a more orderly manner. Count out five to 10 blows, then turn the blade and give it the same amount. Do this until you get into the habit of working the steel equally on both sides.

A common mistake made by beginners is trying to forge after the steel has cooled to the point that it is not moving under the hammer. My students get tired of hearing me yell at them; "Keep it hot!" or "GET IT HOT!" It's not only a waste of time to hammer on steel that does not move under the hammer, but the steel can be damaged by hitting it too hard at a temperature under the forging range. Steel types 1084, 1095 and 5160 should be forged in the range of 1,850 to 2,050F. Keep the material hot and everything will go better.

Good forge theory says that you start the forging at the high end of the forging temperature and each heat would be at a slightly lower temperature until the blade is finished. You won't be able to do this at first but you will eventually be able to do it if you keep at it.

It has taken me 16 years of forging to get to the point where I can use a 4-pound hammer on a regular basis. This makes it possible to shape a 4-inch blade in one heat. That's starting with the method used by the old-time smiths of hot-cutting the end of the bar at an angle. The hot cut section forms the "clip" on the back of the blade

It is important to combat the scale that forms with each heat. To help keep scale at a minimum it is important to keep the fire slightly rich. A fire with excess oxygen will create a lot of unnecessary scale. A "butcher block" brush has very stiff, flat wires and works very well to scrape the scale off each time the blade is taken out of the fire. Obnoxious scale can be scraped off with the flat end of a planer blade or old file.

Wet forging is a Japanese method, it's messy but worth the effort. I started doing it 15 years ago after seeing some Japanese swordsmiths do it on a video. They use a mop made of straw to apply water to the surface of the anvil. The hammer is set in a container of water. When the blade is set on the anvil face and hit with the wet hammer there is a small explosion of steam and that's what loosens the scale. Each additional blow continues the process. Once the blade has been returned to the fire to be heated for the next forging heat, the anvil face is wiped clean of scale and then moistened once more.

I learned another good trick watching this same video. The blade is picked up off of the surface of the anvil after each blow, then rested back on the anvil just as the hammer gets there. It's sort of like you go tap, tap, tap on the anvil with the flat side of the blade and with every tap the hammer meets the blade just as it hits the anvil. This causes the blade to retain heat longer and that means more steel gets moved with each heat. It is the type of thing that takes practice, but it sure is fun when you get it working.

When you are satisfied with the blade shape it is time for the finishing heat.

THE FINISHING HEAT

I can find no references to packing as a forge process in any modern metal working or metallurgical books. I do find the term "finishing heat" and it is a very logical way to end the forging process. That's why I teach the use of a "finishing heat"— some call it packing. I use the words finishing heat because it more accurately describes what is being done. I don't like the word "packing." The only way I pack steel is in a suitcase, and it's in the form of knives and I'm taking them to a knife show.

The way I do a finishing heat is as follows. The blade is brought up to a temperature that is under the point where scale forms. I work the blade over with light and even hammer blows down into the temperature range where there is little or no color visible. It leaves the blade smooth and relatively clean and free of scale. The light blows do not move the steel or change the shape very much, but serve to even out the surface.

FORGING THE TANG

Some bladesmiths forge the tang first and then shape the blade. Others will start with the blade end and then make the tang. If the blade is finished real close to shape and you hold the blade to do the tang, the blade will usually get messed up and need to be redone. I usually rough the blade in, then do the tang. The rough-forged blank is then held by the tang to do the finish forging on the blade.

Most forged blades have narrow tangs and there are several ways to do it. It is not always a neat and clean method, but the edge of the anvil can be used as a bottom tool to start the step-down where the blade meets the tang. To do this, hold the spot where you want the tang to start over the edge of the anvil. The hammer blow should be directly over the edge of the anvil. By turning the blade 180 degrees, the step down on the other side can be forged in with careful hammer blows. It takes skill and power with the hammer to accomplish it this way. One of the following methods is better.

THE SPRING FULLER

An easier way to make the tang step-down is to use a spring fuller. They are easily constructed from any 1/2-inch diameter round bar stock. Mild steel will work but will eventually wear out, coil spring material or a handle for a bumper jack will hold up

A SPRING-FULLER FOR THE HARDIE HOLE

Detail of the spring fuller.

longer. The center section is forged down to about 1/4-inch thick. It is then forged and bent into the shape shown. (See the photo of one made from the handle for a bumper jack.) While there is still some heat in the bottom member arc weld a square shank onto it to fit the hardy hole in your anvil. (Arc welding high carbon steel without it being preheated to at least 200 to 300 degrees F will cause the weld to crack and break.) The spring fuller does not need to be hardened and tempered. Once it is shaped, it should be brought up to the normalizing temperature and then allowed to air cool. This will leave it in a tough condition with plenty of strength and spring.

THE STEP-DOWN HARDY

The step-down hardy will make it easier to get a narrow tang started. (See the drawing.) It can be fabricated out of almost any type steel. Axles or torsion bars from motor vehicles and jack-hammer bits are my favorite materials for hardy tools.

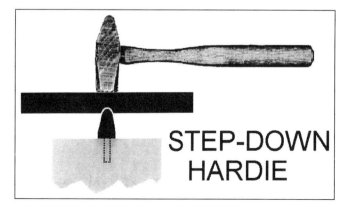

STEP-DOWN HARDIE

The step-down hardy can be used on only one side of the handle to make a full tang shape, or on both sides to form a narrow tang.

The spring fuller in its working position on the makeshift anvil from the $50 Knife Shop.

The wedge hardy is used for either putting curve into or taking it out of a blade or bar. The top edge should be rounded so it won't dig into the steel.

WEDGE HARDIE

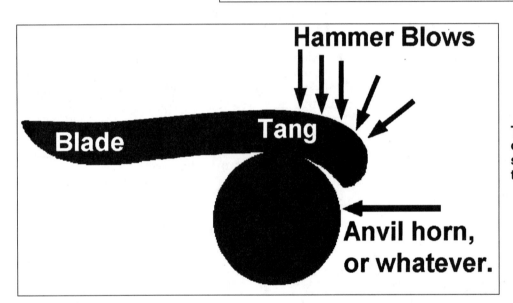

Hammer Blows

Blade　　**Tang**

**Anvil horn,
or whatever.**

The tang is held on the horn of the anvil or any rounded surface and hit just off center to cause a bending blow.

FORGING A FULL-TANG BLADE

Most knife handles are wider at the butt end and curve down from the centerline of the blade. The curve in the handle should be forged in first by either using the wedge tool or by working it over the horn. (See the two drawings.) With the handle profile forged to shape, the taper can then be forged into the tang.

GETTING THE KINKS
AND TWISTS OUT

It took me a lot of years to figure out why most of my forged blades had a slight twist in them. I could never see what I was doing to create the effect, but it was always there when the blade cooled down. It

is easy enough to get the twist out while hot by putting the tang in a vise and using a wrench or fork to work out the kink.

I was sitting down watching a student, and the low angle I was at let me see what was happening. The blade was being presented to the anvil with the tang parallel with the face. This left the partially formed bevel above the surface of the anvil and the first hammer blow would bend the blade down to touch the face. The subsequent forging blows were struck with the edge twisted out of line with the tang. The first blows to forge the bevel are done with the tang parallel with the anvil face. When the second side is started the blade has to be angled so that the hammer blow forges rather than twists the blade. It was simple for me to understand once I could see what was happening. To fix a twist with a hammer it is necessary to go back to the opposite side and carefully work it out by reversing the slight bending process.

Al Bart was an old-time blacksmith from Northern California. One of the tools he always brought to conferences was a hardwood club. The club was used to convince a hot piece of steel to change its shape without moving any metal. My club is made from an old baseball bat from a yard sale. "Schwock" is the sound the club makes on hot steel, that's why I named it a schwocker. When I demonstrate, I will often use the schwocker to put a half-circle in a piece of hot bar stock, then I'll make it straight again. To get long curves out of a blade the face of the anvil will work under the blade. For short bends that need adjustment a small stump of end grain hardwood with a hollow spot will work better to rest the blade on. If the blade drops too much, or is too high in relation to the tang, the schwocker can be used to change the profile.

THAT MYSTERIOUS PROCESS KNOWN AS PACKING

"Packing" is a process that most bladesmiths use in their forging process. The practice came to us out of the 19th century and has been passed down to us by generations of smiths. It is accepted by some, but questioned by others and as far as I know has no basis in modern metallurgical theory. I know of no reference to it in any modern metallurgical books. My 1948 Metals Handbook has a definition of "Mechanical working" which is a process described as follows: Subjecting metal to pressure exerted by rolls, dies, presses, or hammers, to change its form or to affect the structure and consequently the mechanical and physical properties.

Other modern books on forging practice refer to a "finishing heat." It is mentioned in many, but not all of the blacksmithing books written in the late 1800s. When it is mentioned, it is usually in reference to forging chisels, is not mentioned very much when knives are discussed. One reference I can find to packing of blades is in Alex Bealers, *"The Art Of Blacksmithing"*.

When I got into forging, I asked several established bladesmiths to explain their method of packing. There were some differences in the methods used, but the basic formula was something like this. "Hammering the edge portion of the blade with a light hammer as it cools down to the point that the color is barely visible in a dark place." At the same time, I asked two different metallurgists what they thought of "packing" theory. Both explained that the steel recrystallizes during the hardening operation. Their opinion was that the temperature of the hardening operation would undo any grain refinement done in the packing process. So now we have two opinions on the subject, but let's get even more.

Following definitions of packing come from a variety of sources.

1. The edge is packed by hammering it lightly to "jiggle" the carbides into alignment. Forging reduces the size of the carbides along the edge surface, while packing tightens the crystal structure so the molecules remain on the knife's edge longer."

2. In regards to chisels. Just as it is cooling from a bright red-heat to a dull red-heat, strike it two or three sharp blows in a triangular pattern. This will compact the steel molecules yielding them impervious to high speed drill bits or even a new file which is hard for most cutting jobs. Compaction is a bit tricky for the beginner since one blow too many will reach the compaction threshold where the molecules cannot be forced any closer together resulting in splitting.

3. The final refinement of the grain size is referred to as "packing" and is done at the same time that the final shape of the bar is finished. Packing the steel is very important and involves hammering the steel at a dull red color for a long period of time. Grain refinement in parallel rows is essential for strong, high-quality cutting edges. The smaller the grain size, the stronger the material.

4. The hammer blows may appear to be random, but each one is serving a purpose. The grains are being elongated in the direction of maximum stress, somewhat like wood grain. The hammering breaks up large grains and produces a fine-grained, tough, strong structure. As the steel cools out of the red condition, light blows pack the surface and edge. One must be careful at this point, though, because hammering when the steel gets too cool may form cracks.

5. From an old blacksmith book in a section on making chisels: Packing is exactly what its name implies. It is a technique whereby the fibers of the carbon steel are packed tightly with hammer blows to provide an extra degree of density to the chisel or punch point. Packing is done with a light hammer at a sunrise-red heat. So important is the heat, neither too bright nor too dark, that it is wise to provide a dark chamber of some sort, a small keg or box, on the forge so that the red can he judged more accurately. Often in daylight or in the glow of the forge fire it is impossible to ascertain a sunrise red, yet if the metal is much hotter packing will not occur. Actual packing is done with a light hammer, usually a ball pein, about 1-1/2 pounds in weight. When the chisel edge attains sunrise red in the forge it is taken out and is laid across the horn or on the anvil face next to its rounded corner. It is struck rapidly with the hammer at one point on the anvil, the smith turning it from one side to the other while he draws it toward him under

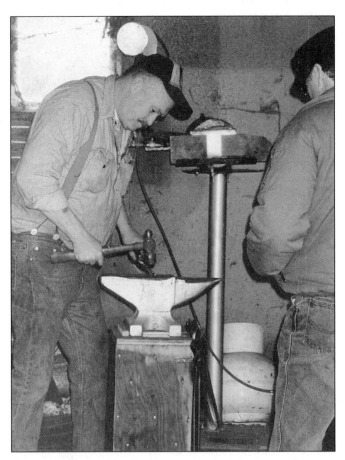

Wendell Fox demonstrates the finer details of a finishing heat.

the blows. This is continued until all red disappears and hammering is stopped. On chisels, the last three hammer blows are important. One should be placed on either side of the edge and the last placed in the middle of the edge at a slightly higher point. These last blows arrange the fibers so as to prevent the chisel edge from breaking in a crescent shape in later use. Wood chisels do not require packing.

6. From Alex Bealer's *The Art Of Blacksmithing:* After blood gutters are formed a fine sword will have its edge packed, to mass the fibers of the steel and enable the weapon to hold its edge longer when used to cut through plate armor. Packing a sword follows exactly the technique of packing a chisel edge. The blade is heated until it turns red when viewed in a shadow perhaps furnished by a barrel set on its side next to the forge. At this heat it is placed on the anvil face and quickly hammered with a 1-1/2-pound hammer. Packing must be done with even blows; otherwise the blade may warp when quenched in brine during hardening. If this happens there is only one way to eliminate the crookedness. The blade is brought to a bright orange-red and tapped smartly with a 4-pound hammer on the end of the tang. Such a blow will rearrange the

molecules throughout the blade and allow it to be hardened without warping on the second trial. Of course, rearranging the molecules also destroys the packing and this must be repeated before hardening and tempering.

Now that you have all of that great information on packing, what will you do with it? I recommend using a finishing heat. I will assume that your blade is pretty well shaped and that proper measures were taken to not overheat it or leave it with a lot of scale hammered into the surface. The finishing heat means working the blade over with light and even hammer blows down into the temperature range where there is little or no color visible. This will leave the blade smooth and relatively clean and free of scale. The light blows do not move the steel or change the shape very much but serve to even out the surface. If there are still rough and uneven places or scale on the surface, heat it up to a temperature that is just under the point where scale forms and do the light hammering once more.

You may call it packing if you like, but always remember that the steel will recrystallize both in the normalizing and quench heats. Call it anything you want, but I'd rather you don't say that you've jiggled, compressed or lined up the molecules.

DECARBURIZATION

I know I have a hot topic when I get three questions in a couple of weeks on the same subject. The questions ranged from curiosity, to a reader being upset over Ed Fowler's statements concerning grinding allowance in "The Trick Is To Forge Thick," *Blade* April '97. Some felt that he was off base in allowing a 1/16 of an inch to grind off to get rid of decarburized material. The issue involved was interesting to me because I can make a very convincing argument for both sides.

First, I will go back in time to 1967 when I first learned about decarburization. I had made a knife for one of my mountain-man friends. After he had used it for awhile, he related that it would not hold an edge when he first got it. After sharpening it three or four times it would hold an edge like it should have. A mutual friend of ours was a metallurgist and he figured out right away what the problem was. I was not taking off enough material after heat treating to get rid off decarburized material. That's when I started leaving a grinding allowance on my blades in order to have enough excess material to take off to get rid of decarburized material. Once I got into forging I allowed even more.

It is the total time at certain temperatures and the atmosphere in the forge or heat treat furnace that determines the amount of decarburization. There are quite a few variables to consider in order to answer the question of exactly how much material is decarburized during forging and/or heat treating. Some of these are the steel type. The specific temperatures used throughout the heating cycles; the amount of time it takes to draw out and forge the blade; the method used (time/temperature) in the heat treat process.

When I consider the methods used by Ed to draw out and heat treat his blades made of 3-inch ball bearings, his allowance of 1/16 of an inch to grind off may be about right. He reduces the 3-inch ball bearings (which are the only steel he uses) with the flat dies on a Beaudry power hammer. This is a long process involving many heats (30 to 40 minutes per ball). This is his "style." He probably has at least five times more decarburized material than I would have on my 2-inch bearings, which I draw out with one heat. When his methods are taken into consideration, my opinion is that his grinding allowance is just about right.

When I draw a bunch of the 2-inch ball bearings, I utilize my friend Dave Thompson's two Beaudry power hammers. (See photos.) The small one is a 150-pound size with real extreme drawing dies and the big one is 300-pound with flat dies. A 2-inch bearing is stretched out to around 18-inches in one heat and there is enough heat left to flatten and straighten it out with the top die of the big Beaudry just idling on it. When I draw the same 2-inch bearings with my hydraulic forging press it takes four heats or more and, because of the extended time, I would naturally have more decarburization.

Many bladesmiths, myself included, use rectangular bar stock to forge some or all of our knives. We forge the end of the bar to the shape we want, hammer the wedge shape down to the edge and also put some taper to the point (distal taper). If we watch our temperature and get the forging accomplished

My friend Dave Thompson's shop. There are five power hammers in this photo. Far left is the 300-pound Beaudry, on the far right is the 150-pound Beaudry. The 50-pound Little Giant that I used to own is behind the Beaudry on the right side of the photo. There are two 25-pound Little Giants in the photo but you have to look to find them.

in a reasonable amount of time, there will not be an excessive amount of decarburization. If we grind off around .020, (which is around a third as much as Ed needs to grind off of his) we will probably get rid of the decarburized material.

The extreme drawing dies on the 150-pound hammer.

A batch of 2-inch ball bearings ready to be drawn out.

The 12-inch-long hammer on the 300-pound just sort of sets down on it and with a tap, tap and a turn or two and the billet is smooth, straight and flat.

Dimension of round or square bar stock	Minimum amount to be removed from each side
up to 1/2"	.016"
1/2 - 1 1/4"	.031"
1 1/4" - 3"	.063"
3" - 5"	.125"

DECARBURIZATION ALLOWANCE

The allowance for rectangular stock would be the same for round bars when the width was less than four times the thickness of the bar. If the width is more than four times the thickness then the allowance from the chart should be doubled. For example: The 5160 bar stock that I make bowie knives from is ¼" X 1 ½". The width is six times the thickness so the amount to grind off would be .032 per side.

From my teaching experiences I have learned that the quality of a blade can be harmed by too much time at the forging temperatures. When a student takes as much as an hour and a half to shape a blade, the steel usually does not get as hard as it should. Before these experiences I was never quite sure how much forging was "too much." The greatest amount of decarburization is on the surface and it gradually decreases to a negligible amount at some point into the steel. As the blade being forged becomes thinner at the edge, the decarburized material from the early stages of the forging could reach completely through the blade.

The stock removal maker also has to allow for decarburization. Hot rolled steel has a "bark" of decarburized material that is a result of the rolling, forging and annealing. Depending on the alloy content and temperatures used, the bark may be anywhere from completely to slightly decarburized. The usual allowance on steel up to 1/2 an inch thick is to allow .016 per side to grind off to get down to good material. (See chart.)

HOW TO FORGE A DAGGER

Jay Lovuolo writes:

I am currently attempting to forge a dagger and am pretty clueless and have been seeking help all over. Do you have any tips for me? Thanks in advance for all your help.

Answer: Forging a double-edged blade has some unique problems associated with it. The first is to try to figure out how much narrower the pre-form needs to be from the finished profile. The second is to hold the rough blade on the anvil at the correct angle to get the bevels even. The final problem is that the forging has to be kept even on all four surfaces of the blade in order for the finished blade to be symmetrical.

All blades start with what I call a pre-form. The bar stock is forged to a certain shape (a pre-form) so that it will have the correct shape and width once the hammer blows spread the edge or edges out. The proper shape and size of a pre-form is something that is learned primarily by experience. A general rule is that the finished blade will be somewhere in the neighborhood of 30 percent to 50 percent wider than the pre-form. The exact width will depend on the thickness of the bar stock and how thin it is forged at the edge.

Let's start by forging a pre-form that is 70 percent of the width that the finished dagger shape should be.

While forging this pre-form some distal taper should be forged into it, otherwise after forging in the bevels the point may be wider than was wanted. The pre-form has to be symmetrical or else the finished piece won't be. If necessary, file or grind it to a symmetrical shape before forging the bevels.

If you look at a dagger blade from the end you will see four facets. For the purpose of this forging lesson you should number them 1, 2, 3, and 4 in a clockwise direction. (See drawing "B.") Start the forging by working a bevel on the surface that will become facet #1 of the blade. It is of the utmost importance to not make any hammer blows past the centerline. You will be forging approximately one third of the bevel into the blade, and remember that you will be bringing the other side down to meet at a centerline. As you do this, note that the forged portion will belly out from the opposite edge; but don't worry, it will straighten itself out with the next forging. Forge the same amount of bevel into facet #3. If you forged both edges equally the shape will be symmetrical. Now go to facet #2, and finally #4. Keep working around the blade in this manner, all the time being aware of where the anvil is under the blade. (See drawing "A.") If you don't keep the anvil under the flat side of the blade you will be putting kinks and bends in the blade and that will make the forging harder.

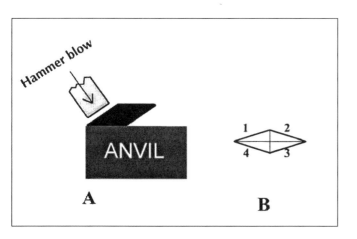

It is easy to tell if you are forging everything equally; as you look at the profile it will be symmetrical, and when you look at it from the point end you will see a diamond shape. (See drawing "B.") Forge and look, forge and look. Take it slow and easy, this is not an easy thing to do. Forge the bevels down to where there is a flat edge approximately 1/16 of an inch thick where the edges meet. You will need this much material in order to clean up the blade prior to heat treating. If you forge the bevels too thin at the edge the dagger will get narrow real fast.

One of the requirements for The American Bladesmith Society, Master Smith rating, is to make a classic European style dagger. I believe that style was chosen because it is the most difficult knife to make perfectly symmetrical.

WILL GAS FORGES MAKE GOOD BLADES?

"Wishing to Remain Anonymous" from Texas writes: (The only time in eight years of the *Blade* Magazine Q&A feature that I had someone request that the name be withheld.)

I want to start making some forged blades. I was considering the purchase of a gas furnace, but was told by a bladesmith who uses only coal that gas would not make good blades because it would not add any carbon to the blade like coal does. What type forge do you use, and what would you recommend for me to start out with?

Answer: Without getting into a lot of complicated chemistry and theory, I will try to explain the commonly accepted and proven-in-use facts about forge fires. Coal, coke, charcoal or gas fires, all can be either reducing (carbon rich), oxidizing (oxygen rich), or neutral. The effect that each of these fires have on a specific steel type will depend on the percentages of the steel's carbon and alloy content.

A bar of iron acts very much like a sponge; it will soak up carbon when at the right temperature in a carbon-rich atmosphere. When placed in an oxygen-rich atmosphere at the right temperature it loses carbon at the same rate of time that it picked it up. This reaction happens at something close to 1/16-inch per hour.

The reducing fire might add carbon to the surface of the blade if left in the fire long enough, but I doubt that most blades are in the fire long enough to gain any real advantage. Once the blade is out in the atmosphere, scale forms and the scale is probably coming off faster

Atmospheric gas furnace by Devin Thomas. Note the digital readout at left center. This is the most efficient and quickest heating furnace I've ever seen.

than the blade can pick up carbon. The stock removal that is done after the forging most likely removes any remaining carbonized material.

When the atmosphere in the forge is oxidizing, scale forms on the blade even while it is in the fire, causing the blade to scale away very rapidly while loosing carbon at the same time. In the neutral fire, the blade neither gains nor loses carbon.

I have used it all; coke, coal, charcoal and finally gas. I see no reason to ever again use anything but gas for forging. Gas is especially efficient when welding large Damascus billets. There is no down time like there is with a coal fire, having to clean out clinker and ash and rebuild the fire. I can make three times as much Damascus material in a given amount of time with gas.

Burner tube detail.

Chapter 7

WHAT IS DAMASCUS STEEL?

It is unlikely that Damascus steel was ever made in Damascus, Syria. It is more likely that Damascus was the trade center where either the steel or blades were obtained and that is how the figured steel came to be named. If you look up Damascus steel in the dictionary, it is defined as "steel with a pattern on the surface." The dictionary also defines "damask" as "a reversible figured fabric…" Damask is also used to describe "peculiar" markings on the surface of steel. This brings up an intriguing question: Could it be that damask cloth was made before the steel was so named? If so, the patterned steel may have gotten its name from the cloth, not the city!

Damascus steel was easy to define back in 1973 when Bill Moran first displayed his pattern-welded blades at the Knifemakers Guild Show. It's not so easy to define today. My list of types keeps growing and growing. Electrical discharge machining, powder-filled patterns, layers made of powder metallurgy steel; there is no limit to the possibilities.

The knife is no longer just a cutting tool or weapon. It can become a "canvas" where the makers of Damascus steel can express their art. Will the future see the development of an art form where patterned steel is simply hung on the wall or made into sculpture? Why not? As it is now, lots of people spend big money for decorated paper and canvas to put on their walls.

A customer once asked me to make up sample pieces of all the different types of Damascus. It would be a collection to admire and study. I never found time to do it, but the idea may be sound. Perhaps bladesmiths should start making up standard-size example pieces to sell to collectors. One inch by 2 inches would be a nice size.

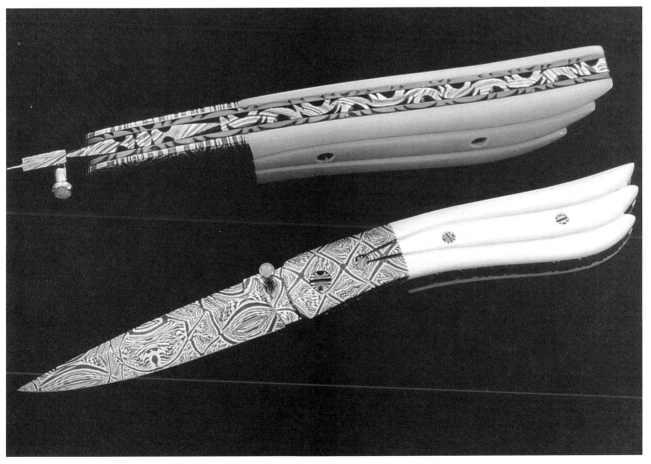

Mosaic damascus folding knife by Barry Gallagher. This defines what an art knife is. Photo by Barry Gallagher.

"Hammer Steel", by J.D. Smith. Mechanical manipulation of the naturally occurring fiber or grain flow in tool steel creates an almost Wootz-like appearance.

I am willing to accept as "Damascus" steel in any form that has either a crystalline or mechanical structure that is visible when brought out by etching. This definition fits Damascus steel into common usage and keeps it in a historical context.

There is a need to call the different Damascus types by a proper and appropriate name and not simply lump them all together as Damascus steel. The patterned blades brought back to Europe by the returning Crusaders, the Viking and Merovingian blades, the Indonesian Kris, the Japanese sword, the German blades of the first half of this century and the current production are, from the mechanical and visual characteristics, very different things. I believe it is time to stop arguing about what is or is not Damascus steel, or what genuine Damascus steel is. The term "Damascus steel" should be used for the whole general class of steel with patterned blades. The specific types should then be identified and referred to by names that accurately describe the origin of their basic metals and their method of manufacture.

CLASSES OF DAMASCUS MATERIAL

The accompanying outline lists all the types of Damascus steel with which I am familiar. The name assigned to a specific class is either one accepted in common usage or something that I felt was appropriate. It is presented for reference and your consideration as a more accurate way to communicate about this material. Modern metallurgists have made the distinction between crystalline and mechanical Damascus. *On Damascus Steel* by Leo S. Figiel M.D., distinguishes between the two. The crystalline type originates from a homogeneous, cast source in either a billet or bar. The mechanical type originates from a heterogeneous source and is laid up by forge welding. Every known type has to fit into one or the other of these two classes.

A specific Damascus blade should be classified and called by a specific name. If you make a blade by forge welding a motorcycle chain together, call it "motorcycle-chain Damascus." If you weld up a bicycle chain by itself and then stack it with a bar that was welded up from cable, then fold it a few times, it becomes composite-bar pattern welded. If your blade was not welded but etched to bring out the crystalline damask, it is either etched bar-stock Damascus or etched cast Damascus.

DAMASCUS STEEL TYPES

I. Crystalline (homogeneous source)

    A. Old Wootz
        1. Indian (crystalline)
        2. Persian (laminar)

    B. Modern Wootz
        1. Crystals arranged in long sheets, laminar grain.
        2. Crystals arranged in a more random pattern.

    C. Etched to bring out dendrites and crystal pattern.
        1. From bar stock
        2. From cast blade shapes

II. Mechanical (forge or furnace welded, heterogeneous source)

    A. Pattern welded
        1. Layered where the individual layers are homogeneous
        2. Layered where the individual layers are hetergeneous
        3. "Turkish," twisted rods
        4. High density

    B. Mosaic
        1. Patterns formed by pipe, wire etc.
        2. Patterns cut by EDM
        3.Combination of powder and pre-forms

    C. Wire
        1. Wire rope source

    a. All steel wires made up of dissimilar alloys
    b. Steel of varying carbon/alloy contents and iron wires
    c. All high carbon steel
    d. Made up combinations, (wires or strands from mixtures of the above)
  2. Other wire sources
    a. Street sweeper
    b. Piano wire
    c. Other wire combinations

  D. Chains
    1. Motorcycle
    2. Bicycle
    3. Timing
    4. Chain saw
    5. Drive chain

III. Particle Metallurgy Or Powder
        Damasteel (Particle Metallurgy)
        Steel and Iron Powder (Pioneered by
          Devin Thomas)

DOES DAMASCUS STEEL HAVE ADVANTAGES?

There is a great deal of difference in the strength and edge-holding ability of blades made by the layered Damascus process. Some variables that affect the performance of the finished product are the starting materials, welding temperature, number of folds, pattern development and heat treatment. These factors are individually important and yet, to a large degree, depend on and affect each other.

If the layered Damascus blade is to have superior strength and cutting ability, it should actually have hard and soft layers in the finished blade. This should give it superior strength and the DCE (Damascus Cutting Effect) would work. DCE theory says that as the soft layers wear away, the hard cutting surfaces are exposed. I have seen DCE work only on blades that had a very fine ladder pattern at the cutting edge. A lot of carbon is lost in the welding process, so it is important to start with steel of at least .95 or more carbon. Up until about 1985 most pattern-welded steel started out with good quality wrought iron or mild steel to make the starting billet. Since that time more and more pattern-welded steel is made of all high carbon steel, the difference in alloy content giving the blade its pattern.

Welded Damascus is possible because combinations of steel and iron will weld together when heated to a certain temperature in a reducing atmosphere. Temperature and atmosphere are the important thing; hammering only pushes all the parts up against all the other parts. The normal temperature for welding steel and iron together is around 2,100 to 2,400 degrees F. At these temperatures the carbon migrates from areas of high to low concentration. This is known as "diffusion" or "carbon migration." The speed at which diffusion takes place is relative to time and temperature; the more time and the higher the temperature, the faster the rate of diffusion. This is why it is important to weld at the lowest temperature possible, get it done quickly and fold the blade material no more than is necessary.

I learn the most about the structure and internal soundness of my welded blades by doing a destructive test of the tip portion of a heat-treated blade. The fracture pattern that a Damascus blade shows when broken is an excellent indication of whether or not the welding was worth the effort. The superior blade is resistant to breakage and shows an irregular pattern when it does give up. As a crack forms across a hard layer, it is stopped by the adjoining soft layer.

The soft layer must be pulled apart before the crack can continue into the next hard layer.

If the blade breaks cleanly and has a crystalline appearance, it is a sign of complete carbon migration. It is possible to have a 500-layer piece of pattern-welded material that shows a nice pattern, yet the carbon is evenly distributed throughout the material with all the layers being close to the same hardness.

Another good indication is the hardness of the blade out of the quench. When too much folding or welding at too high a temperature is done, the blade will not respond well to the hardening process, an indication of excessive carbon loss.

I was disappointed with the strength and cutting ability of my first layered Damascus blades. They

Audra Draper has just passed the 90-degree flex test with her damascus test blade. This is one of the performance requirements for the ABS Master Smith rating.

did not measure up to most of the things I had read about the material. For the first two years of my Damascus making, I tested each new heat-treated blade. I would clamp 1-inch of the point in a vise and flex the blade 90 degrees. Whenever the blades were hard enough to hold an edge well, they would break. If they had very much strength, they would not have edge-holding ability. All of these blades were of the iron/steel, 500-plus layer type.

As I progressed in my bladesmithing skills, I started to look more closely at many of the claims made for Damascus steel and realized that these claims were based on opinion and not on any comparisons made with other knives. My discussions with other bladesmiths verified my opinion that not many comparisons were being made. This brings me back to my first rule of knife testing: No results have any value unless a "same test, same day" comparison is made with another knife of known value. I was chasing a phantom set of attributes and decided then and there to write my own rules for my Damascus steel. The layered steel would be compared to all other types of mechanical Damascus steels for a fair perspective to be determined.

What about the ancient blades that were said to have cut a silk scarf floating in air and then cut through swords, armor, rocks and anvils? When I put it in perspective it seems that the fame of Damascus steel was gained at a time when most blades were iron, or steel that would be inferior to present-day low-quality materials. It is my opinion that the strength and cutting ability of the ancient blades will not equal the best selectively hardened and tempered modern non-Damascus blades. My opinion will be hard to prove because of the lack of ancient blades available for testing.

If we classify modern mechanical (welded) blades made from wires, chains, etc., as different types of Damascus, then how do these blades measure up when their physical characteristics are compared in fair tests?

The strength of a welded Damascus blade depends on a number of variables. The most important is that there are alternating hard and soft layers running throughout the blade. The study of the

Wade Colter can't help smiling. That's because his damascus blade just passed the ABS Master Smith flex test. He got to do his test in public at the Oregon Knife Collectors Association annual show in 1999.

fractured surface of a layered blade that had superior strength shows that there is an uneven breaking in the fracture. Think of a crack trying to work its way through a layered blade; the hard layers are easy to fracture but when the crack comes to a soft layer it has to tear the soft layer apart before the fracturing can continue. In most layered steels there are occasional flaws that also provide an easy path into which the crack can spread.

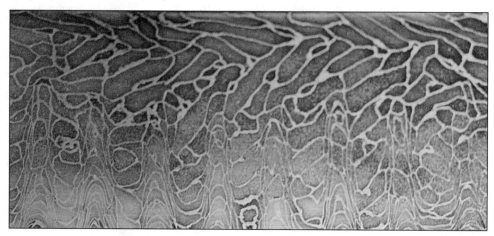

Close-up view of a wire damascus blade that has been manipulated to create a "ladder" pattern at the edge.

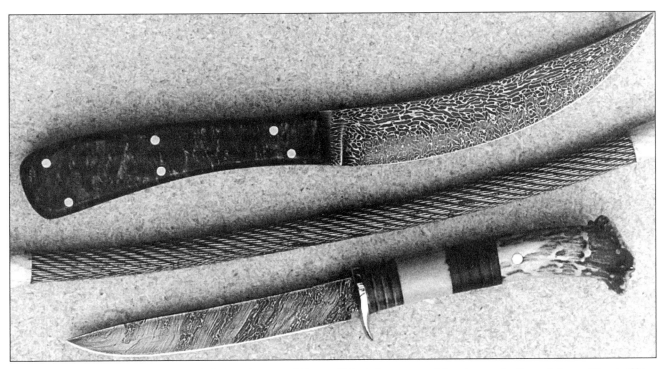

The top knife was made out of eight pieces of the anti-twist crane cable shown in the picture. The knife at the bottom has a blade of twisted wire damascus.

When a welded Damascus blade breaks clean with a crystalline appearance, it indicates that something went wrong. The usual cause is too much folding. Such a blade will often show a beautiful pattern but will have no more strength or cutting ability than an average homogeneous blade.

Some of the problems encountered when making layered steel are eliminated when wire rope is used to make Damascus. Wire rope should be used that is all high carbon material (whether it is high carbon can be determined by a quench test of the rope before welding). The diameter of the individual wires will, to a large degree, determine the strength and cutting ability of the welded-up blade. The high carbon wire decarburizes to a depth of approximately .005 inches during the welding process. The decarburized outer portion of the wire becomes nearly pure iron. This effect is what causes the pattern and other Damascus properties in blades welded up from wire.

If the starting billet is made of 3/8-inch cable which usually has wires that are .015 inches in diameter, the finished blade will have just one third or less of the total carbon with which it started. (.85 carbon to start, less than .30 when finished). This blade would be strong and beautiful but would have little cutting ability when compared to a blade made of wires .040 to .060 in diameter. The proportion of remaining high carbon material is much greater as the wires get larger. This is useful in controlling the physical properties and appearance of the billet by using different-size wires in the core, edge, back or outer skin.

The layers in a finished wire Damascus blade do not run in straight lines; they instead twist through the blade, alternating their twist from one side to the other. The best blades that I have tested are made by starting with a large enough bundle to make the finished blade with no folding. When correctly done, the material known as wire Damascus will always be stronger than the layered material.

DAMASCUS MADE FROM CHAIN MATERIALS

I compared bicycle chain, motorcycle chain, various assortments of timing chains and chain-saw

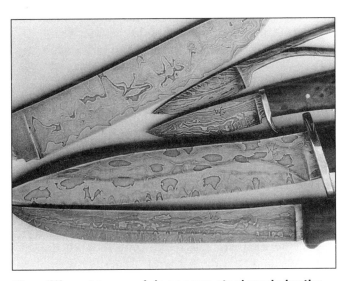

Five different types of damascus steel made by the author. Top left, bicycle chain. Right side top to bottom: wire damascus, pattern-welded, chain saw chain, and motorcycle chain.

chain. I got the best cutting ability from chain-saw Damascus. It takes a lot more work to prepare a billet for welding but it is worth the effort. Most modern chain-saw chains have chrome-plated cutting teeth. I have not been successful at welding chrome-plated parts, so I grind off the portion of the cutting tooth that is plated. It would seem from quench tests on the chain before welding and the appearance of the etched blade that there are three different alloys of high-carbon material in the chain with which I have worked. This fact, along with the shape of the pieces of chain, gives chain-saw Damascus blades their exceptional beauty and cutting ability.

A NEW GENERATION OF DAMASCUS MATERIALS

In the last 10 years there have been three advances in techniques and equipment that have eliminated many variables that have a negative impact on the quality of making the layer-welded material. The first advance was the development of a new generation of gas furnaces specifically designed for welding layered Damascus steel. These furnaces are rapidly replacing coal forges as the heat source used by the bladesmith for welding. Welding is usually accomplished at a lower temperature in a gas furnace and that is beneficial for the quality of the blade. It is very easy to overheat or even burn up a billet in a coal forge. When welding in a properly regulated gas furnace, it is nearly impossible to overheat the billet.

The second development that has improved the quality of layered Damascus is the elimination of the folding process by starting with enough layers of material to make the finished blade. I call it one-weld Damascus. The first time I saw this done was in 1983 by artist/blacksmith David Thompson and his uncle, Ron Thompson. They made some billets of layered Damascus by stacking layers of metal-cutting band-saw blade material mixed with steel-strapping material. The billet was welded, drawn out and forged into blades with no folding.

"Twisted nickel" as made by Jim Ferguson is another one-weld layered Damascus. He combines nickel with spring steel and welds it under a large press, twists it and then forges it flat, creating a billet with a large, distinctive twist pattern.

A.J. Hubbard has developed the one-weld welding of layered material to a high degree by using his patented process known as Precision Engineered Damascus (PED). His process encapsulates very thin, alternating layers of differing types of steel in a metallic wrapper. The total number of layers required for the blade is then welded in one process with no folding.

Devin Thomas uses a different method to "dry" weld layers of stainless and other steel. He also produces mokume with his method. "Dry" welding

Two damascus blades made by the author. The top blade is my version of all high-carbon damascus. It has approximately 200 layers of Sandvik band saw steel and 1095. I start with up to 40 layers and get the total layer count in three welds or less. All welding and drawing is done with the hydraulic forging press. The bottom blade is stainless damascus by Devin Thomas. I like his stainless damascus because of the crisp, clean and precise patterns.

means that no flux is used. I have examined numerous blades made by this process and it is the cleanest layered material that I have seen. Devin is currently developing Damascus made with a combination of pattern pieces and metal powders.

When a mixture of high- and low-alloy steels are welded together, the resulting billet is not always compatible to a lot of drawing out. In eliminating the multiple stretching, folding and re-welding, the one-weld Damascus process makes the welding of stainless steel and other difficult-to-weld steels much more feasible.

DAMASTEEL, PARTICLE METALLURGY DAMASCUS

In November 1992, a cooperation began between Söderfors Powder AB and Kaj Embretsen, Bladesmith, Edsbyn, Sweden. A successful method to produce patterned material by use of the powder metallurgy (PM) was developed during 1993. Patent was received June 1996 regarding methods to produce patterned billets from PM. The premier award for "Innovation of the Year" was received at the EPMA Congress in Paris in June 1994. A new company, DAMASTEEL AB, was formed in August 1995, to serve the market with Damascene steel billets and bars.

CONCLUSION

The combination of modern technology with better and more suitable starting materials will guarantee that Damascus materials will continue to

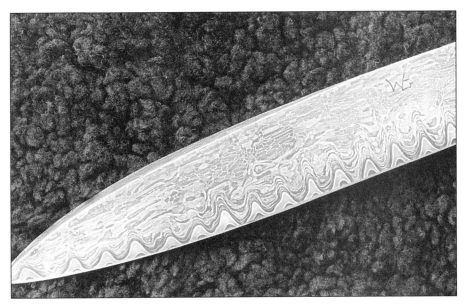

The author made this blade as an experiment in putting a hard piece of material between two springy sides. It creates an interesting "tooth" effect.

improve. With each passing year the odds of making a finished blade of better quality improves.

THE DAMASCUS ADVANTAGE

Paul Trudel of Ottawa, Ontario, Canada writes:

Can you tell me what are the advantages of having a Damascus blade? I have all kinds of information describing and showing how different patterns are obtained. I believe that there must be something else than just good looks and intricate designs.

Your answer will be greatly appreciated.

Answer: I will assume that your question concerns pattern-welded material and so my answers will have to do with Damascus material made by the forge welding process. There are both physical and artistic aspects of the Damascus blade to consider. It is said that art should bring out some emotion in the observer. I can speak from experience about the emotional affect of Damascus steel on the human mind. It was at the Knifemakers Guild Show in 1974 when I first saw Bill Moran's Damascus steel. The Damascus virus quickly infected me. It took me another eight years to get worked up enough to get into making Damascus steel. I've been making the material for 16 years now. I've still got the bug, and if I may quote Damascus steel pioneer Daryl Meier, "...and there is no known cure".

Some folks describe a magical, incomprehensible attraction to the Damascus blade. As for myself, I can feel strong emotions about a beautiful Damascus blade. On the other hand, a shiny hollow-ground blade usually leaves me pretty calm.

A beautiful Damascus blade can be the most interesting component of a knife. The handle material, fittings and design become secondary when there is a beautiful Damascus blade involved. The Damascus blade dominates all the other design elements. In my opinion, most Damascus knives are purchased to get the blade.

When it comes to the mechanical properties of pattern-welded Damascus there are wide differences in the strength and edge-holding ability of blades. This is a result of the many variables that exist in the process of making a Damascus blade. There is an interlocking of causes and effects between the variables.

Some of these variables are as follows:

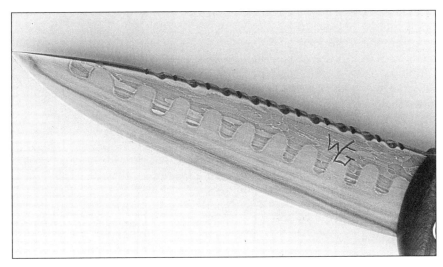

Another of the author's experiments with composite blades. The edge piece of heavy saw plate was formed with a die made for the hydraulic press. The edge piece was then pressed down into the hot wire damascus material. When everything cooled down the pieces were cleaned of scale; tack welded in place and then forge welded. The edge quench line, which could have been deeper, confuses the visual effect of this method of construction.

1. The starting materials; for example: the alloy content, number and thickness of the layers.
2. The temperature and atmosphere in the welding fire.
3. Total time at each welding heat.
4. Total number of doubling welds.
5. The forging time and temperature to shape the blade after the billet is forge welded.
6. Quality of the heat treating.

How do you choose a quality blade? The more experience a Damascus maker has, the better the chance is that he will have eliminated the things that can and do go wrong in the process of getting a finished blade.

If you want a Damascus blade in a working knife, ask the maker what type of Damascus he would recommend for the intended use. Ask him what comparisons were done to support the opinion. Finally, ask what type of guarantee will be given on the blade.

If beauty is the only criteria, buy the prettiest blade you can find, and then take whatever strength and cutting ability comes with it.

ALL HIGH-CARBON, PATTERN-WELDED STEEL

Mike Sweany of Sand Springs, Oklahoma writes:

My question has to do with pattern-welded steel. Is it necessary when using two types of high-carbon steel to weld up more layers than what gives a good pattern? Pattern welding in the old days was more of a way to refine the material, working impurities out of the iron and working the carbon from the steel into the iron. (Or so I have read.) My theory is if you start with two different high-carbon steels, only a pleasing pattern is required. Is making 500 layers or more a waste of time? I would appreciate your thoughts on this.

Answer: That's a good question and your "all high-carbon steel" theory is a good one. In order to answer the question of number of layers and percentages of high-carbon material I would first have to ask an important question. The question is: What do we expect of the finished blade? If beauty was the only criteria, I would do something radically different than if cutting ability or strength was wanted. The starting materials, number of layers and manipulation of the layers would be totally different depending on the results hoped for. I faced the question of layers back in 1983. I was looking for magic strength and cutting ability with blades. I welded up billets using 500 layers of wrought iron and high-carbon steel, but I wasn't finding any special properties. When I broke the tips off of these blades the grain structure was nearly homogeneous. The only real indication of layering was the occasional flaw. I finally decided to create my own rules.

I welded up layered steel with many combinations of materials and numbers of layers. Testing showed me that strength was lost by the material becoming homogeneous after 200 layers. I am getting excellent

beauty, strength and cutting ability with what I call "No Rules, High-Low Damascus." (It's called High-Low because it is all high-carbon, yet has a low layer count.) I start with bandsaw steel (sort of like L-6) and 1095. I work my billet up to 100 to 200 layers in three welds or less. The thickness of the blade will determine the layer count. A thin folding knife does not need as many layers to look as good as a thicker hunting knife. A 100-layer blade with full ladder pattern is much more interesting than a random layer blade with the same layer count.

HOW TO MAKE A LADDER PATTERN IN DAMASCUS

Matthew Butterly of Busselton, Western Australia writes:

With a ladder pattern in Damascus, do the grooves have to be cut in with a grinder or can they be cut in with a hardie or hot chisel? I recently saw a picture of a ladder pattern die being used. Would this be the same as hot cutting?

(Author's note) My original answer created two more questions so I have expanded my reply from the way it originally appeared in *Blade*.

Answer: I make the blade pre-form twice as thick as it will be when finished and the edge is straight. It will curve up more than enough as the grooves are forged out. I use a narrow grinding wheel to cut the grooves to form a ladder pattern. The grooves are cut approximately 60 percent of the way through the blade and alternate from one side to the other. (See drawing.) I have a specially shaped straight-pein hammer for spreading the grooves. A hammer with a flat face will often push the surface of the steel down into the groove, and that's not good.

I've adopted a style where the ladder pattern is only on the edge portion up to about half of the width of the blade. I find the random pattern at the back a nice con-

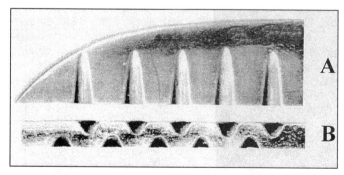

"A" illustrates the side view of the blade preform. "B" shows the edge portion of the preform. (Remember that is twice the thickness the finished blade will be.) As the grooves are forged out, the straight bottom edge will take on a lot more curve than is wanted. The thick back portion of the blade is then forged down to the finished thickness, with the addition of some distal taper. This will cause the point of the blade to drop down from the excess curve.

This picture from the shop of Devin Thomas shows how shaped die blocks in a large hydraulic press forge grooves into a hot billet of stainless damascus.

trast with the ladder pattern at the edge. I edge quench my Damascus blades and the contrast in the pattern seems to work well with the difference in appearance caused by the quench. I would rather make a blade that was unbreakable than one that had a uniform appearance because it was fully hardened.

I tried hot-forming and then grinding the high parts off but settled on grinding because I have better control in keeping the pattern uniform. With a die setup in a press or large power hammer there is absolute uniformity in the pattern. (See photo.) Several makers that I know use a milling machine to cut the grooves. Regardless of the method used, there is not much difference in the pattern of the finished blade.

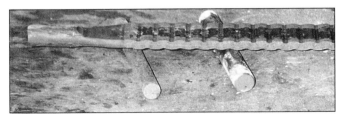

A freshly "squeezed" bar. Note that the grooves alternate from one side to the other.

ETCHING DAMASCUS

Phil Chiu of Marlborough, New Hampshire writes:

What type of acid is used to etch Damascus? I've been using Archer etchant for printed circuit boards. I don't like the results. What little etching I can get wipes off easily, even after soaking in the etchant for some time.

Answer: I use Archer etchant (a ferric chloride Solution) and it gives me good results, but it took me awhile to figure it out. Here is how I do it. The fresh etchant is mixed with three or four parts of water. The temperature of the etch bath should be maintained around 60-70 degrees F. I get the best results by starting with a hand-rubbed 400-grit finish. I put the bare blade (that means no fingerprints) into the etchant by hanging it on a wire. I allow the etch to work for five to eight minutes, then take it out and put it into a strong solution of TSP (trisodium phosphate) and water. TSP is sold in the paint department of most stores. It is a chemical neutralizer for ferric chloride. I allow the etched blade to neutralize for several minutes, then wash the carbon deposit off of the surface with soapy water and some fine steel wool. I then give the blade a quick hand rub with 1,000-grit wet or dry paper to check the progress of the etch. Most blades of cable and motorcycle chain need anywhere from two to four cycles of the five- to eight-minute etch/rub followed by the TSP. Some pattern-welded blades respond well to one eight- to 12-minute etch. The process of etch and rub, etch and rub gives a depth and appearance that I have not been able to get any other way.

As it comes out of the bottle, the etchant is too strong and it eats all the layers at the same rate. This usually results in a poor appearance because there is little delineation between the layers. Other times the appearance will be granular and pitted looking. A slower etch always brings out more pattern.

You didn't mention what type of Damascus you were working with. Some commercial Damascus does not have much pattern to it. I've had lots of questions about this, but little experience etching the commercially available Damascus. Try the method I recommend and if you still are having trouble it may be the material.

EMERGENCY WELDING FLUX

Gene Martin of Williams, Oregon writes:

What about the puddle of borax that came out of my forge today? I realize the puddle of molten flux will have impurities in it, but I am thinking of using it sometime when borax might be unavailable.

Answer: I always wondered about that burnt, glassy looking, black stuff myself. Most homemade dragon breath furnaces are made with a trough made of fire brick and fire clay in the bottom to catch the borax. To keep it from building up and melting the liner, I scrape the excess borax out as my furnace is cooling down after a welding party. At just the right tempera-

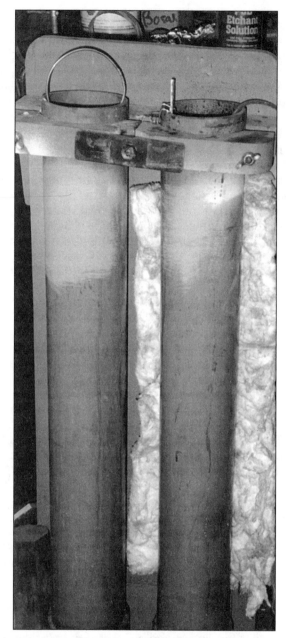

This is my etching setup. The two sections
of PVC tube are 4 inches in diameter and
34 inches long. The tube is electrical con-
duit and came to me as scrap from a construction job. It cost me $28 for plugs and
glue to cap the bottom ends. The left tube
is neutralizer (TSP) solution; the right tube
contains the Archer Etchant, mixed with
three parts of water. Note the bottle of
etchant at the top right of the photo. A
stainless steel ring that is made too large
to fall down into the tube is affixed to a
wire that goes through the tang of the
blade. (The ring is visible in the neutralizer
tube.) The wooden holder is bolted to the
steel workbench behind the etching setup.

This photo has nothing to do with the puddle of
borax in the bottom of a gas welding furnace. It does
show Gene Martin and Todd Logsdon with something they dug out of the bottom of a coal forge, it's
the largest clinker I ever saw. This type of clinker can
happen when coal is stored on loose gravel and
some of it gets into the fire pot. ABS School, 1995.

oxide (scale from the steel), and contents of the fire
clay and brick bottom of my furnace.

It would probably have some fluxing action but
might not be as active as the fresh borax.

The chemical action of fresh borax on steel at high
temperatures is that of a strong acid. It dissolves scale
and allows it to melt back into the surface of the steel
or drip off. I believe some of the cleaning action would
probably be lost by the impurities in the residue from
the forge.

You might conduct an experiment by scaling up a
piece of steel. Use the black residue for flux and time it
to see how long it takes to dissolve the scale. Fresh
borax will take about two minutes to dissolve the
scale, then hammer the steel lightly and let cool. Once
the experiment has cooled grind into it to see what
impurities were hammered into the surface.

ture it balls up and can be raked out. It will have all of
the following in it: melted Kaowool (liner material), iron

Based on my experience, anhydrous borax is the best bargain there is for the bladesmith. It does not take that much borax and the result in good welds is worth the small expense.

QUESTIONS ABOUT WIRE DAMASCUS

Nels Nelson of Tucson, Arizona writes:

I have been trying to make cable Damascus blades with no positive results as yet. I have tried welding and tying the ends of the cable which is 5/8-inch New Improved. I heated it in a coal forge and used Borax before scale formed, then tried hammering it into a square shape, then flattened and quenched in oil. Can cable that has rope in the middle be used for Damascus blades? I burn the cable in a wood fire to get rid of the rope, then soak in muriatic acid. I end up with hollow cable. Will this work?

Answer: You didn't say what type of borax you are using. Because of the large surface area in cable, the more positive fluxing action of anhydrous borax is necessary. Many problems with forge welding are solved with a switch to anhydrous borax. If you are now using household borax a switch to anhydrous will give you better results. At the welding temperature, borax acts like a powerful acid to clean the surface of the material being welded. Anhydrous borax gives better coverage as the billet is heating and that means less scale in between all those wires.

I've been very successful with just burning out the lubricating oil/grease from the cable and have not found any need to soak it in acid. I would recommend taking the cable apart and taking the rope core out, then assembling the cable again, then burn out the lubrication. It is usually only necessary to unwind several strands in order to get the core out. It is necessary to get the rope out before the welding heat so that ash from the burned rope will not be trapped inside the billet.

The way I do it is to cut the cable into 12-inch pieces. An abrasive chop saw is used for this operation. Then the lubrication is burned out and then the ends are fused with a torch. The piece is then heated and twisted up tight. I then cut the

twisted cable into three or four pieces. These are stacked up two by two or two by three, wired together and then welded onto a handle. The purpose of this is to get a big enough stack so that I will not have to double it (cut and fold or re-stack) to get a billet large enough to make a blade.

When I had photomicrographs made of the cross-section of welded up high-carbon steel cable it showed a decarburized zone around each wire. The metallurgist who did the picture said the decarburized material was nearly pure iron. This soft part of the wire was approximately .010 inch thick.

The carbon left the surface during the welding heat. The higher the heat — plus time, the more loss there is. The thickness of the shell of decarburized material around a small wire will be the same as in a large wire. The remaining percentage of high-carbon material is much greater as the diameter of the wires increases. (See drawing.)

A lot of reduction in cross section at the welding heat is necessary in order for cable to weld up without flaws . Without folding, 5/8-inch cable does not have enough mass to weld up solid and have a large

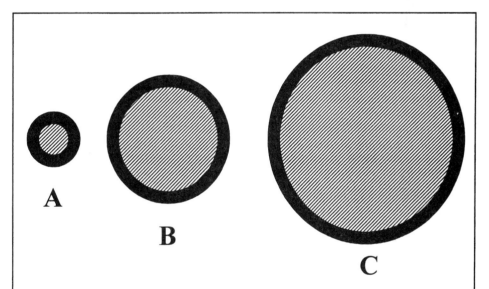

Each circle illustrates the cross section of a single wire from a welded up blade made of high carbon cable. The dark band is decarburized material.

"A" is a small wire from 1/4" cable. When welded, it has more iron than steel in it.

"B" is a medium size wire from 1" cable. It has a lot more steel than iron, that makes a good balance of carbon content and pattern.

"C" is an extra-large wire from a bridge cable. It has the maximum amount of steel remaining but doesn't show much pattern or other characteristics expected in a damascus blade.

Wire cross-sections.

enough piece for a knife. Because of the amount of decarburization, 5/8-inch cable will usually not make knives that are very hard. It is not as much the diameter of the cable but the size of the individual wires. Small wires have a smaller percentage of carbon left after the welding process. I start with usually 3/4-inch or 1-inch cable that has large wires in it. Blades made from these billets always have a higher hardness than if smaller diameter cable (with small wires) is used.

I once had some new and unused cable that was giving me problems. Every blade I made out of it was full of tiny little flaws. I knew it had something to do with that specific cable because I wasn't having trouble with any other cable I used. I discovered the problem when I was taking a piece of it apart to use the single strands for a special project. (I get real wild patterns by making billets by combining strands from many different types and sizes of cable.) Wrapped around the core of the problem cable was a piece of waxed paper that had printed on it "Made In Korea - Made In Korea - Made In Korea - Made In Korea." I took the remainder of the cable apart, removed the paper and had no more unexplained flaws with that cable.

WASHED OUT PATTERN ON THE EDGE OF A DAGGER BLADE

Skip Snyder of Helena, Montana writes:

I sell Damascus material and one of my customers had a problem with a dagger blade. The pattern along the edges is looking washed-out, but the pattern in the center of the blade is just fine. The mix of materials used usually gives a nice pattern. What do you think caused the irregular etch?

Answer: When different areas of a blade are not the same types of structure they will not react to the etching process in the same way. The differences may be in the grain size or a difference in hardness. Either way, the cause is usually from uneven heating in the normalizing, annealing or hardening phases.

A dagger blade is very different in cross section from a single-blade knife. Because of the thickness of the center rib in relation to the edge it is easy to over-

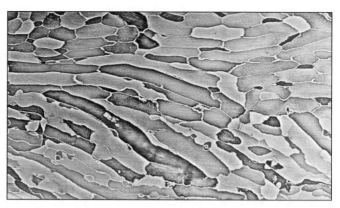

This close-up photo shows the variety of patterns in a blade welded up from cable containing three or four different types of wires. Things to note: The welded wires show up in everything from side to end. The different alloy content in the wires causes the etch to go deeper on some wires. Decarburized material shows up as the light colored web-work, some wires show a lot of it, a few show very little.

heat the edge. My opinion is that the edge of the dagger blade was overheated going into the quenching oil. I would suggest that the blade be annealed and hardened again. Take care that you get an even heat and see if the blade etches out more even.

It is undesirable for the thin sections of a blade to go above the hardening temperature and then drop back when the rest of the blade catches up. The overheated sections will have a more coarse grain and there will be unequal stresses in the blade from the uneven heating. It is always best to heat slow and easy and quench the blade on the rising heat.

It is important to have the heat source for hardening running not too much hotter than the hardening temperature of the blade. This allows a slow even rise to the quenching temperature without overheating the thinnest sections of the blade.

The fact that the edge of a double-edged blade comes up to temperature before the center can be used to your advantage. You can use it to make a selectively hardened blade, assuming that the evenness of the pattern is not important. I call it the "Wiener Roasting" System. (See drawing.)

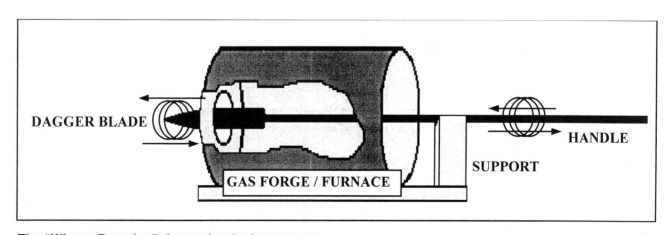

DAGGER BLADE

HANDLE

SUPPORT

GAS FORGE / FURNACE

The "Wiener Roasting" dagger hardening system.

Here is how I do it. The heat source is a homemade gas furnace with a hole in the back end large enough to stick the point of the dagger blade through. The blade is welded onto a handle so that it is centered and balanced. It is necessary to be able to spin the blade and at the same time move the point through the opening in the back so that it does not overheat. The fire is regulated so that it is much hotter than the normal hardening fire. This is necessary to bring the edge up to temperature before the center rib absorbs enough heat to harden. It is wise to practice on a dummy blade to refine the technique. (Any new hardening system should be practiced.)

You will have to work fast and not make any wrong moves. When the edge is up to the hardening temperature the blade is quickly stuck point first into the quenchant. Take care to go straight in and you'll have less chance for a warped blade. If you can't get the edge hot enough to harden before the center of the blade comes up to temperature it means you do not have the furnace running hot enough.

HOW TO CLEAN A DAMASCUS BLADE

Questions often come up about how to clean up a Damascus blade. Some owners fear that cleaning may ruin the pattern.

First check with the maker and see what he recommends. Many makers, as I do, will clean blades of their own making for either no charge or a minimal fee.

If you want to tackle it yourself, here is how you should do it. Obtain some 1,500-grit or finer wet-or-dry paper. Back it up with a flat piece of hard rubber, Pink Pearl-type eraser, leather or etc. The paper is used dry and can be rubbed on a piece of wood to clog it up somewhat and slow up the cutting action. A piece of old cloth placed on a small block of wood the same length as the blade it is an excellent work surface. The blade is laid flat on the block with the cutting edge just inside of the edge. This setup is necessary so that the blade can be cleaned right down to the edge. It also may keep you from getting tangled up with the cutting edge. Use a light touch, with a wiping motion, and work towards the tip taking one long stroke at a time. This is continued until the blade is free of the rust and tarnish. As the abrasive paper gets clogged up it will give a finer finish.

Keep using the same area on the paper unless it quits working before the blade is cleaned to your satisfaction. This process is called "hand-finishing" or a "hand-rubbed finish".

Some Damascus blades respond well to a cold-blue treatment. Clean up as above, and then go over the blade with the finest steel wool that you can find. Apply the cold blue solution as directed on the container. After the rinse, dry the blade and rub down with light oil, WD-40 or similar product. Let set awhile, wipe off the excess oil and give it a final rub with your tired wet or dry paper. This will remove the cold-blue from the surface of the blade, but leave the color in the deep portion of the pattern. Blades with an adequate depth of etch to start with can be cleaned up many times without ruining the pattern.

HOW TO MAKE MOKUME

Thomas J. Janstrom, Townsville, Australia writes:

I would like to know how to make mokume to help embellish my knives. If you could tell me how to make this material I would be most happy.

Answer: Mokume is a Japanese word that means burl or wood-grain and it can apply to layered iron, steel, or non-ferrous laminates. The mokume that you are interested in is the non-ferrous type that is made by a fusion-welding process. If we were to use the word correctly it would always include the type of materials used for the laminations.

Contemporary mokume is usually made of combinations of the following; copper, nickel silver, brass, bronze alloys and pure nickel. My favorite is copper and nickel silver as made by Devin Thomas. I purchase the bar stock then saw and forge it to shape. At times I carve grooves in it before forging to develop a pattern. After finishing the mokume parts, I will etch them, then develop a patina by using either cold blue or a commercial antique finish for silver working. Mokume parts do not have to be etched to delineate the layers but I find they stay nice looking longer when etched and given a patina treatment. Devin will furnish straight-layered, ladder or dot pattern mokume in a variety of materials and number of layers.

To make your own you will need the following:

1. Thin sheet stock of the chosen contrasting materials.
2. A pressure plate (See drawing).

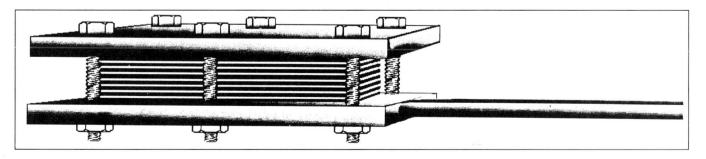

3. Clay / water mixture.

4. Heat source: charcoal, coal, electric or gas. Temperature range 1,500 to 1,600 degrees F.

A good size for your first batch of mokume would be 1 inch wide and 2 inches long. Start with copper and nickel silver sheet, .030 thick, 15 pieces of each. Cut the pieces to size, flatten as necessary and then hand-sand the surfaces down to bare metal. Wear rubber gloves so that the pieces are not contaminated with oily fingerprints. Wash with acetone or lacquer thinner, and stack the alternating pieces up nice and neat. Work in a dust-free area, any dust or oil between the layers will cause a flaw. Sometimes a thicker piece of copper is used on the bottom of the stack which will make the base for a part that will have only one side visible such as a bracelet, belt buckle or pommel cap.

The pressure plate is prepared by coating the inside surface with the clay mixture. This keeps the mokume from welding to the pressure plate. I believe that stainless steel heat treating foil would also work in place of the clay/water mix. With the stack bolted securely in the pressure plate the whole works is put in a nice easy fire and slowly and uniformly brought up to the temperature at which fusion takes place, (1,500-1,600 F). Fusion and welding are the same thing. The way it works is as follows: as the metals to be joined are heated, the atomic particles begin moving faster and faster. As the heat is increased the particles move faster until they reach a point that they will interchange with any compatible material that is touching.

As the stack of alternating materials in the pressure plate reach the point of fusion, a shadow or shimmer is visible on the surface. Welding should be complete. However, most of the time the pressure plate is removed from the heat source and lightly worked with a hand hammer to assure the weld. Success of the welding will depend on the flatness and cleanliness of the laminations and that the whole stack reached the correct temperature. Copper, brass and nickel silver melt at around 2,000 F; therefore, the danger of melting all or part of the billet is always present.

After cooling, the billet is removed and the rough and uneven edges are ground in order to check the quality of the weld. The billet can then be sawed into rough shapes for pattern development and forging. Mokume can be forged somewhat at room temperature if it is annealed. It is safer to forge it hot because there is less chance of questionable welds coming apart. Non-ferrous materials are forged at a low temperature. If there is much color in the billet it may be too hot, 1,100 F is about right. Forge your mokume easy and slow. It is easy to tell when you have worked it too hot because it will start coming apart in large crystalline pieces.

I finish mokume by hand sanding to 800-grit without any buffing. I believe I get a better etch with the open grain of the hand-sanded finish. (This also applies to forge welded steel.) After the etch to delineate the layers, I rub it out with 2,000-grit paper then treat with an oxidizer to give the color contrast patina.

Chapter 8

HOW TO SHARPEN KNIVES

It was in the August '91 issue of *Blade Magazine* that I answered a question on sharpening. It was the fourth question to come in and an important one, too. Sharpening is one part of knives and knife-making that is confusing and misunderstood. Most knives are not sharp the majority of the time. Some of this is because they were never truly sharp in the first place. A blade being too thick at the edge can cause this. Some knives are dull most of the time because the user simply does not take the time to keep the blade sharp.

Before we discuss sharpening technique it will be necessary to understand a few very important factors in the sharpening process. First of all, and the most important is, the sharpening process should be thought of as two distinct and different operations. First roughing and then finishing. It takes either two different stones or one combination stone with the two correct types and sizes of grit to do the total job.

For the roughing process a stone is required that will quickly remove material from the hardest blade. This stone should have grit made of silicon carbide as there is nothing else that cuts quite so fast. The grit size will be around 150 to 240. I use the Norton Medium Crystalon (silicon carbide) for the roughing operation. The roughing stone leaves a coarse and ragged edge that will saw through fibrous materials, but will not be suitable for any type of fine cutting. The finish stone smoothes up the edge and is used to take the wire edge off, leaving a true sharp edge. The finish stone is the Fine India (aluminum oxide). The grit size of 320 is fine enough to give a hair-shaving edge yet leaves enough micro-teeth to give superior slicing ability.

I use odorless kerosene for a sharpening fluid. (WD-40 will work also, but clogs the stones up over a period of time.) Kerosene keeps the stone clean, creates the quickest cutting action and is economical. Oil will work, but is slow-cutting.

I use an angle of 12 to 15 degrees per side. The angle varies with the type of knife. Less angle for light use, more angle for heavy use. Leatherwork and wood-carving knives are sharpened by laying them nearly flat on the stone. The thinner edge will cut the soft materials better, and the strength of the edge isn't a factor. At the other extreme is the survival-type knife blade where strength is required. In this case, the sharpening angle should be greater. The knife edge must have enough material in it to handle the particular type of work for which it is

intended. The best angle for your own knives is best worked out by trial and error.

There are many types of sharpening systems. I rate them by the time it takes to remove the necessary steel and refine the edge. Many bench stones are made with inferior and irregular grit sizes. These are usually attractively priced, but they are slow-cutting and wear out quickly.

I prefer the Norton India/Crystalon stone because of the uniformity of grit size and the purity of the grit. This gives them a superior ability to remove even the hardest metal. Silicon carbide will cut the hardest knife blades, no questions asked. I have often said that there is no such thing as a hard-to-sharpen knife. There are knives that have blades that are too thick to be easily sharpened on any stone. What they need is re-grinding. Crystalon is the Norton trade name for silicon carbide, and India is their trade name for aluminum oxide.

Arkansas stones have a very slow cutting action. I have better things to do with my time. They will give a very good edge if you don't mind spending the extra time involved.

The sharpening process is started by taking cuts across the stone in the direction of the arrows. Do five strokes, and then reverse the direction for the other side of the blade. To maintain the correct angle for the full length of the blade it is necessary to lift the handle of the knife as you get towards the tip; it's a compound angle. Count the strokes and be sure to do the same amount on each side. I start with five passes on each side and then look for the wire edge. Take a red marking pen and run a line of

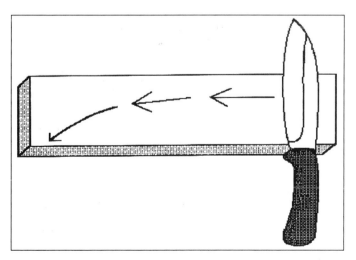

The arrows show the action of the blade on the stone.

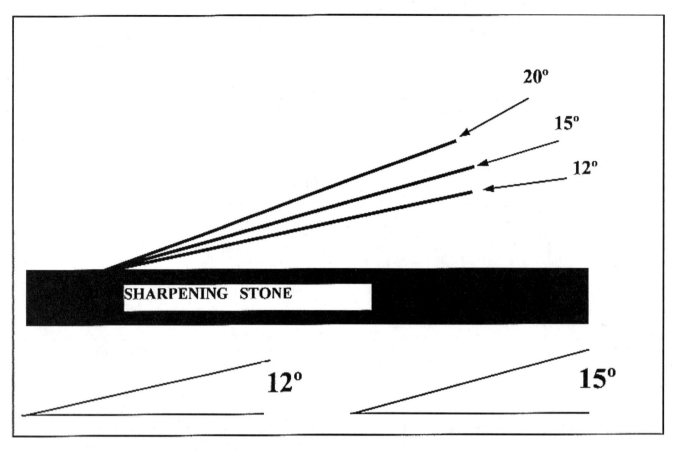

Sharpening angles. Use the ones at the bottom as a pattern to make a wedge to place under the blade in order to train your eyes and hands to the proper angle.

ink down both sides of edge before starting. This gives a visible indication of where you are contacting the edge on the stone. To help yourself learn the correct angle, make a wedge out of wood the shape of the sharpening angle. (See the pattern.) Place the wedge on the stone with the knife on it to give yourself a visible reminder of the sharpening angle. An edge will not be truly sharp unless the bevels are true and flat. It takes good control to achieve this. Practice is the key.

THE WIRE EDGE

It is important to understand the wire edge and how to get it off of the freshly sharpened blade. The wire edge is formed as the two sharpening bevels meet at the edge. What I call a wire is a thin piece of blade material that bends back and forth from the action on the stone and is not removed. (See drawing.)When the wire edge is not lined up the knife will not appear to be sharp, yet sufficient material may have already been removed. Since the edge does not feel sharp, it is often worked some more on the stone and many knives are worn out prematurely from this overworking. When the wire edge is lined up, the blade will seem to be sharp. I refer to this phenomenon as "false sharp." The blade may shave hair and slice paper, but when the edge con-

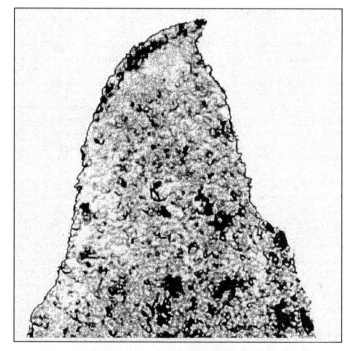

This is a photomicrograph, magnified 1,000 times, of the cross-section of a blade that shows the effect of buffing a blade and not getting the wire off. The section shown is about the thickness of two sheets of paper. The blade was sharp, but not as sharp as it could have been.

122

tacts any type of hard substance the wire edge bends over and the knife will quit cutting.

REMOVING THE WIRE EDGE

My favorite way to remove the wire edge is to stroke the edge very lightly on the finish stone at an angle of around 30 degrees. The strokes are alternated from one side to the other and are very light. You will feel the hook of the wire with a fingernail and it will be on the opposite side from the last stroke. As the blade is stroked with the light cuts the wire is abraded off, leaving the true sharp edge. It might seem that the steep angle used to get the wire edge off would slow down the cutting ability of the knife, but it doesn't because not that much material is removed when it is correctly done. With the wire edge removed you will have a superior and long-lasting edge.

It is very easy to lose the sharp cutting angle at the edge when trying to get the wire edge off by buffing or stropping. If you like to finish an edge this way, do it after removing the wire on a stone. The angle on the strop or buff is critical; if too steep, the edge gets rounded off and the edge loses its true sharpness. I recommend getting the wire edge off on the stone, then buffing or stropping to polish the edge when that is wanted or needed.

THE STROP STICK

A very excellent strop stick can be made as follows. You will need a strip of wood 1 inch wide and about a foot long, also a strip of leather as wide as the wood and about eight inches long. Glue the leather to the wood, leaving a handle at one end. I use the same green polishing compound on the strop that I use for buffing blades. The leather is lightly coated with the green compound and your strop is ready to use. A little stropping goes a long way; don't overdo it. Several passes down each side will refine the edge without losing its bite. Experiment with your knives to see how much "polish" you want on your edge.

If you appreciate fine knives, it is worth the time to practice sharpening until it is mastered.

THE CONVEX EDGE

A convex edge can be thick or thin or somewhere in between. Flat-ground, hollow-ground or convex-ground blades may have either a convex edge or conventional edge.

The advantage of the convex edge, when it is properly done, is the extremely thin cutting edge. When properly established on a convex-ground blade it gives the maximum in cutting ability, and yet it has more strength than the flat or hollow-ground blade. A convex blade profile is developed by using the slack belt section on the belt grinder to form the sides of the blade into a convex shape. The true form of a convex-ground blade has the sides of

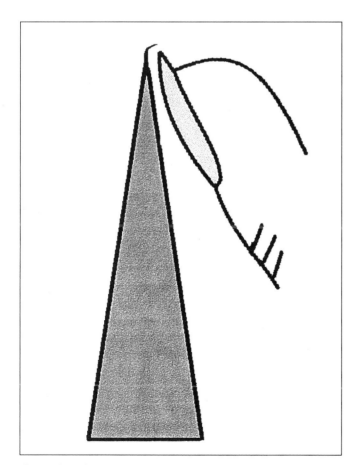

Checking for the wire edge.

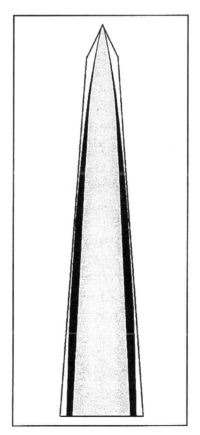

The outside profile shows a flat-ground knife that is a little too thick at the edge. The dark band outlines a medium-thick convex blade, the gray area a thin one. A flat-ground blade could fit inside the profile of the thin convex blade, it's all in the style of the one who grinds it.

123

the blade carried right out to a sharp cutting edge. A high degree of sharpness is achieved by buffing or stropping the edge. The polished-convex is a slashing type edge, perfect for cutting free-hanging rope. The true potential of the convex blade is not realized unless the whole blade is polished to a high degree. The slick surface of the blade reduces friction against the material being cut and increases the depth of penetration in the chopping tests. The true convex edge has no advantage in an endurance cutting test when compared to a flat-ground blade that is correctly ground and not left with a thick edge. I do not recommend a polished edge on a working-type knife. The hard-use knife needs to be capable of sawing through tough materials. This is not possible with a polished edge.

Many of the (so-called) convex edges being put on production knives are rather fat and slow-cutting in comparison to the edges put on knives made by knowledgeable custom makers. By actual micrometer measurement, the fat blades have as much as two or three times more material at the cutting edge.

Please refer to the cross-section drawing to see the actual physical differences in three blades. The drawing makes it very clear why some blades do so much better in the cutting and chopping tests.

HOLLOW-GROUND OR CONVEX, WHICH IS BEST?

A reader once wanted to know which grind is best, hollow or convex. He said he had a new hollow-ground knife that would not saw through a single strand from a 1-inch rope. He indicated that he had another new knife with a convex grind that cut the rope easily. He was confused because hollow-ground knives are supposed to cut well because they are thinner. I had him send me the hollow-ground knife in question so I could analyze it for him.

When the knife came, I could see why it did not have much chance of slicing through a rope. It was not that sharp to start with and even though the hollow-ground blade was thin at the edge, the sharpening angle was quite steep. The knife was a

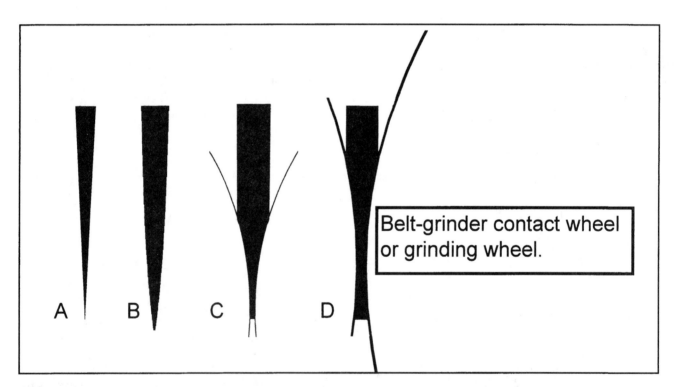

Shown are four cross-section drawings of blades. Flat, convex, and two versions of hollow-ground are represented. Any of the three types can be made either too thin or too fat. It's not simply a matter of what type of grind it is but how it is applied to a certain thickness of blade material that will determine what it will do in cutting tests. "A" represents a flat-ground blade that is relatively thin, (1/8 of an inch) at the spine and with the grind carried out to infinity. It cuts good but may be too weak for rough use. "B" is a convex cross-section that's not real thin but not fat either, it is a good all-around cross-section. Note the difference in the thickness at the edge and mid point of "C" and "D". "C" represents a typical stainless blade with a spine of 1/4 inch and a short hollow-grind. This is exactly the type of grind that brought up the original question. It's almost too thin at the edge for a heavy knife and the thickness at the mid-point makes it slow when trying to chop wood or slice tomatoes. "D" is the same thickness material as "C" but the grind is carried up farther on the blade. It has a better cross-section but the edge was left too thick by the position of the hollow-ground portion on the blade.

heavy survival-type knife and yet it had a short, thin hollow grind as illustrated by "C" in the drawing. After looking the knife over and thinking about it for awhile I decided that I did not understand it at all. The grind in relation to the type of knife made no sense to me.

When the rope slicing is over, the sharpest and thinnest blade will win every time. Is this the best type blade for all uses? Certainly not! There may be as many different types of grinds as there are states in the U.S.A. Each knifemaker will have to work out what is best for the knives he or she makes.

See the accompanying blade cross-section drawings and explanation to help understand that any type of grind can be either too fat or too thin for its intended purpose.

HOW TO SHARPEN
A CONVEX EDGE

Gary Friedman of Goshen, Massachusetts writes:

What is the correct way to sharpen a blade with a convex edge?

Answer: The convex edge is sharpened like any other edge. The exception being that the sharpening angle may be less, depending on how the blade was ground. Most makers seem to have their own version of this edge. In fact, there are almost as many names for it as there are ideas about what exactly it is. Some of the different names given to it are pumpkin seed, apple seed, rolled, Moran, Japanese sword, and of course convex. There are a lot of different combinations. It could have a flat- or hollow-ground blade with a convex shape at the cutting edge. The other possibility is to have the cross-section of the blade to be convex. The advantage of the convex blade, when properly done, is the thin cutting edge. However, it will gain little if the blade is too thick in the cross section. Some of the best cutting blades I have tested were flat-ground with only the last 1/8 of an inch or so being convex in shape. The thickness of the blade and the quality of the edge have more to do with the ability of a blade to penetrate rope and wood than the particular type of cross section.

WHY WOULD A SOFT
KNIFE CUT BETTER?

Matthew Butterly of Australia writes:

An article in another knife magazine stated that ABS mastersmith Jerry Fisk had drawn his camp knife to less of a temper to make it cut better. Would you explain why his method works?

Answer: Everything I've learned about edge-holding indicates that hardness is usually the prerequisite for edge-holding ability. My opinions are based on the way I sharpen and test knives. Jerry has said the same thing about his opinion on softer blades.

I often find that differences of opinion come about when two people are in the same game but with different rules. I believe that's what's happening here.

Jerry wrote, "On my personal knives I prefer a softer draw than what is the current accepted norm. Most people seem to prefer a 59-60 Rockwell hardness. I prefer a softer draw of 52-54 for several reasons. With the steel being softer, it gives a more aggressive cutting edge by making long microscopic teeth when sharpening. When I want to cut something, I want it cut with as little effort as possible. When the blade is on the harder side, the shorter microscopic teeth 'break off.' The 'longer' teeth of the softer blade cut longer before breaking off or laying more to one side. Butchers use a 'butcher's steel' to stand the teeth back up straight and start cutting again without going to a sharpening stone. It makes sense that the softer teeth can be bent over and straightened back up more times than the teeth on the harder steel. The teeth on the harder steels break off quicker when bent over."

I've got it figured out. Jerry uses knives with a wire edge on them and that is not uncommon. Butchers, cooks and many old-time outdoors people use knives with such a wire edge. That's why the sharpening steel is used; it lines up the wire edge once it's bent over. A butcher or cook will usually have nothing to do with a blade that's as hard as most handmade hunting knives are. The reason is that the wire edge on a soft knife cuts wickedly in meat, vegetables and fruit. In my experience, this is not the edge I prefer on a working knife.

I prefer a harder knife that has the two sides of the blade meeting at infinity. There's no wire edge to bend over, break off or in need of alignment. A knife with a Rockwell hardness of 59-60 RC sharpened the way I like it may not cut as well on soft materials, but I do believe it works best for everyday work and hunting-type applications.

Knifemakers are different from each other in many respects. Their motives, designs, materials, equipment and methods are rarely the same. This is as it should be.

I CAN'T GET MY FAVORITE
KNIFE SHARP ANYMORE

Howard McFetridge of Oregon writes:

I can't get my old-favorite hunting knife sharp any more. The more I work on it the more frustrated I get. I am using a fine grit white ceramic stone that was guaranteed to give a razor edge. Any suggestions?

Answer: Your knife blade has more than likely gotten thick at the edge from the years of use and sharpening. The blade cross-section drawing illustrates how the edge gets thick as the blade is sharpened. "A" is the edge when the blade is new; "B" indicates the new position of the edge after much sharpening. The single sharpening angle of 15 degrees no longer gives an adequately thin edge. "C" indicates the shoulder of material that has to be removed with the roughing stone in order to re-establish the thinness required at the edge.

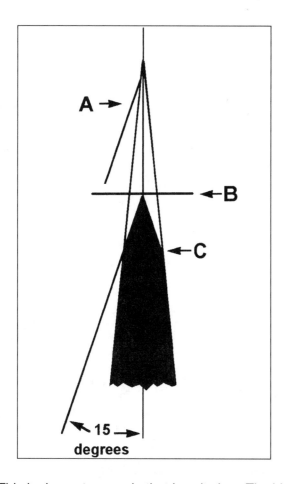

15 degrees

This is done at an angle that is quite low. The blade in the drawing has an included angle of 10 degrees, or 5 degrees on each side of the centerline. A secondary sharpening angle of around 10 degrees will remove the shoulder and allow the primary sharpening angle of 15 degrees to be effective.

Think of sharpening as a two-step procedure. The first step is metal removal with a coarse or medium stone. This removes small chipped-out, flat and dull places. It is also necessary to remove the shoulder of material that develops from the blade being touched up with a steel or fine stone. The blade that is touched up with a sharpening steel or an ultra-fine ceramic rod develops a shoulder quickly. Once the edge is thinned down, you should be able to get your knife sharp. The fine ceramic stone is good for touching-up the edge, but will not remove enough metal to keep the edge thinned down properly.

TAKING THE MYSTERY OUT OF CHISEL GRINDS

Jamie Coffey writes:

What is the rationale for the single-bevel edges seen lately on blades like the CQC7 by Ernie Emerson? It seems to me that they would be harder to sharpen, especially if you're trying to take out "dings" that damage both sides of the edge. It also seems that the off-center angle would shift the best cutting angle away from the plane of the overall blade, making it *necessary to slice at a veering angle for best efficiency. I don't see any offsetting advantages for this odd blade shape. Is it done for image or is there a reason for it?*

Answer: Ernie Emerson, who makes the CQC7 (CQC stands for Close Quarters Combat) folding knife, says that the blade shape and cross-section style is what his customers, Navy SEALS, prefer. They want a strong prying- and stabbing-type blade. Their preferences were determined from actual tests of different blade styles.

The chisel grind, in its several forms, seems to be gaining in popularity and that makes your question very timely. It follows several other questions I've received on the same subject from phone calls or conversations at knife shows.

Some chisel-ground blades are for image only; others are for a specific purpose. I had suspected this and verified it at the 1996 New York Custom Knife Show. While there, I talked with knifemakers about the chisel edge, and that series of conversations was most informative. I learned some advantages of the chisel edge that I had not considered. I also found some differences of opinion as to what a chisel edge is and what it does. (That's exactly the way it was when the convex edge became popular and many makers had their own version of it.)

Note blade cross sections "A" and "B" in the accompanying illustration. I'll call "A" the wedge grind and "B" the full chisel. Both blades have the same included angle. However, "B" has the back at 90 degrees to one side. Blades "A" and "B" have the same amount of material at the cutting edge and the same cutting ability. The amount of metal to be removed in order to work out a chip in a knife-edge depends on the thickness of the edge. I believe the same amount of metal will have to be removed. One way, it is all removed from one side. The other way, half of it is removed from each side. In my opinion, one would not be any harder to sharpen than the other.

Blade "E" is the same as "B" but with a secondary-sharpening bevel. The sharpening angle, when it excessively thickens the edge, will prevent the blade from cutting in a straight line.

The blade type that you call the single-bevel is what I call the part-chisel-ground blade. It has a cross section with a parallel section at the back. One side is at 90 degrees to the back with the chisel grind being one-third to one-half the width of the blade. When done with a chisel-type point as in blade "C1", the tip has great strength because it has more material than a conventional tip.

I made a "C1" style blade in order to have an answer based on actual cutting tests. Cutting a variety of materials would give me a hands-on answer to the issue of whether the offset angle of the chisel-ground blade would cause it to veer away from the direction of cut. The bevel on this blade was brought down to meet the back side at infinity. (Refer to blade "C".) As a result of the thin edge, this blade was wickedly sharp and showed no tendency to veer away from the line of

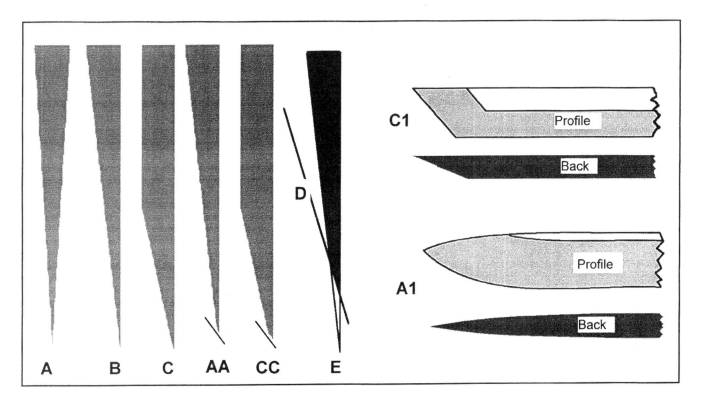

This drawing shows three views of the common wedge-ground blade shape. See figures and A and A1 (profile and back view). B is flat-ground, all on one side. The chisel-ground blade is shown in C and C1. Note the effect that the sharpening angle, line D, will have as seen in AA, CC and E.

cut. I performed cutting tests on vegetables, soft and hard wood, paper and leather. If this type of blade has a sharpening angle as per blade "CC", then it becomes difficult to keep it cutting in a straight line.

There is a mixture of sharpening styles on this type of blade. Some are a true chisel edge and some have the secondary sharpening angle. Blade "CC" is stronger than "C", but "C" has the best penetration in soft materials.

Figure "A1" shows the conventional wedge-ground blade with distal taper at the tip formed by the grind lines curving in a line parallel with the cutting edge. This tip has less material in it and would naturally be weaker than the "C1" blade.

ABS Mastersmith J.D. Smith was the first to explain to me that the "C1" blade makes a larger hole when stuck into a soft object. It cuts a hole, whereas the wedge action of the "A1" blade pushes material out of the way. (Some call it an armor-piercing tip.) I've recently seen some chisel-point knives that had either a false or sharpened back at the tip. This causes the profile to become more like "A1" and negates some of the strength of the chisel tip.

"A" shows the pierced pattern of a chisel-point knife with a straight back. The corners at "AA" will often be cut when the back of the blade is square. "B" shows the pierced pattern of a conventional knife blade. The hole has the tendency to "heal" or close up. Test this for yourself on paper, cardboard or leather.

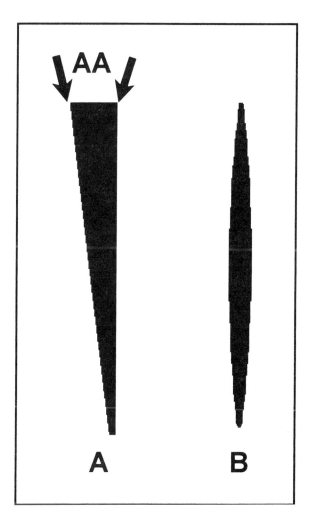

Whether made for looks or a specific purpose, the thickness of the back combined with the cross-section shape of the blade determines the knife's strength and cutting ability. (I assume that first-class steel, heat treated to perfection, was used in the blade.)

More on chisel-grinds.

Ivan de A. Campos writes:

I have had in my possession a number of chisel-ground blades and they are all different at the edge. Some have a heavier grind, others are ground thinner. Some have no secondary edge, others do. Some have a slightly convex edge on the ground side. I have noticed that some cut very well, but it is not easy to control the direction of the cut. This would not be trouble in a fighter, though.

When the blade has no secondary edge, is it possible to sharpen it at home without damaging it? It seems very complicated, though I have read it is even simpler than the conventional grinds, which puzzles me even more.

Chisel-ground blades are very stout looking and I think they should be easier to make than a full flat or even a hollow-ground blade. Chisel grinding should produce a cheaper knife for the same materials, but these knives are usually more expensive than similar knives with regular flat- or hollow-grinds. How can it be? I am sure your answer will be of great help. Thanks in advance and keep up your great work.

Answer: Chisel-ground knives with a true flat-grind and a point, such as illustration "C1," have a distinct purpose. That is to do the maximum damage when used as slashing and thrusting weapons. Such a blade has one straight side with the bevel on the opposite side. The bevel has to be brought down to the edge in a flat plane or else there is no cutting advantage. The thin profile of the true chisel edge is the secret of the extreme sharpness. The only way to sharpen such a blade to maintain it's keen cutting ability is to lay the whole flat bevel on the stone and work it all down until the edge is sharp. This will change the finish of the blade, but will not damage it. The same dilemma faces the owners of true convex-ground blades. The final edge is usually finished on a slack belt grinder, then buffed. There is no way for the average knife user to easily duplicate this edge.

I can't explain the price differences. In my opinion a chisel-grind is perhaps the easiest and quickest grind to make. All that is needed is a guide that will locate the blade at the correct angle to the abrasive belt or wheel. With the back and bottom of the blade located against the guide, the blade is then pressed against an abrasive wheel or belt. The correct cross section is then generated without any variance. (See drawings.)

The true chisel point has a different function than the chisel cutting edge. The back of a chisel-ground knife should be left square to make it more deadly. The point that is formed by a true flat-grind punches a hole in any material that is pierced. The conventional knife-point wedges its way into the material. (See drawing at the bottom of page 127.)

Differences in cross section and sharpening angle are also found on hollow- and convex- ground blades. Even the flat-grind will vary depending on how thick it is left at the edge. It appears that most makers of handmade and factory knives all have their own idea of what the cross section and secondary sharpening angle should be.

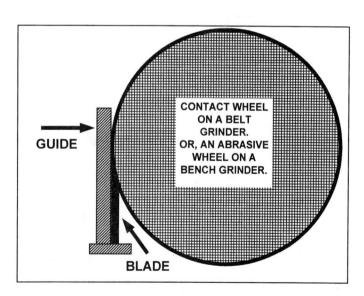

Two jigs to make chisel grinding as easy as 1,2,3.

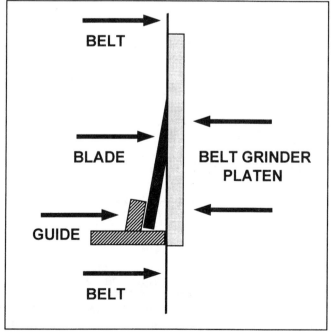

Two jigs to make chisel grinding as easy as 1,2,3.

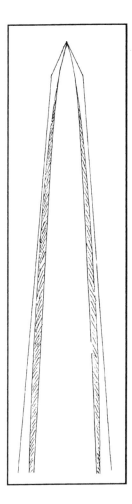

Measurements taken off of actual blades are used to illustrate three blade cross-sections.

HOW TO CREATE CROSS-SECTION DRAWINGS OF BLADES

This is the easiest way to make a graphic of different blade cross sections. Use lay-out dye or marking pen to coat a section of the blade about one inch wide extending from the edge to the back. Scribe lines every .025 inch over the blade's width. A sharp, hard pencil line will do. The important thing is to not scratch the surface of the blade. Using a micrometer or vernier caliper, carefully measure the thickness at these points. On a piece of graph paper that has 1/4-inch squares, plot the points of measurement. Draw a vertical line from top to bottom, space in at least 2 inches from the edge. Each measurement going up the width of the blade will be marked with a dot on each side of the centerline. When all the dots are on the paper it is time to connect them. The width of one square equals .025 on the blade. Your finished drawing will be 10 times wider than the knife blade.

This visual comparison helps see why some blades are superior to others in cutting things. For example, a thin blade with a dull edge will chop wood better than a sharp, thick-edged blade.

(See the actual blade profile.) The outside profile is of a factory knife; the inside profile is a full convex grind on a 3/16-inch-thick blade. The shaded area is the cross section of a slightly thicker, full convex, compromise-grind.

Chapter 9

GRINDING

Robert Bizzell of Butte, Montana writes:

I don't really know how much of a question this is, but here goes. I have been a part-time maker since 1993 and am self-taught except for a week spent with Keith Gipson at TSJC in Trinidad, Colorado. The only real problem I have is to consistently get good bevels on my blades. It is getting easier, but boy have I burned some steel along the way. Does everyone have a hard time with this part? Is it something that your hands have to learn through repetition? It looks like it would be easier to flat-grind on a 6-inch belt instead of a 2-inch belt, is this the case?

Answer: After 36 years it is less frustrating but not easy for me to grind good blades. Repetition does help build skill, but for me it takes great concentration at the same time. With your own two hands you will stick the blade against the belt and grind where you didn't want to remove anything. All I can say is, "Just don't do it."

Here are some things that have helped me.

1. Use sharp belts and keep the blade cool.
2. Have good lighting that comes in from both sides of the belt.
3. Experiment with the height of the grinder so that you can work without neck and arm strain.
4. If you have been standing up to grind, try sitting on a stool, this works out good for some makers.
5. Start a light cut and go the full length of the blade before looking at it.
6. Practice. When I was a kid I took piano lessons for a while. My teacher was always telling me that practice didn't make perfect, but perfect practice makes perfect.

I don't know of anyone who uses a 6-inch belt for flat grinding. With a belt that wide it takes a lot more pressure on the blade and that makes accurate control difficult to achieve. Holding the blade without grinding the fingers is difficult with the wide belt. Some makers prefer a 1-inch belt for hollow grinding. I've got one of my homemade grinders set up so that I can use either a 1- or 2-inch-wide contact wheel. I prefer the 1-inch-wide belt for grinding really small blades.

Grinding Long Blades

Garrett Clark of Kenai, Alaska writes:

As a beginner I am in the process of grinding a sword blank. As I reposition my hands I am having a problem keeping my grind line straight. Is there a method which will make it easier? The grinder I am using is a Burr King 960.

Answer: Here is how I do it. The flats in the guard area are cleaned up using a horizontal 6-inch by 48-inch belt sander. An 8-inch-long grinding magnet is used to hold the blade. Once I get the flats established I go to a 2-inch by 72-inch belt grinder to take off 80 percent of the material to form the bevels. At this time I'm not too worried about making sure it is really straight. When I go back to the platen on the 6 x 48 I've got nearly 18 inches of abrasive to contact the blade.

I bought the 6 x 48 machine used and had in mind using it primarily for woodworking. An 18-inch Damascus blade was giving me trouble with my 2 x 72 belt grinder. I decided to try the wide belt machine and it worked so well that I've utilized it on long blades ever since. The platen of the wide belt sander is at approximately waist level, making it quite easy to swing the whole length of a long blade over the grinding surface. Using the grinding magnet to hold the blade is essential. Being in the horizontal position, the blade sort of floats over the platen.

The longest blade I have done was a full-tang wire Damascus blade that was nearly 26 inches long, including the tang. I've done half a dozen other blades that run from 15 to 18 inches. I would not want to be without the 6 x 48 for grinding long blades.

BLADE FINISHES

Hand-finishing, when well done, results in a crisp and clean definition of the surfaces that gives a more true appearance than a mirror-finish does. The reflections from the surface of a buffed and mirror-finished blade can cause a visible distortion of the lines and the actual surfaces are usually not kept as flat and true. Reflections from the surface of a mirror-polished blade make it difficult to photograph. Many years ago I made a large double-edged Bolo-style knife that was buffed to perfection. To photograph it I stood it upright against a background. When I got the pictures back there was a perfect image of the camera, tripod and myself; all perfectly reflected from the center of the blade. The reflection was almost more interesting than the knife.

Blades that are not stainless steel benefit from a high polish because the surface is smoother and more resistant to rust and staining. I rarely mirror polish because I prefer the appearance and practicality of a satin or hand-rubbed finish. They don't show every little scratch like a mirror-polished blade and are very easy to touch up. Many years of dealing with well-used and sometimes abused knives have taught me the disadvantages of a high polish.

I made a lot of stock-removal, highly polished blades back in the 70s. I often saw how traumatic it was to a customer when a shiny blade was accidentally scratched. I was in the shop one evening about 9:30 when I got a call from a local customer. While sharpening his mirror-finished 154-CM blade he had slipped off the stone and put an ugly scrape down the side of the blade. He was very upset with himself and said he wouldn't be able to sleep until it was fixed. I had him bring it over and I refinished it with a satin finish. The customer went home with a blade he wasn't afraid to sharpen and use; and that was about the time I started putting a satin finish on most all of my working knife blades. When making knives for the collector market it is probably desirable to learn to mirror polish blades or else refine hand rubbing to a high degree. For working knives though, I'd stick to finishes that are easy to touch up or redo.

THE HAND-RUBBED FINISH

A close look at the surface of a finely finished Japanese sword blade will reveal a lot of information about its construction, age and quality. Perfection in the polish makes the grain structure of the steel clearly visible. It has always amazed me that such a high degree of blade finishing was accomplished without the use of belt grinders and buffing wheels. The whole process is done by hand using natural stones and abrasives.

The high degree of finish allowed the swordsmith to see if his blade was free of visible defects. The finish made the grain structure visible and that would show if the heat treatment was correct. The fine finish would also allow the purchaser to see the quality of his purchase. It was only natural that a high degree of polish became one of the characteristics of a quality blade.

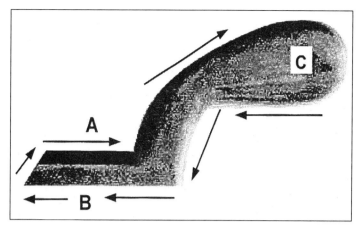

A side view of the push stick.

Hand-finishing, when well done, results in a crisp and clean definition of the surfaces that gives a more true appearance than a mirror finish does. The reflections from the surface of a buffed and mirror-finished blade can cause a visible distortion of the lines and the actual surfaces are usually not kept as flat and true.

I use what I call a quick-rubbed finish on many forged blades. It's quick because the strokes are all lengthwise with the blade. The quick-rubbed finish results in a nice, although not perfect, finish because there are usually some coarser lines under the final finish.

I use what I call a push stick for hand rubbing. (See drawing.) It is necessary to have a firm and flat surface backing the paper; the one shown is made of Micarta®. The abrasive paper is wrapped around the push stick and held with the hand at "C" and the index finger at "A". Surface "B" is what contacts the knife blade. The push stick can be 1/2 inch or 1 inch wide, the abrasive paper is cut accordingly. A narrow face allows more pressure to be applied; the wide one will work out divots better.

When using a belt grinder to start the finishing process the blade can be taken anywhere from 300 to 600 grit before the hand finishing starts. I stop at 320. Whatever the final belt grit size, the hand finishing would start by dropping back one grit-size to start. The scratch pattern from the belt will be in direction "B" and the first rub will be lengthwise "A." (See drawing.)

The hand-rubbing process may be accomplished by alternating directions "A" and "B" only.

If you were doing it all by hand the sequence would be as

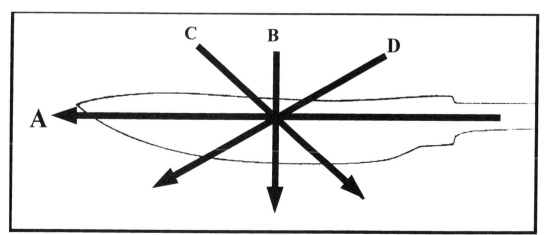

The proper sequence of directions for hand-rubbing a blade.

follows. "A" would be 100 grit, "B" would be 200, back to "A" for 300, "B" would be 400 and so on till the desired degree of finish is achieved. To further refine the final steps "C" and "D" can also be utilized. With the quick-rub method, all the work is done in direction "A".

The final step is always in direction "A" with all the strokes starting at the tang and going towards the point. A fresh section of paper is used for each stroke to get the finest finish. Silicon carbide wet or dry paper is used. Some makers use water and some use it dry. Dry is always best for the final steps. Grit sizes are rounded off to the nearest hundred-something, use whatever you can get. See the chart for a comparison of U.S. and import grit sizes.

HOW TO DO A BRUSHED FINISH

Doug McKellar of Amherst, New Hampshire writes:

What is meant by a "brushed finish" and how is it done? I hand-rub some of my blades down to 800-grit, is this a brushed finish?

Answer: I think a brushed finish is what I call a satin finish. Usually the hand-rubbed finish is simply called "hand-rubbed." One distinction between a hand-rubbed finish and the satin or brushed finish is the direction the scratch pattern runs. The satin finish shows its pattern at a 90-degree angle to the edge and is usually not much finer than 300- or 400-grit with light buffing. A hand-rubbed finish has the scratch pattern running parallel with the cutting edge and is usually taken to a much finer degree of finish.

Here's how I do my version of a satin finish. Get the blade down to a half-dull, 240-grit finish or, if you prefer, use a sharp 320 belt. The blade can be flat-, convex- or hollow-ground. Carefully buff the blade with No. SF (satin finishing) 300 (grit) compound. I use the compound on a 10-inch sewn muslin wheel that runs 1,750 RPM. It takes practice to get a uniform scratch pattern. At this point the surface will be fairly open and not too smooth. Once you have a uniform finish, buff the blade lightly with a medium cutting compound. Easy does it with this step, once or twice down each side is enough. Finish the blade by buffing lightly once or twice down each side with a finish compound like RCH Green Chrome. Over buffing with the final finish compound will wipe out the scratch pattern that sets up the satin finish. The result will be a shiny blade. The finish buffing is done on the 10-inch sewn muslin wheel at 1,750 RPM. With practice you will be able to get a nice satin finish that is not too shiny.

Satin finishing compound is a water-based glue product that is also called greaseless compound. It is applied to the wheel while it is turning. The wheel is left running and the glue hardens. I turn the buffer on, then turn it off and apply the compound as the wheel runs down. Not too much is required. If the compound is applied in a thick layer when it hardens the buff acts more like a grinding wheel and it will not make a satin finish.

These compounds are available from most knifemaker supply companies.

U.S. (CAMI)	EUROPEAN (FEPA)	MICRON	NEW STRUCTURED	AVERAGE PARTICLE SIZE IN INCHES
600	P 1200	15	/	.00060
500	P 1000	/	/	.00071
400	P 800	30	A 25	.00085
360	P 600	/	A 35	.00100
320	P 400	40	A 45	.00137
/	P 320	/	A 60	.00180
240	/	/	A 65	.00209
/	P 240	60	A 75	.00254
220	/	/	A 90	.00257
180	P 180	80	A 110	.00304
150	/	100	/	.00378
120	/	/	A 160	.00452
/	P 100	/	A 200	.00608
80	P 80	/	/	.00768
60	60	/	/	.01014

GRIT SIZE COMPARISON

Chapter 10

THE TANG

"Out of sight, Out of mind", is not the way to think of your knife tang. The strength of the knife tang is often overlooked as a design element. After seeing many knives and a couple of swords that had their handles broken off, I've formed some strong opinions about how a tang should be constructed. Broken tangs can result from any of the following; defective heat treatment (either too hard or too soft... spring temper is good), not being large enough, stress risers, handle material too weak for the intended purpose, or air space between the tang and handle material.

TROUBLE SHOOTING

When a handle breaks at the junction of the blade and guard it is usually because of a stress riser. It's an accident waiting to happen when the junction of tang and blade is square. This corner should have as large a radius as is feasible. When the tang breaks up inside the handle it was either too small or too hard. See the comments below concerning handles made of spacers. When a spacer-type handle is constructed it is imperative that the tang be of the utmost strength. I've worked out a formula for tang size that gives the maximum strength. See the drawing in the chapter "The Combat-Quality Blade."

The practice of arc or gas welding tangs is very popular, but I don't recommend it unless the tang is thoroughly tested before the knife is assembled. Most welds are somewhere between 80 percent and 90 percent the strength of the surrounding material. The trouble with arc welding is that the grain structure in the areas around the weld is left extremely coarse from the heat required to make the weld. My own experience with arc welded joints was most unfavorable with blades made of 52100. Arc welding creates a very large and weak grain structure in the weld zone. This steel has the tendency to air harden and I never could get the strength I wanted in the tang.

I prefer a silver-brazed joint because the strength of the joint is always stronger than the surrounding material. The heat involved is much less when properly done and therefore the grain enlargement found with arc or gas welding is not present. I learned to silver-braze many years ago when I worked in the saw manufacturing and repair business. My first job was silver-brazing carbide bits into saws and cutters of all descriptions.

Saws often developed cracks around the expansion slots or at the bottom of the gullets. Sometimes whole sections were broken out and would be repaired by welding in a new section. The welder used was an old Atomic/Hydrogen type. The operator, a guy named Sam, was very good at what he did. After the weld was made and while it was still hot, he would use a ball pein hammer to forge the weld. He would then use an acetylene torch to heat the area that was just welded, then turn off the oxygen and let the gas flame form a layer of soot on the weld. The saw would then be placed in a container of kitty litter that had been preheated with a heat lamp. I remember the problems his replacement had when Sam was on vacation. His replacement had been shown very carefully how to do it; however he didn't think the forging step was necessary so he skipped it. Guess what? Almost every weld he made failed. The break in each case showed a very coarse grain in the weld zone. The point of that story is this: The coarse grain from welding needs to be refined by forging in order for it to have anything close to the strength of the material in the tang.

NARROW-TANG VERSUS FULL-TANG

Several years ago Steve Shackleford, editor of *Blade Magazine*, asked me to participate in a point-counterpoint article on the subject of full-tang versus narrow-tang knife construction. I remember telling him that the only way I would do it was if I could argue for both sides. I have used both methods for 36 years because neither method by itself is most suitable for the many differing styles of knives I make.

Most of the opinions I've seen in print that advocate one method or the other missed two points that I consider the most important of all. Those points are these: The simplicity of tools required to make the narrow tang, and the strength and durability of the narrow tang when it is properly constructed. My opinions were formed from how well the different methods held up on knives I've made and from what I've observed about other knives, both newly made and old.

The majority of knives throughout history have had narrow tangs. The many advantages of that method became clear from my experiments with primitive knifemaking methods. Probably most important is the frugality of blade material. It takes almost twice as much steel to make a full-tang knife

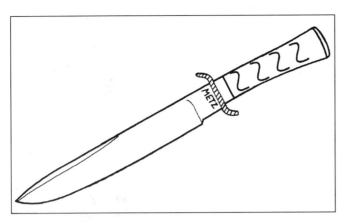

Drawing by *BLADE* reader Greg Metz.

as it does to make one with a narrow tang. Narrow-tang construction has always been common because few tools were required. The narrow tang is contained within the handle material so there is less metal to be finished when compared to a full tang.

A handle that is made of stacked spacers is weak in as much as the handle itself does not have much strength against breaking in the transverse section. The strength of the handle will depend totally on the tang. As an example of this, recently there was a discussion on the WWW about a sword with a broken handle. A photo of the broken handle showed a round tang that, in my opinion, was much too small for the diameter of the handle. The tang appeared to be approximately 25 percent of the diameter of the handle. The handle separated at a place where the tang should have been rectangular and at least 80 percent the width of the handle. The handle of bronze, bone and marble spacers had little actual strength against sideways pressure. The tang that supports a spacer type handle for sword or a knife that will receive rough use should be of the maximum in size and strength. In my opinion a sword handle should be of one-piece construction and a fairly strong piece of material at that.

I explained handle construction in *Blade* Q & A March '97. Greg Metz of Cascade, Idaho wrote: What is the best procedure for assembling this handle? (See drawing enclosed.) I am concerned with the joint between the guard and ferrule. Do I epoxy the ferrule and handle together, then shape them? Or is it better to solder the ferrule to the guard and then fit the handle to it? I am concerned about scratching the exposed back side of the guard when attaching the ferrule. I would also like to know if there is a way I could attach the butt cap that doesn't have the tang sticking through it.

I recommended the following sequence for a narrow-tang knife: First, solder the guard to the blade. Use a 430 F, lead-free soft silver solder. (See "Guard Soldering" that follows.) Then fit the handle into the ferrule, use epoxy or super glue to hold it together.

Then use epoxy to join the handle-ferrule assembly to the tang.

There are several ways to attach the butt cap so that the tang does not have to go through it. The method I use is to silver-braze a nut to the underside of the butt cap. The nut/butt cap assembly threads onto the end of the tang and when tightened it draws the whole handle up tight. In my opinion, this is the strongest way to assemble a narrow-tang knife. A method I use on small knives is to silver braze a large wood screw to the butt cap. The butt cap with the screw attached is then screwed and glued into the handle. A good silver solder job would probably hold the screw to the pommel cap on light duty knives, but I wouldn't trust it on a heavy use knife like the Bowie style in your drawing. I've also seen several knives where the butt cap was simply epoxied on and it eventually fell off.

Another factor to consider is the fact that the narrow-tang knife is more of a sealed unit than where slab handles are affixed to the full tang. There is no doubt in my mind that there are fewer things to go wrong with a properly constructed narrow-tang knife.

When the guard is fitted onto the tang and a stub tang is silver brazed or welded, a gain in strength is made. For example, if the blade is 1/4-inch thick and the tang is threaded, the end of the tang is 1/4-inch. If a stub tang is added it can be as large as is needed for strength. See details in "The Combat Quality Blade."

There should be no air space between a handle and the tang. If the handle can move on the tang then the tang is not supported and can be bent. The strongest handle construction is where a through-bolt is used with either a threaded pommel cap or a nut on the end to draw everything up tight.

GUARD SOLDERING

A question was raised about what causes corrosion, rusting and sometimes pitting at the joint where the guard or bolsters are soldered to the blade? How can it be fixed?

Several versions of this question come from collectors and knifemakers. I can relate to the problem because I recently had to deal with it on an ivory-handled folder I'd made.

The problem is caused when acid-type flux is trapped in the solder joint. The neutralizing and cleaning process was not efficient in killing the acid flux. The flux eventually eats its way out and can nearly ruin a blade if not caught in the early stages. A fine line of rust is usually the first indication of the problem and pitting follows if the acid is not completely neutralized. When the acid flux residue works out and eats into the blade it is hard to fix the damage.

There are several things to try that may eliminate the problem. The first is to improve the solder-

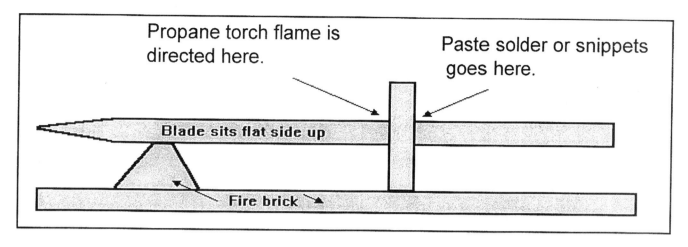

Guard soldering jig.

ing method so that pockets or bubbles of trapped flux are eliminated. The second step is to use a multiple-step neutralizing process. A final solution may be to use an acid-free flux.

For many years I had no problems with soldered joints. After soldering I would wash the soldered parts in warm water and then let them soak in a warm soda water solution for several hours. This was followed by a clear-water rinse. In the last three or four years I have noticed that this process does not seem to work as well. I am of the opinion that something has changed in the flux that makes it more difficult to neutralize. It is interesting to me that when I first noticed the problem it wasn't long before I started hearing and seeing about the same thing on other knives.

There are acid-free fluxes available that may be more suitable than what is furnished with the silver-bearing, lead-free solder commonly used in knife work. The method used for soldering guards may be trapping flux in the joint. Many makers put the blade point up and apply the solder to the blade side of the guard. This pushes the solder and flux into the joint and usually results in too much solder being used. When too much solder is used it takes more heat and also makes the cleaning of the joint more difficult. With this method the temperature may not be sufficiently hot to cause 100 percent solder flow through the joint and that may trap flux in the joint.

I believe a more trouble-free method is to lay the blade down on a jig. (See drawing.)

The guard should be fitted very close because the solder will not hide a poor fit. The blade/guard area should be heated slowly and some liquid flux applied. This etches the surface of the stainless and prepares it for the solder. Apply a small amount of the paste solder or a few snippets of stick solder to the area of the guard on the handle side. If you feed stick solder into the heated joint I can almost guarantee that there will be too much used. Too much heat will destroy the action of the flux, resulting in a poor bond. If the flux turns black and the solder

won't flow, then you will know that you have too much heat. The torch flame should be pulled back every so often. Just watch and wait for the solder to flow. This method assures the whole guard area is up to temperature or else the solder will not flow through the joint. Use only enough heat to cause the solder to flow. Too much heat can actually cause the solder to boil and that can cause bubbles in the joint. These bubbles will usually have flux in them. Capillary action will draw the solder through the joint, towards the heat source. Turn the blade "other side up" occasionally during heating. Use a piece of stainless wire that is slightly sharpened and polished to help the solder flow completely around the joint. While still liquefied, wipe the excess solder off with a flux brush or a piece of leather.

Never use a file on a solder joint. If you do you will surely leave a mark on the blade or guard. Use a sharpened copper or brass rod as you would use an engraving tool and scrape out the excess solder. There will not be much cleanup once you master the above method. Use 600-grit backed up by a piece of stiff leather to polish the surface of the blade and guard, then buff.

Make yourself a "dummy" blade to practice on, then practice until you have mastered the process.

EPOXY AND MICARTA®

Part of the reward I get for my job as Q&A answer person for *Blade* is all the things I learn that otherwise I would miss out on. The following is from a letter the magazine received after I wrote about Micarta without a capitol "M."

"Regarding Q & A answer regarding Micarta in October, 1995 *Blade*. Your readers could be better informed on this particular subject. Let me qualify that I am a retired Westinghouse Micarta Engineering Manager with 35 years experience at Westinghouse Micarta in R & D and management.

A sailor's knife made by the author. The blade is made of saw steel. It has a bronze guard and a Micarta® handle. This knife has had two lives. In 1986 I traveled to Palestine, Texas to the shop of the late Don Hastings for my ABS Journeyman Smith cutting and flex test. I passed the test and then used the knife in demonstrations for several years. It had been flexed 90 degrees quite a few times before the tip finally broke off. I had a customer with a limited budget who wanted a knife in a hurry. He was first mate on an ocean-going tug boat and had a long trip coming up. I was digging around in my "Project" file and found the test blade. I proposed making his knife out of the test blade and he agreed.

The most severe test the knife faced was being hammered through the wall of earthmover tires so they could become bumpers for a barge. There was no other way to do the job and it had to be done. It's often that way in the real world and a selectively hardened blade with an indestructible Micarta® handle saved the day. The knife has stood up to many years of hard use and is still going as far as I know.

Incidentally, **Micarta** is a registered trade name and as such should be capitalized.

"I take exception to Mr. Goddard's selection of the quick-cure epoxy for slab-type handles. I use a 24-hour system I formulate myself. I use the slow-curing system to gain the toughness developed in the adhesive line cure during a slower reaction rate. The faster the system cures the harder and more brittle the adhesion line or layer. Thus the lower the impact strength of the Epoxy adhesive."

Answer: I have used the fast-cure Devcon® epoxy for more than 15 years, and when it is carefully mixed while warm (80ºF) it is tough enough and does not fail. This is not the case with many other brands of the fast-cure epoxy that I have tried. In the course of 32 years of knife making I have tested nearly every type of epoxy and super glue that is commercially available. My conclusions are based on results.

Update: As I process this for the book you are reading it's 36 years now and I'm still using quick-cure epoxy. The brand I am using now is Duro® Quick Set™, made by Loctite Corporation.

I make sure that the handle material is dry and flat and I do let it cure under clamp pressure for 24 hours. I use riveted pins to hold my handles in place, therefore the epoxy is actually more of a seal than an adhesive. If I were to decide to put knives together where I needed an adhesive to hold them together I would perhaps look for another product. One of my favorite rules is, "If it ain't broke, don't fix it."

There is one more factor to consider with slab-type handles. I use vulcanized fiber spacer material between the slab and tang. (The spacer material is sold by knifemaker supply companies) The spacer acts as a shock absorber as well as an expansion / contraction buffer. Natural materials that aren't stabilized or sealed against moisture will expand and contract with the seasons of the year. Without this material in the glue line the handle slabs are prone to work loose.

(See photo.)

WELDED GUARDS

When I answered a question about the feasibility of welding a stainless-steel guard onto a stainless-steel blade in the Q&A of the March 1994 *Blade*, my answer was not very positive because I thought it might not be a practical thing to do. After reading my reply, Dick Kiefer of Belton, Missouri sent in his method for welding guards, which appeared in the Q&A of the July/August 1994 issue.

Dick wrote: I make about 30 knives per year as a part-time maker. Certainly more for enjoyment than profit. In my experience I have found I prefer a welded guard to a soldered guard. I use 440-C, 154-CM and some David Boye's steel bar stock and occasionally some forged Damascus. I always use the same material for the blade and guard. I cut strips of matching steel approximately 1/16 of an inch thick by 12 inches long to use as welding rods. The

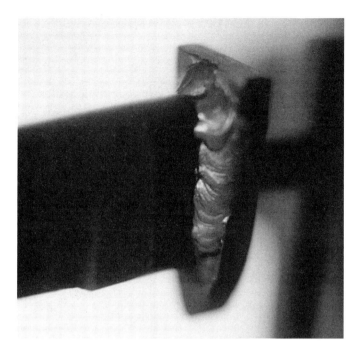 

Photo #1 shows the guard welded in position, #2 Shows how it looks after it is cleaned up. Very nice work!

guards are welded on, ground and polished prior to heat treatment. The resulting shaped fit of the guard is smooth, esthetically appealing and much stronger than a soldered joint.

That seems like a straightforward approach. If you want to try the Kiefer method, Crucible Specialty Metals recommends the following procedure for welding on 154-CM. The same recommendations should work for ATS-34 and 440-C.

Welding or brazing should be done in the annealed condition whenever possible. Welding in the heat-treated condition results in poor weldability and requires careful preheating and post-heating at just below the tempering temperature. Welding-rod of austenitic (non-hardenable) stainless steel can be used if the weld needn't be hard or abrasive-resistant.

TITANIUM FOR GUARDS AND BOLSTERS

Chris Vidito of Bound Brook, New Jersey writes:

What is the best way to attach titanium guards and bolsters to blades?

Answer: Titanium is commonly used for folder liners and bolsters but I can't remember seeing a guard made of it. As far as I know, the common welding, brazing and soldering methods will not join titanium to steel or other common folder liner materials. Titanium can be welded to titanium by several methods. Spot welding works well for joining titanium folding knife bolsters to titanium liners. In order to join titanium to other metals it will have to be a mechanical joint using either screws or pins. Most titanium folders are assembled with screws that hold the bolsters to the liners.

A titanium guard would have to be fitted to a fixed-blade knife using pressure only to hold it in place. That's not a problem on narrow tang knives. The guard would have to be secured with pins on a full-tang knife.

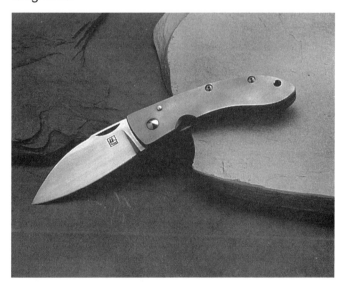

Folder by Bob Lum, titanium sides with screw-together construction. Photo by Bob Lum.

LEATHER WASHER HANDLES

Albert Abdulky of Stocton, California writes:

I would like information on how to construct a leather washer handle. Are the washers glued together or just compressed or both? What types of leather are used?

Answer: My experience is limited to a half dozen knives I made using leather spacers for either the whole handle or the Scagel style, which is half leather, half antler. I cut the spacers into rough rectangles that were slightly oversize of the finished handle size. I used scraps of the oak-tanned leather I use to make my sheaths from. I dipped the spacers in warm water for about 30 seconds; the spacers were damp but not saturated. I stacked them up about four or five at a time and compressed them in a large vise. I separated the stacks and then let the spacers dry. Sometimes I stained them with brown leather dye and allowed them to dry again. The spacers were then glued together, four or five at a time with Barge cement. Each stack of four or five was then clamped tightly in a large "C" clamp until the glue dried.

Once dry, the stack of spacers was drilled to fit the tang. When I had enough stacks of spacers drilled for the whole handle I would compress them again. There is not much reduction at this time. When the leather handle is epoxied in place on the tang it is essential that there are no air spaces left. I use slow-cure epoxy for handles so that I can work any bubbles out of the space between the tang and handle material.

A screwed-on butt cap is necessary for any spacer type handle. The strength in the handle depends on everything being sucked up really tight so that nothing can slip out of place. Once the epoxy has cured the handle can be sanded down and finished with a good quality wax. Kiwi brand shoe polish is my favorite for leather spacer handles (and shoes).

A note of caution on any spacer-type handle. The tang is the only real strength against the handle bending or breaking so it should be the maximum in size and spring tempered.

WOOD FOR HANDLES

Recently there has been talk that wood is "dead" as a handle material. I can't agree entirely with that statement. I will agree that stag, ivory and pearl are very desirable and probably help sell knives in the collector market. If the dealers in collectible knives don't want knives with wood handles that is fine and good. Back in the real world, many knifemakers keep busy making working knives as part or perhaps all of their production. Wood or Micarta® are very appropriate for working knives.

The thing that I find wrong with wood is often the type of wood being used. I see a lot of wood handles that look cheap and that won't help sell a knife. Quality wood will help sell knives when everything else about the knife is "working".

My personal preference has been totally warped by having an excellent supply of really good desert ironwood and snakewood. I can't visualize most of the fixed blade knives I want to make with any other wood on them.

Wood on folding knives is another story. I rarely use wood on a folder; it just does not wear well in the pocket.

If you think that you can't afford select, rare and beautiful wood you need an attitude adjustment and it goes like this. Buying good wood is an investment that helps you guarantee that you will be paid well for the labor you put in a knife. In the end, the customer pays for the wood and they pay gladly for high quality material.

Guard soldering jig.

MATERIAL FOR PINS

Michael in California and Paul in Oregon both asked:

Where does one purchase material for pins, and how are they set or riveted? How about obtaining drill bits the correct size?

Answer: I purchase 90 percent of my pin material from a local welding supply store. I use nickel-alloy and bronze brazing rod and stainless steel TIG welding rod. Most of the knifemaker supply companies sell wire for pins. Wire will come in gauge size or by standard fraction sizes. I purchase the gauge size wire from the different knifemaker supply firms for use in repairing old knives. Most commercial knives use gauge size wire rather than fractional. It is important to have drill bits to match the diameter of the pin stock you want to use. It's not much fun to discover you have holes in the tang of a hardened blade with no pin stock to fit.

It was in 1955 and High School Arts and Crafts class where I learned to use copper harness rivets for leatherwork. When I made my first knives in shop class I didn't have harness rivets long enough so I used welding wire that I riveted on each side of the handle. In 1963 when I started making knives to sell I continued to use pins.

I purchase high-speed steel drill bits from several local firms. They are nothing fancy, just whatever brand they have in stock. There are three systems of drill sizes: letter, number and fraction. Between the three systems I can usually find a drill the correct size. When I buy pin stock I usually get enough to last several years. I use a micrometer to measure the exact diameter and then make sure that I have the right drills for it.

I use drills that are approximately .002 oversize. That figures out like this: 1/16-inch #52, 3/32-inch #41, 1/8-inch #30 and 5/32-inch #21. After I sharpen a drill bit I usually drill a test hole to make sure it is not cutting oversize.

PROBLEMS WITH SHRINKING HANDLE MATERIAL

John Cornett of Etowna, Tennessee writes:

I am a new knifemaker. I enjoy it more than any other hobby I have ever had. I have a thousand questions and I know you are a busy man. Here is one of my questions.

How do I keep my handles from shrinking away from the joints? Am I going too fast on my grinding, finishing, or maybe the material is not cured or dry.

Answer: It is best to keep the heat from grinding belts and buffing wheels down to a minimum. Excess heat can cause discoloration, cracking or raised grain in some woods. However, I think it is much more likely that your handle material wasn't dry. Most hardwoods used for handle material should be cut to just oversize of the finished handle and then allowed to set in a dry place for a minimum of six months. A year is better.

The wood in the center of a 2-inch x 4-inch chunk of hardwood will have quite a bit of moisture in it compared to the outside layer. Like almost everything else, I learned this the hard way. About 20 years ago I bought a beautiful piece of Macassar Ebony that was 2 inches thick, 8 inches wide and about 18 inches long. I got it from a wood dealer who had had it more than 15 years and I had no reason to suspect that it wasn't ready to use. I brought it home and sawed off enough pieces for a matching Bowie and Toothpick set I was working on. The set was finished and delivered. Within four months one of the slabs had shrunk enough to cause cracks to develop around the end-pins of the five-pin pattern. One slab had shrunk very little; the other three slabs had shrunk to varying degrees. I had to replace three of the four handle slabs. Let's pretend that I numbered those slabs from one to four. Number one was the first one off the outside of the chunk. Number four was closest to the center and it was the one that shrunk enough to crack the handle slab. I had cut my slabs off of the end that was fresh cut by the wood dealer. The other end was sealed with wax so there was no way for the wood to be free of excess moisture.

I check the moisture content of new wood by weighing a small piece on my reloading powder scale. I write the weight on it with pencil and then put it under my epoxy curing light. The light is adjusted so that the temperature is around 120 degrees F. The wood sample is weighed every 4-6 hours until such a time, as there is no more loss in weight. This shows how much moisture it has to give up. At this point the material is drier than it should be. If put on a knife it would probably swell as it became normalized to the normal humidity and temperature of it's home. The trick is having the material with average moisture content. With luck it will stay close to the same size as the knife tang.

THE STAG DOCTOR

With each passing year I get more enthused about making something useful out of what otherwise would end up in a landfill. That's why I chose an ugly, sun-bleached, and cracked piece of elk antler for the handle of the friction folder I made for the *Blade* Workshop series. There was a time when I would not have considered it as usable material. As I write this the year is 1999 and we're running out of a lot of stuff, so let's all make the most out of what we have to work with.

It's said that you can't judge a book by its cover. If we judge a piece of material only from the outward appearance we can miss finding a beautiful handle waiting to be discovered. The surface of this antler looked like rotten chalk, but underneath it had the appearance of antique ivory. Here is how I made the reject elk antler into usable handle material.

1.   The antler side for a friction folder needs to be a minimum of 3/16 of an inch thick, solid

and strong. With a design that used a liner, the strength of the handle material is not as important. The usable part of the antler does not include the soft core. If you choose to leave some of the core exposed it should be sealed with super glue. If left unsealed it will quickly rot out when exposed to working knife conditions, (first wet, then dry). Elk antler is superior to deer antler because it is white under the colored crust. The colored crust is usually shallow but occasionally runs deeper. A mature bull elk will grow antlers with the darkest and deepest colors. The texture of the antler from these bulls is also the best looking of all. The color of deer antler runs from light shades of gray to brown.

2.   Antler should be split and stored in a very dry place until completely cured. I use a heated storage locker to keep my materials dry. It's a big wood box with shelves made of pegboard to allow air circulation. The heat source is a 100 W light bulb that runs on a thermostat set at 75 degrees.

3.   Cracks should not go completely through the material.

4.   Shape the handle material close to the finished size.

5.   Use dye to color the whole surface of the handle piece. (Practice on a small piece of scrap from the antler you want to use to see what happens.) Be sure to get the dye in the cracks and allow it to thoroughly dry. Depending on the density of the antler material, the dye may only fill the cracks. Other times the antler is more porous and some color will go into all or other parts of the surface. (Note the color variation on the handle.) I used potassium permanganate crystals dissolved in water for dye. Water-base dye may not penetrate as deeply as leather dye and that's good for this application. Brown leather dye has the tendency to appear somewhat red when applied to stag. The potassium permanganate dye gives the most natural brown color of any dye I've found.

6.   Fill the cracks with super glue; also seal the inside of the handle slab with the glue.

7.   When the glue is dry, sand to the final shape and fit to the pattern.

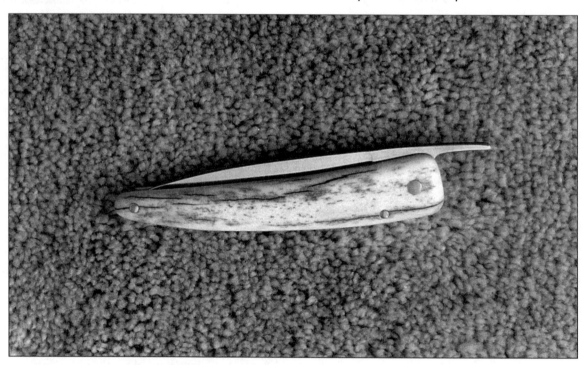

Friction folder by the author with "doctored" elk antler handle.

Chapter 11

HOW TO MAKE A FRICTION FOLDER

It was around 1969 when I started a collection named "The Evolution of the Folding Knife." I didn't know much when I started except that primitive and old folding knives were very interesting to me. My chronology of evolution was arbitrarily decided upon by the complexity of the action and construction. Primitive folders are difficult to date because some places in the world the same style folders with the same materials have been made for hundreds of years. I got tired of the collection when I felt I had learned as much as possible from studying the knives. I had examples of most of the major development steps that brought the folding knife from the most basic up to about 1840. After that, most folders were factory made and I didn't have much to learn from them.

I made my first friction folder in about 1981. I suppose I got the idea from the primitive friction folders in my evolution collection. Folding knives without springs have been around for a long time. There is an often-told story about one of the artifacts discovered under a stone wall that was torn down in England. The remains of a folding knife were found in what was supposedly a Roman campsite. The crude drawing I've seen of it makes it look like it had no spring.

The old friction folders I've studied are of three general types. Most of these have a handle made of one piece of wood, antler or horn that has been slotted for the blade. I've classified them as follows.

Type 1. Two-pin, pin-Stop. There is one pin for the blade pivot, the other pin serves as a blade stop in the open (and sometimes closed position). This is the simplest of all folding knives, one handle piece, one blade and two pins. The ancient craftsman who invented the folding knife probably only used one pin for the pivot with nothing to stop the blade but the handle material. A change was needed when the handle material split from the pressure exerted by the tang when the knife was in use. The first evolutionary step would have been to build the next model with a second pin to stop the blade.

Type 2. Tang Extension Stop: One-, two- or three-pin construction.

Type 3. Ferrule-Stop: The blade pivot area is round in cross section with a sheet metal band around it. In the open position the blade stops on the edge of the ferrule. Some have the metal that makes the ferrule bent in making a bearing surface for the blade. Gene Chapman's booklet "Penny Knife" shows how to make this style of knife complete with details for fabricating the ferrule that makes a bearing surface for the tang. (See Photo)

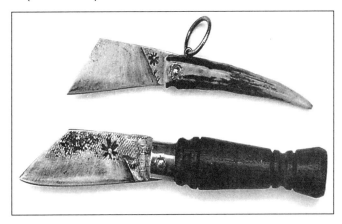

Two modern friction folders by Gene Chapman. Both are slotted for the blade. #1 would be classed as a tang-extension stop with one pin . #2 is the ferrule-stop-type commonly known as a Penny Knife. A penny is supposedly what they cost during the Revolutionary War.
I remember seeing an advertisement for pocket-knives that said they were "like the ones your Grandfather had," Whenever I handle one of Gene Chapman's folding knives I feel that these "are" the knives that my Great-great-grandfather had.

I find it difficult and time-consuming to slot antler and horn so I usually split it and make a spacer of steel. This gives me more area to do file work or engrave and it also gives me the option to forge a thong holder on the end of the spacer.

MATERIALS NEEDED

1. Handle material: An antler tip or chunk of wood 4 inches long will contain a 3 1/2-inch blade. An antler tip handle piece should be symmetrical in cross-section and straight in the plane that the blade will set. It's really difficult to order stag through the mail and get ones that will work. All my particularly beautiful and well-matched tip handles were hand-picked from suppliers at knife shows or saved from elk antlers that I cut up for handles. Because of curves in both directions, not all elk antlers will have usable tips for anything other than very small folders.

2. Blade and spacer material: Saw steel or O-1 precision-ground flat stock, 1/8 of an inch thick, 3/4 of an inch or more wide for the blade and 1/4 of an inch wide for the spacer type. The critical thing is that the material is flat and parallel. Folding knives of any type will have a smoother action when the blade material is absolutely parallel in the pivot area. Precision-ground flat stock (O-1) may appear expensive but by the time you finish the project you will have saved more than enough time to count it money well spent.

3. Pin stock, 3/32 of an inch and 1/8 of an inch. Welding wire, brazing rod, nails, an old-style metal clothes hanger or whatever you have or can find, just make sure you have a drill bit the size for your pin stock.

THE DESIGN

You will have to figure out the pivot point for a specific handle width only one time. Keep a pattern of it and the next time you will have the action figured out beforehand. I have something more than 120 patterns for folders I have made since 1972. What that means is I have a pattern for the action for just about any size of design that comes along.

The best way to design a folding knife of any type is to first decide on the blade size and shape, and then work out the handle to contain the blade. The exception is when a crown stag or antler tip is used, then the handle shape and size becomes the starting point.

Most friction folders are slotted for the blade. I like the style with a spacer because it gives me freedom for forged details at the end, and also space to do file work or engraving on both the inner and outer surfaces of the spacer. I also find it less time-consuming. I can make several spacers in the time it takes to slot a handle by hand.

What follows is the step-by-step sequence for designing and making a spacer-style friction folder from an antler tip. If an antler tip is not available, use wood or Micarta®; shape it as you want and jump ahead to step #4.

STEP 1: Cut the antler tip to length and split it down the middle.

STEP 2: Grind the inside surfaces flat and make both sides the same thickness.

STEP 3: The two sides are usually not symmetrical in cross section to each other. Some material may need to be removed from the outline of one of the handle pieces in order to keep both pieces the same profile.

STEP 4: Designing the action, I call it the "action" because it is the mechanical part of a folding knife. It always starts with the pivot point and the top and bottom edges of the blade. Trace the profile of the handle piece onto cardboard.

STEP 5: Cut another piece of cardboard that is large enough to make the blade pattern.

STEP 6: Locate the centerline of the handle pattern, and mark where it is an equal distance from the end and both the top and bottom.

STEP 7: Align the cardboard blade piece with the handle and push a map tack through the handle pattern into it. This creates the pivot pin location.

STEP 8: Swing the blade pattern piece (B) through an arc that will show the open and closed positions, and mark it as to length and width to fit in the handle pattern (A). Finish the blade pattern by refining the outline of the blade. Some adjustment of the pivot-hole location of blade and handle may be needed to position the blade properly in both the open and closed positions. I do not have a formula to give you. I find it by trial and error on the first pattern in a certain width handle. (See the drawing showing the pattern pieces.

Three folding knives by the author. Top to bottom: Single-blade jackknife with filework and a forged thong holder. Center, single-blade jack-knife with filework, no forged details. Bottom, crown stag, friction folder with filework and a forged scroll on the tang extension.

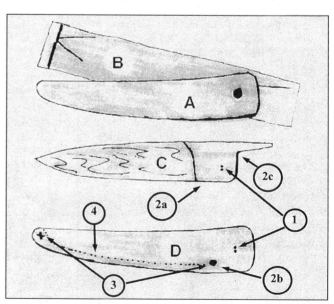

Pattern parts and locator points for the spacer-type friction folder.

Note that it took me two tries to get the proper pivot location.)

STEP 9: This project is a spacer-type friction folder, so the location for the stop pin is worked out at this time. This point is not negotiable but is determined by the three points designated 2a, 2b, and 2c on the pattern design illustration. The location may not make sense until the blade pattern is rotated on the handle pattern.

STEP 10: The spacer-style handle will require three holes in each side. The holes for the spacer are 3/32 of an inch; the blade pivot pin is 1/8 of an inch. For pin material on this type of folder I use mild-steel welding wire. I can then use cold blue solution to color the heads of the pins for an antique look.

STEP 11: With the cardboard pattern pieces for both handle and blade working properly, it is time to drill the holes in either pattern piece of the actual knife parts. Masonite®, plastic, aluminum or steel will all work to keep a master pattern. The handle holes that go through the spacer can be a little oversize and it will not matter much, but the hole in the blade must fit the pin precisely. Even a properly sharpened drill bit may drill an oversize hole. Here is how I do it. Drill a hole that is smaller than the finished size, and then open it up with a drill bit of the size you want. The fin-

ished hole will be very close to the correct size. As an example, first drill with a 3/32-inch bit to finish and with a 1/8-inch bit for the pivot holes.

Pattern Parts & Location Points

See the drawing mentioned above. "A" is the cardboard pattern traced from the pre-shaped handle. "B" is the oversize cardboard piece used to design the blade. Note the pencil marks that show the outer limits of the blade shape. "C" and "D" are the finished pattern pieces. Note that there are two sets of holes at position "1." This is from the trial-and-error method of determining the correct location of the blade in the handle. The position marked by the "2" on the end of the tang is where it stops at point "2" up against the spacer in the handle when the blade is in the open position. Point "2" on the bottom of the tang stops against the spacer and keeps the edge portion of the blade from bottoming out when the blade is closed. The spacer-type handle is held together by two through pins indicated by "3"; "4" indicates the position and shape of the spacer. Now is the time to transfer that pattern to the materials used to make the knife.

Drilling the Handle Material

1. Trace the pattern onto the handle material with a sharp pencil. Do not use anything other than a lead pencil when working with any natural handle material, especially stag or ivory. Stag and ivory are porous and the ink can go deep into the surface. One dot from a felt-tip marker may ruin a good handle slab. Saw, grind or file to the rough shape. At this stage I usually take the shape to the outside of the line. The excess material will be removed when the parts are stacked together.

2. The steel for the spacer and blade can be coated with layout dye (available from knife-maker and industrial supply companies), or use a red or black marking pen. Be sure to keep the layout dye or marking-pen ink away from your handle material. Clamp the pattern piece securely onto the material and carefully trace around it with a sharp scribe. Sharpen-

Left, to right: Stag drilling jig. Locking pliers that have been modified to work as a clamping device for half-round surfaces. Drill press platform for holding

Pattern piece clamped to handle side for drilling.

One side of the handle being used as a guide to drill the pivot hole in the opposite side.

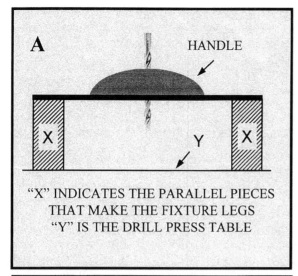

"X" INDICATES THE PARALLEL PIECES
THAT MAKE THE FIXTURE LEGS
"Y" IS THE DRILL PRESS TABLE

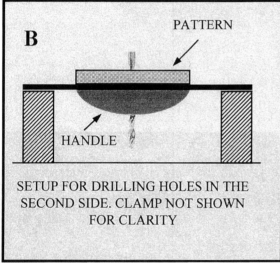

SETUP FOR DRILLING HOLES IN THE
SECOND SIDE. CLAMP NOT SHOWN
FOR CLARITY

Drawings to clarify the purpose of the jig in the previous photographs.

ing the end of a worn-out triangular or round file will make a quick scribe. Needles for the old-fashioned wind-up record players are still available. The steel they are made of is very hard and, when Super-Glued® into the end of a piece of wood or antler, they make a nice scribe for marking steel.

3.   With the outline of the handle material shaped, it is time to drill the three holes in each handle side. (See drawings and photo of the drill jig that makes it easier to drill the rounded stag slabs.)
The jig allows the slab to be drilled upside down with the flat side kept parallel with the steel plate. If the handle slabs were parallel, they could be placed on the table of the drill press and that would make the jig unnecessary. The cross section of stag slabs of the type used for friction folders are often more half round than rectangular. The first side is easy to drill because the flat side is down.
To use the pattern for a guide to drill the second side, the pattern is placed on the top of

the plate with the slab to be drilled on the under side. The alignment of the first hole is by eye and the two are then clamped in position on the jig. The plate will have some oversize holes drilled in it for clearance on the drill bit. This is the best way I have found to get the holes in both halves at 90 degrees to the inside of the knife. An alternate method is to use a flat piece of steel placed on two parallel pieces of material. A drill-press vise will work if the jaws are parallel with the base and are also deep enough to get the clamp in while clamped to the handle slab. Note the modified clamping-type pliers in the photo. It provides a perfect clamp for holding half-round materials. Also note the trial pin in place so that one half of the folder can be used as a jig to drill the other half. This is how I do it with one-of-a-kind folders where a pattern is not being saved for future use; these are usually the type made with an antler crown for the handle.

4.   Clamp the handle pattern onto the blade blank and drill the 1/8-inch pivot hole as indicated by the No. 1 in drawing "C."

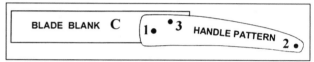

Handle drilling sequence.

5.   Clamp the handle pattern on the spacer material and drill the 3/32-inch holes indicated by "2" and "3."

6.   Grind the blade and spacer to the rough shape. When the blade profile is ground, take care to not grind beyond the drilled hole and stay outside the scribed line in the area of fit-up. (See arrows on drawing "D.")

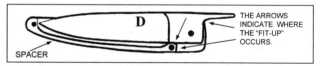

This drawing shows the finished shapes of the spacer, handle and blade. It shows the proper position of the final fit-up in the closed position.

7.   Assemble the back-side handle slab with the spacer and blade in position with trial pins as shown in drawing "D." Rotate the blade between the open and closed positions and work down the material for the final "fit-up."

8.   Work slow and easy to get the blade to sit correctly in the open and closed positions.

9.   Once you are satisfied with the fit-up, it is time to grind the bevels on the blade.

10.   Heat treat and finish the blade and make the final fit and finish. The spacer for this type folder can be left in the soft condition.

11. The two handle pieces are assembled with trial pins and shaped on the "round". (That means rounding off the rectangular edges.) The inside surfaces are also finished and relief is given to the area where the tang will rub. (See drawing.)

The shaded area shows where relief is necessary so that the blade tang does not show rub marks from the handle.

The relief is necessary so that the tang does not show rub marks when in the open position. I mark the arc with a divider, then remove the material with files, scrapers and sandpaper. The handle sides are 90 percent finished before assembly.

Final assembly starts with setting the pins that hold the handle together. This is the last chance to check the fit-up on the action. (See photos.)

The finished knife parts assembled with trial pins; the open position.

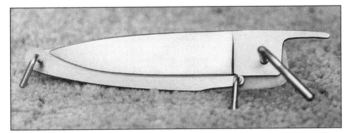

The finished knife parts assembled with trial pins; the closed position.

12. Riveting the friction folder together should be done only after some "pin-setting practice" on scrap materials. The rivet is simply a pin that has been "headed" on both sides. I form the recess for the head by hand turning a countersink made from a conical-shaped mounted point. (See the photo.) Any kind of power or speed on the countersink and the results will often be more than is needed. I do not have a formula for how large the countersink should be made. Start with a recess that is approximately 20 percent larger than the pin size.

Turning the counter sink tool by hand.

See the photo for a simple angle-iron jig that will grip the pins tightly without smashing them. The jig is made by placing the angle iron pieces in a vise with a thin piece of cardboard between them. Holes are drilled down the center, one for each size of the pin stock to be held. With the cardboard removed, jig in the vise jaws; a tight grip is applied to the pin stock.

Pin-holding jig for the bench vise.

The first practice exercise is to form a head on a piece of the pin material you will be using. Make a series of light hammer blows around the edge of the pin. The hammer should have a slightly rounded face. Note the shape of the hammer face in the photo of the pin stock in the jig. As you pein the head, observe the action of the hammer on the pin. Note the high spot formed in the center of the pin and work it off with a file. Make another round of light hammer blows on the end of the pin. With careful and even blows, a perfect head can be made. Next, practice on making a head on the pin stock while it is in a piece of wood or scrap stag. The trick is to make the head big enough so that it will not pull out but not so big that it splits the handle material. It's your choice to make a flush-headed pin or one with a dome sticking up above the surface.

I use a jig to grind the back of the folder square with the spacer or spring. See the photo of the jig with a small crown folder in

Jig for grinding the back of a folding knife square with the sides.

Grinding jig in place on the table of the belt grinder.

grinding position.

See photo of the project folder in position on the table of the belt grinder.

Final assembly starts by riveting the two handle halves and spacer together. A little peining is done on one side of the pin then a little on the other end and then back to the front. It's better to start with a little more pin stock than

needed because it can always be filed off. Once that is done, a final cleanup is done around the edges of the handle. Wipe out the inside of the handle to get rid of dust and grit and then it is time to rivet the blade in position. Take care to not get the pivot pin too tight. A piece of .002 shim stock with a notch in it can be inserted between the blade and handle piece. As the peining progresses, the shim is checked from time to time to see when the handles start to grip it. Don't set the pivot pin so tight that you can't get the shim out. I only did that one time.

I use all hand work to finish the outside surfaces of a folder. Sandpaper backed up with a firm surface will work the heads of the pins down. Finish with fine-grit paper and 0000 steel wool.

Sharpen the knife and you are almost ready to put it in your pocket. Because there is no spring to hold the blade shut, I recommend that friction folders intended for use as pocket-knives should be carried in a leather pouch.

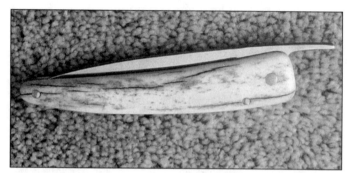

The finished friction folder in the resting position.

See the photos of the finished project.

The finished folding knife in the working position.

PINS AND SCREWS FOR FOLDING KNIVES

Don Snedden sent three questions pertaining to folding knife construction.

Question #1: *I've been using 6061 aluminum and 308 stainless steel welding rod for pins. What do you feel is the strongest material for peining that is still fairly malleable?*

146

Answer: Stainless steel is the strongest and it can be peined, although the head can not be made as large as with aluminum. For maximum strength I use stainless TIG rod for all the pins in my folders. It's 304, which is a rod for universal applications. The 304 may be softer than 308 and as such may be more suitable for making pins that are peined to make a head. For fixed-blade handles I use brazing rod and nickel-silver wire for pins. On most small to medium fixed-blade knives I don't pein anymore but rely on super glue to hold the pins in place. The secret to making it look good is to have the hole very close to the size of the pin.

Question #2: *How do you get a really wide looking pin at your pivot such as the crown folders you make?*

Answer: I make the nickel-silver "birds-eye" washers on my old-fashioned metal lathe. (It was made in 1908.) The washers are laid out, drilled and reamed on one long strip of material, then cut apart, stacked up on a small mandrel made from a machine screw and then turned to the correct diameter. They are set down into a counter-bored recess in order to create a peining surface on the wood bolsters I use on crown folders. The birds-eye washers are also necessary when I use stag for the sides of folders without bolsters. (See photo)

Question #3: *Do you feel there are any advantages of using screws? I feel they are mostly for looks, which is cool. But for strength I can't see any advantages.*

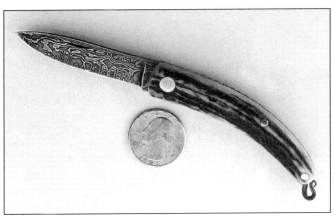

Stag tip folder with "bird's-eye" washer.

Answer: The modern locking-liner is the type of mechanism that may need to be tuned up, adjusted and occasionally repaired. I look at screws as being necessary to make them easy to work on. If some part gets worn or out of whack the screws are necessary in order to be able to easily disassemble and fix the problem. I can't see how screws would be any stronger than pins of the same diameter. I'm assuming the pinning was done correctly.

Note: Peen (pein), to draw, bend or flatten by hammering with the peen/pein end of a hammer. Pein is an alternate to peen and the use that I prefer.

Chapter 12

MODIFIED VISE-GRIP® PLIERS AS CLAMPS FOR THE KNIFEMAKER

Vise-Grips® are the wrong tool for the right job. (A tool man told me that.) That's because there are times when nothing else will work even if it means marking up the object being gripped. I've worked past that and have become very fond of my modified "clamping pliers." I have 10 pairs of these modified Vise-Grip® pliers. They have replaced most of the other clamps in my shop. Some are the large size, but most are the middle size.

To modify them I first grind out the pipe jaws and wire cutters in order to give clearance for the work being held. I then use super glue to attach thick sole leather or Micarta® pads. The pads have a radius, which is necessary to grip rounded surfaces. It also keeps the area of contact small and that, in turn, puts less strain on the pad. Super glue is applied around the jaw and Micarta® dust is sprinkled on it to build up a fillet for strength. If the pad breaks loose stick it back on with more super glue.

The modified Vise-Grip® clamp is the perfect work holder for small parts when held in a bench vise. Note the rivet heads that hold the pliers together. On 2, 3 and 4 they have been ground flat so the Vise-Grip clamp can be held securely in the vise jaws.

See the drawing.

1. This pair is fitted with slip-on leather grippers, as shown it clamps half-round to flat real good.

2. Copper tube, fitted and shaped, holds steel and other metal stuff without scratching it.

3. Hard sole-leather affixed with super glue and Micarta dust for glue. It grips stag, ivory and pearl without cracking or marking it.

4. This version holds one side of a miniature folding knife for handwork or machine polishing. A bigger pair like this holds guards for full-size knives for shaping and polishing. I got the idea for these when I found a pair with one broken jaw.

GODDARD'S RULE OF BUYING VISE-GRIPS

Yard sales, flea markets or junk shops only. The pliers must be rusty but in good shape and also less than $2. If they are nice and shiny the price is usually too high for me.

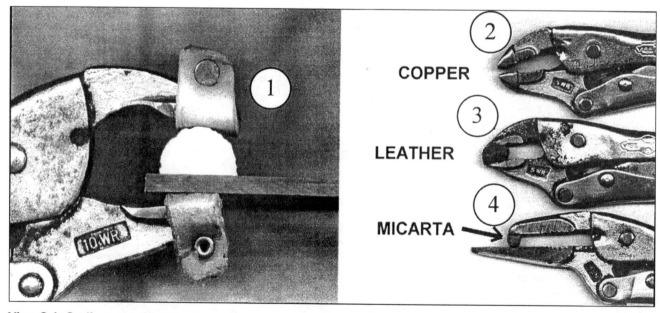

Vise-Grip® pliers modified by the author for use as clamps for knifemaking.

SAND-BLASTED FINISHES

Eric Shaver of Moscow, Idaho writes:

I was wondering how much finishing should be done to a blade before having it sand-blasted. Should all the scratches be removed before I have the blade sand-blasted?

Answer: Heavy sand blasting with coarse sand will blend in some scratches. Fine or dull sand will have less effect on the surface finish. It will depend somewhat on the visual effect that you want for the blade. A tactical folder might look better with a fine satin finish lightly blasted. A rough and ready survival knife might look just fine with a 120- or 220-grit belt finish with a heavy blast job. In any case, the finish prior to sand blasting should be uniform over the surface of the blade.

PLASMA CUTTING BLADE BLANKS

Garrett Clark of Alaska writes:

Is there a problem using a plasma cutter on blade blanks for stock removal? At this time I am using O-1 steel. Is there a better steel type to use? I find using a band saw is quite time-consuming and a plasma cutter would be much faster.

Answer: O-1 steel has the tendency to air harden. The heat from the plasma cutter would leave a very hard skin at the edge. Although the hard skin is very thin, it would have to be ground off. My own experiments with plasma-cut blanks showed that the skin at the cut edge was so hard that a file would not touch it, and it would surely ruin a band saw blade.

O-1 is an excellent steel when heat treated correctly. In my opinion it has the potential to equal 52100 in edge-holding ability. Just like with 52100 it takes more care to get a superior blade than with some of the more simple steels like 1095 or 5160.

HEAT BLUED FITTINGS

Matthew Butterly of Busselton, Western Australia writes:

Would you explain the term fire-blued fittings?

Answer: I don't use the term "fire-blued." I call it heat bluing which means the same thing. When non stainless-steels are heated through the range of approximately 300 to 900 degrees F they show "temper colors." The color is the result of a layer of oxide forming on the surface. Each steel has its own color at a specific temperature. Approximate colors are as follows: at around 300 to 400 degrees F the first faint color shows as pale yellow. As the temperature rises the colors change from yellow to brown, then purple, blue and then silver gray at around 700 degrees F. There are many shades in between those listed. The oxide is a thin, easily removed layer of color.

A tough black finish is possible on steel parts by working them over with a wire brush as they cool below 1,400 degrees F. The brushing is continued as the part cools to around 500 degrees F when a paste wax is rubbed in while hot. Several layers of wax are applied as the part continues cooling. I have found Johnson's Paste Wax to be very good for this process. This is a finish that will not easily wear off like oxide colors do.

LOGO ETCHING WITH SALT WATER

I learned about salt water etching with direct current in 1973 from a very wild looking person. I was selling my knives at an open-air craft market and he stopped to look. He asked how I put my logo on the blades and I explained that I applied a wax mixture to the blade with a hot iron, then scratched my logo through the wax and then applied acid to etch the mark. He told me that instead of using acid I should use salt water and a 6-volt battery. I have to admit it was a couple of years before I tried it.

I always had to mix the acid a little different to get consistent results with the variety of steels I was working with. The acid mix that worked on one type of steel would not work that well on another and the acid wouldn't touch Stellite at all. Salt water and good quality direct current will etch every metal I've tried, including Stellite 6K, copper, brass and nickel-silver. I haven't tried it on titanium.

The wax mixture is applied to the clean blade with a hot iron. When the wax cools the logo is scratched into it and then it is treated with the salt-water etchant. It took me awhile to get it working smoothly but I have now been using this process for 22 years.

It takes a real good source of 6-volt direct current. A variable voltage power supply for electronic work will work; mine is from Radio Shack. Toy transformers and battery eliminators for radios and such won't work too well because the direct current they put out is not a pure form. A power supply from an obsolete computer will work very well. Most of those that I've modified put out two different voltages with 6V being the lowest. Just test the output leads and use the ones that are 6V.

I worked up a demo at a handles and guard class I taught and used red ski wax for the resist and it worked just fine. The only DC we had was an automobile battery charger set on 6 volts. Because the DC wasn't very pure, the etch came out somewhat ragged and uneven. For some reason the DC has to be real good or the etch isn't crisp.

I mix my salt-water etchant in an old-style half-ounce India-ink bottle. However much salt you can get between the tip of your finger and the end of your thumb is all that is necessary, too much salt in the water and the etch gets uneven and may even eat the wax away. Oregon has good water, but if your tap water doesn't work try the distilled variety.

The negative wire goes to a holder that grabs a Q-tip® by the end. (Cotton swab means Q-tip®, that's important because the cheap ones won't work very well.) Here is how to make the holder for the cotton swab. You will need a small steel rod, not over 5/32 of an inch in diameter and 5 or 6 inches long. Stainless steel would be good. Ask for 5/32-inch stainless TIG wire at your local welding supply store. (TIG wire is also good to use for pin stock for holding handles on knives.) Cut a slot in the end of the rod and pry it apart just far enough so that it will grip the cotton swab by the cotton covered end. Leave about half of the cotton part sticking out and pull the cotton out to make it fluffy. Make a holder for the rod so that you can adjust it so that the fluffed up end of the cotton swab will just contact the knife blade.

My resist is beeswax and microcrystalline wax, about 50/50. I apply it with a hot iron. (Like clothes were ironed with before perma-press.) It will take some practice to be able to apply a nice even layer of wax. It can be either too thick or too thin; practice is the key to make this process work. (Polycrystalline or microcrystalline wax is used in the lost-wax casting process.) My jewelry making instructor got me 5 pounds back when I started with this type of etching and I'm still using from that batch because a little of the wax mix goes a long way. The reason for the mixture on the wax is so it will be consistent in hardness over a wider temperature range. The wax can be either too hard or too soft; it needs to be workable. When too hard it will lift off with the stylus, scribe or whatever you want to call it. When too

soft the voltage can melt it, or if the voltage is too high it can eat holes in the resist. Keep the resist free of lint and dust because they will cause the etchant to eat holes wherever the contaminant is. The stylus tool needs to have a well-polished ball end on it so it does not dig into the blade; it needs to slide on the surface. A fine tip is used for small delicate logos like on a miniature. A wider tip will make a bolder mark for the larger knives.

The positive is put on the blade with an alligator clamp with the negative going to the swab holder. I use the dropper from the ink bottle to put a little puddle of the etchant on the blade. The cotton swab is soaked with salt water and lowered down till it just rests in the puddle. Be careful not to jam the cotton swab into the wax or you can ruin the mark. The 6 volts DC is then applied, etch for five minutes to start. Too much voltage will melt the wax, or it may eat holes in the resist. The results of that happening are awful because it looks like the logo was shot with a tiny little shotgun. The only fix is to regrind and finish the blade. I use tap water because it works. I wear my OptiVISOR full time in the shop and this is good for checking to see if the etch is getting started correctly.

The versatility of the size and styles that are possible make it valuable for me. This is a great way to mark blades but not easy to learn. Practice a lot before you try it on a finished blade and stick with it until you get it all figured out.

Chapter 13

KNIFE TESTING

While just about everyone "tests" their knives, most are not uniform or scientific. This leaves a number of questions floating around about the performance of knives. Here are a few of the important ones:

Does one type of steel have a particular advantage over another in specific applications?

How strong must a blade be for different types of use?

What would a realistic strength test consist of?

How sharp is sharp?

Are there different types of sharpness and if so does one have an advantage over another?

It might seem that these questions would take an impossible amount of time and effort to answer. It is my hope that these simple tests will take some of the mystery out the questions listed above.

THE THREE BASIC TESTS

#1 Endurance cutting ability. The ability to stay sharp.

#2 Chopping ability, comparing and evaluating the efficiency of different blade cross-sections.

#3 Strength testing is divided into two parts. The first is edge strength, the ability to resist chipping or cracking at the edge. The second is total blade strength, the ability to be flexed without damage.

THE RULES FOR TESTING

Always compare the test blade with a blade of known value at the same time and on the same material. It has very little value to state what a particular blade will do if a fair comparison was not made with another blade of known value.

A blade made of a specific steel must be tested at the highest hardness at which it will have adequate strength for it's intended use. It is assumed that the test blade was given a proper heat-treatment.

Great care must be taken to see that the test blades have the same cross section geometry. In order to get a fair comparison the blade thickness and length must be the same. With the rules out of the way we will get down to some common sense observations about test procedures.

HOW SHARP IS SHARP?

Before accurate test results can be arrived at it will be necessary to discuss sharpening and to define, exactly, a sharp edge. A perfect edge is one that has the primary included angle coming to a crisp and exact point. The cross section of the blade must be quite thin in order to cut the rope in the endurance test. This edge may be a polished edge from a buffing wheel or leather strop, or it might be put on with a sharpening stone. Either type must have the wire edge removed in order to have a long-lasting and testable edge. The ability of a knife to shave hair is not a valid test if the edge has a wire on it.

DEFINING THE WIRE EDGE AND REMOVING IT.

As the blade is abraded on the sharpening stone the edge gets thinner and thinner until the straight lines that form the included angle of the blade meet. At this point there is a thin wire or burr of blade material that simply bends back and forth under the pressure of the stone, or buffing wheel. The wire edge may be perfectly lined up from light pressure on the stone, or by careful use of the buffing wheel or strop. This edge will shave hair and slice paper but will fail quickly when the edge contacts wood, rope, hide or other hard objects. As the wire edge contacts hard materials it bends back and forth and finally breaks out, leaving a microscopic flat where the wire of steel pulled away from the edge. At other times the wire will bend over causing the knife to appear dull, actually the blade material that was doing the cutting is bent over. The best way to be assured that the wire edge is off and that you have a true sharp edge is to draw the edge across a smooth metal rod. Use a back-stroke at an angle somewhat greater than the sharpening angle. You will be able to feel the wire by running a fingernail down the side of the blade opposite the side that was stroked on the rod. If the wire or burr is still there, the fingernail will hook on it. Once the wire edge is removed and the true sharp edge is properly set up, accurate testing can begin.
(See the chapter on sharpening.)

THE HISTORY OF THE GODDARD ENDURANCE TESTING PROGRAM

I started out cutting cardboard as an edge-holding test 28 years ago. It was a boring and time-wasting process simply because a superior blade would cut until your arm was sore, and you were up to your knees in cut off pieces of cardboard. The first tests on rope were done in 1972; the purpose was to determine the difference between 440C and 154CM. My friend and customer, Maynard Meadows, had suggested using sisal rope, and very successful and time efficient tests were achieved. We started out cutting the full 1-inch rope, but soon switched to the single strands as they dulled the test blades quick enough to make the testing time-efficient. (See photo.)

A test knife with some rope that's been cut. A narrow-tang test blade is held in this handle with a set screw. A full-sized handle is necessary to get an accurate test.

Over the next eight years I made several dozen test-knives to compare different steels, and also to compare the same steels with different heat-treatments. Maynard, being an avid big game hunter would take the test knives on hunting trips in order to get a comparison in actual use. The field tests re-enforced the results that we were getting with our rope cutting tests. I obtained abrasive resistance charts from two different steel companies and, by comparing their bar charts with my rope cutting tests when the hardness of the steel was the same, realized that I was within 5 percent of their ratings. I gained more confidence in my endurance testing as time went along.

THE EFFECT OF HARDNESS ON EDGE-HOLDING ABILITY

One of the tests that I did early on, with the help of Paul Bos, was to determine the effect on edge-holding as the hardness changed. Paul is a profes-

sional heat-treater and was interested in helping in these tests. We ran test batches of D-5, 154CM, and 440C, giving half the blades their normal working hardness, the other half were drawn back two points on the Rockwell C scale. The blades drawn back two points would cut 15 percent to 20 percent less, which surprised both of us. Later when comparing a blade with a hardness of 54RC to a blade of 60RC, I found the percentage loss held up. The steel that did 40 cuts at 60RC would do 30 cuts at 58RC, 20 cuts at 56RC, 10 cuts at 54RC and at a hardness of 52RC, would hardly cut the rope one time.

ENDURANCE TESTING

Test blades are prepared having a width of 1-inch, a thickness of 1/8 of an inch and length of 3-3/4 inches. Blades are flat-ground to .020 inches at the edge. Sharpening is done on the Norton Fine India Stone, the wire edge being worked off with the stone. This gives a hair-shaving, long-lasting edge that has what I refer to as micro teeth. Slicing cuts are made on a single strand from the 1-inch rope. Care is taken to use an equal section of blade from one knife to the other. The edge will bite into the rope strand when freshly sharpened, but as slicing continues there comes a point when the edge no longer is biting into the fibers. This is the point at which slicing is stopped and the number of cuts is recorded. The edge looses its ability to shave hair at about the same time as it loses its bite into the rope. Each blade is tested at least three times and the results are averaged.

The author cutting rope at the 1999 Oregon Knife Show – Symposium of Knife Technology. Photo by Bob Lum.

Update: The last five years or so I've been cutting on a scale. (See photo.) I quit cutting when the pressure reaches a certain point, usually 35 pounds. I had a normal variance of 10 percent and that has dropped to 5 percent by using the scale.

THE SLICING CUT COMPARED TO THE PUSH

The blade with a buffed edge will push through the rope strand with much less pressure than if it has the micro-tooth type of edge. The limiting factor to the number of cuts with the polished edge is the amount of strength required. It is harder to determine when the edge actually quits working. Depending on how hard you wish to push, it uses four to 10 times more rope. The blade with micro-teeth will slice through the rope better than the polished edge. The slicing test is faster and more accurate for the type of edge that I advocate. Over the years I have learned that the micro-tooth edge is superior for a working knife.

THE DIFFERENCES IN ROPE

I currently have a 154CM knife that is what I call a "check blade." When I get a new supply of rope, I always do a cutting test with this knife. That way I will be aware of any change in the number of cuts expected. There are big differences in rope. Some will dull a blade three times faster than others will. Using my 154CM check-blade and the original rope that testing was started with, I would get around 44 cuts on the average test. The last two batches of rope have been much more abrasive and the number of cuts has dropped to around 20. When testing on the rope from my Knife-Expo demonstrations, the number of cuts dropped even more, to around 15 or 17. The fibers in it are large, it is very stiff, and I had noticed that it was very hard to cut during the free-hanging rope cutting demonstration I did at the show. A knife that would easily do three at a time on most of the ropes that I have cut would do only two at a time on that hard rope.

For future testing I am advocating the use of 1/2-inch rope. It will be easier to find and very comparable results were found when I compared it to using the single strands out of 1-inch rope.

THE SHARPENING STONE

The condition of the stone that the edge is finished on will have a great effect on test results. A new stone is always more aggressive than one that has been used for some time. My finish stone, the Norton Fine India needs to be lapped about every 18 months. By this time the cutting is starting to get slow and the stone is showing some wear, and the number of cuts that a test blade will make will become less. Accurate comparisons between blades can still be made as long as the testing is done with the stone in the same condition. Those test results should not be compared to any done when the stone was fresh.

THE FREE-HANGING ROPE TEST

The free-hanging rope cut is primarily a test of the knife's sharpness. I do not use it as part of my testing because it has so many variables. The test has secondary value as a gauge of blade strength. I had a stock-removal blade break into several pieces while attempting to make one cut at a time on free-hanging 1-inch rope. It was hard all the way through, no soft-back. A blade with too much soft-back will bend in the test. Cutting free-hanging rope is a very effective way to demonstrate, as a comparison, the cutting ability of different knives. It takes a blade with good geometry, made from good steel, correctly hardened and tempered and with a nearly perfect edge to easily complete the cut. It does not matter if the blade is forged or made by the stock removal method.

TESTING THE CHOPPING ABILITY OF A KNIFE

At a knife show in Oklahoma I was asked to do a 2x4 chopping demonstration. I had just passed my ABS Journeyman Smith requirements. The only knife I had with me that was long enough was one of my test blades. The 10-inch blade, which was forged from a Nicholsen Black Diamond file, weighed only 12 ounces. Regardless of the weight, it was a very efficient wood chopping and free-hanging rope knife. The narrow tang put the weight mostly in the blade, a real advantage in a chopping test. As I finished chopping through the 2x4 I heard someone say, "18 seconds!" Although I had never thought of timing myself on the 2x4 chop, it is a good comparison to make when testing a chopping knife. When I returned home and timed myself on some Oregon 2x4s, I never could beat that time. That Oklahoma wood was very soft and there was no double check of the timing, so I cannot claim a record of some sort.

Another comparison to make is to count the number of swings it takes to chop through a wood 2x4. The number can vary a lot with a specific blade, depending on the force of the arm swing, offset of the handle, wrist action, accuracy of the cut, and hardness of the 2x4. A knife with good steel, having at least a 10-inch blade, and weighing 12 ounces or more, will chop a 2x4 of average hardness in half with around 25 swings.

In order to get as many comparisons as possible, I started measuring the depth of penetration into a piece of wood with a single blow, however, and this did not seem to be very consistent. I did a series of tests to determine the largest piece of wood that could be cut with a single blow. A pine or fir board 3/4 of an inch by 1-1/2 inches (actual measurement) is a good size to start with for this comparison test. The knives with a dropped handle would always out-chop the straight broom-handle designs.

These were useful comparisons, but I wanted to eliminate the human arm and the advantage of good handle design. I wanted to be able to test only the efficiency of the grind (blade cross section geometry). This is how the Chop-O-Mattic penetration test machine came to be built.

The Chop-O-Mattic edge testing machine.

THE CHOP-O-MATTIC EDGE TESTER

As you can see in the photo, sets screws hold the blade horizontally with it's back secured against a pivoting arm. The arm is raised a given distance, then allowed to fall free, and the knife-edge penetrates the edge of a piece of test material held by a clamp. The depth of penetration is measured with a vernier caliper and recorded. Accurate and uniform results are reached, and the human element is eliminated. The specifications for the machine are as follows. The arm weighs 3-3/4 pounds. The distance from the pivot point to the striking point is 23 inches. The arm is dropped from a point that will give 14 inches of blade travel. Initial testing was done with no adjustment for the weight of the knife, which gave the heaviest knives an advantage. One chop was done on each of three different materials with each knife. The total penetration on all three materials

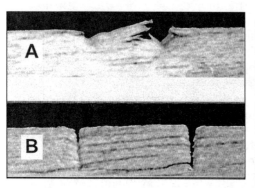

Actual pictures of test results from the Chop-O-Mattic machine. The wood is mahogany, "A" shows the results of two tests with a factory knife edge. "B" shows the results after the blade was thinned and correctly sharpened. Depth of penetration on "B" was nearly 1/8 of an inch.

was totaled. The materials used were 3/4-inch Mahogany, 3/4-inch cedar, and 3/8-inch Delrin®.

The knives were mounted to give a square hit on the test material. When there was a difference in the depth of the cut from one side to the other, the two measurements were averaged.

TESTING EDGE STRENGTH

The stock-removal makers trust their heat-treater to return blades with the hardness that was specified. If this degree of hardness has proven to give superior edge-holding ability, and yet be strong enough to resist chipping out, then all is well. The maker doing his own heat treating will need to establish some type of testing process in order to insure the integrity of the blades. Bladesmiths do their own heat-treating and often work with a larger selection of steels than a stock-removal maker. The best possible heat treatment must be worked out for each steel type. This starts by using the correct temperatures during the forging operation, continues with proper normalizing and annealing, and is finished by using the correct hardening temperature to gain maximum hardness with a fine grain structure.

Determining the tempering temperature for a new steel type is like walking a tightrope. On one side, the blade may be too hard and break; on the other side it may not hold an edge. The tempering temperature is very critical, 25 degrees F one way or the other will make a difference whether the edge will chip out or not. The fine line between too hard and too soft should not be left to chance and should be worked out carefully with actual tests.

THE BRASS ROD TEST

The Brass Rod Test was shown to me 40 years ago by a blacksmith who said he made knives in the 1920s and 30s. It is the best test of edge strength I have found. Clamp a brass rod 1/4-inch in diameter horizontally in a vise with the top third above the jaws. Lay the edge of the knife on the rod at the same angle used for sharpening. Apply enough pressure so that you can see the edge deflect from the pressure on the rod. This pressure works out to 35 to 40 pounds. Use a good light source behind the vise so that you can see the deflection. If the edge chips out with moderate pressure on the rod, the edge will chip out in use. If the edge stays bent over in the deflected area, it will bend in use and be too soft to hold an edge. The superior blade will deflect and yet spring back.

I go one step further in testing camp knives and combat blades by chopping knots out of 2x4s. The grind I use for a big, rough-use blade is a compromise between a thin blade that is good for rope cutting and a thick, maxi-strength blade.

THE 90-DEGREE FLEX TEST

When a knife dulls it can be sharpened and a blade that takes a bend can be straightened and put back to work. When a blade stains, it will still work. A broken blade can spell disaster in a life-or-death situation where a blade of maximum strength is absolutely essential. The 90-degree flex test is a good way to determine the ultimate strength of a blade. The test was originated to prove the strength of a blade that is given the hard edge / soft back treatment. Though criticized by some as being too severe a test, it is useful and proves the worth of the soft back. My testing procedures, including the flex test, give me a confidence that I otherwise would not have.

If the blade has too much soft back, it may bend in normal use and won't have sufficient stiffness to be useful. If the hard edge extends too far up the blade, or if the body of the blade was not given the proper thermal treatments before hardening, the blade will break. It is reasonable to expect that a blade with the proper ratio of hard edge to soft back will be capable of being bent 45 degrees, and will "return to straight" with no cracking or breaking at the edge.

Often, when flexing a blade held in a vise, it will be so strong that the vise jaw cutting into the steel will cause the blade to break at that point. When this happens, a true measurement of the strength of the blade is not possible. In order to get a true test of strength; I adopted the practice of placing a piece of hardwood with a rounded edge in the vise for the blade to be bent over.

THE KNIFE BREAKER

This photo shows the Knife Breaker. It was built in order to have a standard test of the effectiveness of different thermal treatments on the strength of blades. I named the machine "Knife Breaker," not because breaking blades was the purpose, but because it easily broke blades that could not be broken with maximum hand pressure. The purpose was to make it possible to deflect the blade a preset amount over a fixed distance. A heavy "U" bolt holds the point of the knife securely and the blade support is adjusted for the length of blade to be tested. A wood block to give the desired deflex is placed under the blade. The photograph of The Knife Breaker shows it set up to test a blade. The wood block plus the 1/2-inch steel bar under the blade will test a deflection of 1/2 an inch. By pushing down on the lever-arm, up to 1,500 Pounds of pressure can be put on the blade. To test the blade, the arm is pushed down until the underside of the blade contacts the block. That puts an exact amount of pressure on the blade. A good test is a deflection of 1 inch over a length of 7 inches.

Demonstrating the knife breaker at a knife show in 1991.

These are the tests I have worked out to determine the overall efficiency of different steels, selective heat treatments, blade cross sections, sharpening methods, blade thickness, and etc.

Close-up view of the setup for a preset flex test.

CONCLUSIONS

#1. Sharpening procedures that will give maximum cutting ability are largely misunderstood.

#2. There are three types of "sharp." They are: false sharp (the wire edge), polished sharp, and micro-tooth sharp.

155

#3. The polished edge has an advantage in the type of cutting where the knife is pushed through the material.

#4. The edge with micro-teeth cuts better with a slicing cut, and will last longer in the average cutting application.

#5. There is no such thing as "hard-to-sharpen steel." Fat edges and thick blades cause this belief in some cases. Most of the time it is caused because the sharpening stone being used is inferior and lacks the ability to work down the edge in a reasonable amount of time.

#6. Hardness has more influence on edge-holding ability than alloy content. The highest alloyed steel will not perform unless it is at its full working hardness.

#7. In the chopping tests, inferior steel with good cross-section geometry will out-cut superior steel with bad geometry.

#8. The weight of a heavy knife is of little value if it has a fat edge.

#9. Handle shape, size, and the angle to the blade are very critical to the performance of the chopping knives.

#10. The blade with a high polish will chop wood and cut free-hanging rope better than one with a satin or sand blasted finish.

#11. Superior knives will be developed if more accurate comparisons of performance are made and the product modified in order to make it better.

#12. If there must be a contest or challenge, it would be wise to remember the following facts: Any knife can be beaten in either specific tests or overall testing by any or all of the following; better design, superior steel, more effective heat treating procedures, superlative sharpening technique, or by utilizing the ultimate in blade cross-section geometry.

#13. A particular type of steel has a certain potential in cutting ability and strength. It matters not so much that the blade is forged or created by stock-removal methods, but that it was given the proper thermal treatments to bring out the maximum in performance.

It is my hope that handmade and production makers alike will take time to consider the factors tested and think of how they can apply these to their products. If you disagree with my tests or conclusions I hope that you will prove me wrong by designing better tests and by making more and better comparisons. Do not keep a secret of what you have learned.

THE FREE-HANGING ROPE TEST

The free-hanging rope cut is primarily a test of the sharpness of a knife. It does not matter if the blade was forged or made by the stock-removal method. To cut one free-hanging rope the knife needs only to be sharp and swung with authority. This was proven accidentally when student Bill Nease used metal from the wrong steel pile and made his test blade of mild steel. He was having a hard time getting it sharp so I buffed the edge and was able to cut the rope with it. I handed the knife to Bill, he completed the cut, and history was made. He discovered that the knife was soft when the edge curled over when cutting the 2x4 in that part of the test.

Recently there were two free-hanging rope cutting contests. I didn't get to see the first one that took place at a hammer-in in California. That contest was won with a knife made by Al Barton and swung by Tim Hancock. The number of ropes cut was eight. I was going to compete in the second contest so I really wanted to see what the "eight-rope" knife was like.

My best effort in the past was three ropes and so when I heard about the knife that cut eight I was very impressed. I then applied my rule. "Same test, same rope, same day, same person swinging the knife." I thought to myself that I should just wait and see what the eight-rope knife was like. When I had cut three ropes it was with a knife that was made for normal use.

I had my knife finished for the contest at the Oregon Knife show when I first saw the knife that cut eight in California. Once I saw what it was like it gave me confidence because I didn't see anything that was magic. I thought that my knife would cut at least whatever his would. That knife out-weighed mine by nine ounces, but I believed that I had a sharper knife.

Seven of us tried our knives during the first ever free-hanging rope cutting contest held at a knife

Ed Schempp shows masterful form in the free-hanging rope-cutting contest. Photo by Ken Kailey.

show. I got six at once but went out on seven. That was good for third place. The knife, considering its length, was the thinnest at the edge that I ever dared make. Imagine a blade that was 12 inches long and 2 inches wide but as thin at the edge as any hunting knife I ever made.

I was the only one in the contest with a stock-removal blade. It was my old favorite D-2 worked in the hard state out of a planer blade. (I only used stock-removal because I didn't have time to make a forged one, but I did give it a soft-back draw.) I was very pleased with my straight-edged blade, even though at 17 ounces it was light for this type of contest. My cut on four was not smooth and I felt the shock of the rope being cut. Five and six were smooth with very little shock. Those watching a video of the event say I choked up on seven... stopped my swing in the rope. Don't ask me why I would do that, I figured that big bundle of ropes stopped me.

Ed Schempp and Bob Kramer. On the right is Ed who won the contest by cutting eight ropes at once. He then did another with nine and cut all but one thread of the rope. Bob finished second with seven ropes.

A QUICK METALLURGY LESSON FROM THE SCHOOL OF HARD KNOCKS

In 1983 I started testing my selectively heat treated blades with the 90-degree flex test. These were a mixture of Damascus and forged. Some of those first test blades broke between 45 and 90 degrees and the fracture showed a medium to coarse grain. I had read just enough metallurgy to

realize that a coarse grain usually meant that the blade was overheated going into the quenchant. I had heard of using a magnet to test for the hardening temperature but had never tried it. I started using it and no longer had broken blades. The magnet taught me that I could not judge the hardening temperature by eye.

Breaking the tips off of knife blades is not a total waste of good material... that's where I get the material for those little friction folder blades!

An interesting thing happened about that same time. I was ready to test two heat treated blades that I had forged from Nicholsen Black Diamond files. I had judged the hardening temperature by eye on the first blade. The second blade was hardened using a magnet. I had gotten them mixed up and did not know which one was which. I tried them with a file and one seemed a little harder than the other was. I'm still not sure why I did it but I hit the two blades together edge to edge. One blade notched the other with little damage to itself. This was puzzling because the blade that was notched seemed to be the harder of the two. I broke off the tips of the two blades and studied the grain size. The notched blade showed a medium to coarse grain and the undamaged one had a nice fine grain. Learn to think of the heat treating process as necessary to end up with a fine grain in the knife blade. At the same time it is hardened and tempered to perfection.

A VERY SAD STORY
(A test with an unhappy ending.)

The cutting, chopping and flex tests for ABS Journeyman Smith have to be accomplished by the applicant with his/her own hand. One day, a journeyman applicant was in my shop bright and early, the 1-inch rope for the rope-cutting test was hung with care. The applicant easily passed the first test when he stepped up and neatly cut a piece from the free-hanging end.

Chopping a wood 2x4 in half two times is the second test. This test of edge-holding ability requires the blade to shave hair after making the cuts. As the applicant started chopping, his test knife broke at the junction of tang and blade.

A visual inspection of the break showed a very coarse grain, and a cut made with a file indicated the steel was harder than it should have been in that area. My experience led me to believe that something had gone wrong in the heat treatment. There are numerous small details to be worked out with one's own equipment and methods. The broken blade showed the applicant's lack of experience with his equipment and methods. It'll usually take quite a bit of practice to completely master the heat treating process.

I relate this story to make the point that knowledge without practice and experience can be of little value. The applicant knew the fundamentals of selective hardening and yet the knife unexpectedly broke.

EXPERIENCE THE INCREDIBLE
CRAFTSMANSHIP OF A CUSTOM KNIFE

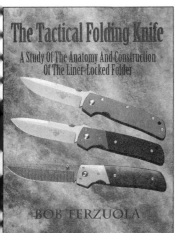
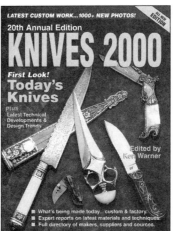

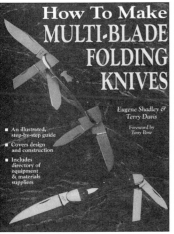
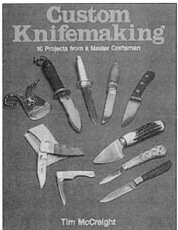

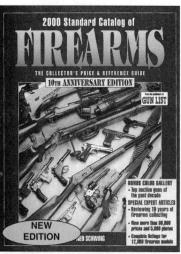

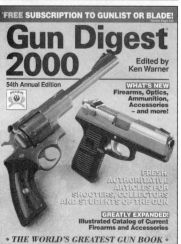
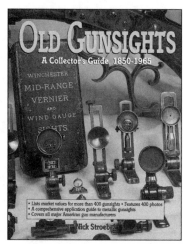